D0384876

ROMAN CULTURE

Weapons and the Man

The Cultures of Mankind

GREEK CULTURE: The Adventure of the Human Spirit
Edited by Alice von Hildebrand

ROMAN CULTURE: Weapons and the Man
Edited by Garry Wills

MEDIEVAL CULTURE: The Image and the City
Edited by Ruth Brantl

RENAISSANCE CULTURE: A New Sense of Order
Edited by Julian Mates and Eugene Cantelupe

THE AGE OF REASON: The Culture of the Seventeenth Century
Edited by Leo Weinstein

THE ENLIGHTENMENT: The Culture of the Eighteenth Century
Edited by Isidor Schneider

ROMANTICISM: The Culture of the Nineteenth Century
Edited by Morse Peckham

TWENTIETH-CENTURY CULTURE: The Breaking Up
Edited by Robert Phelps

Roman Culture

Weapons and the Man

Edited by Garry Wills

George Braziller · New York

Copyright © 1966, by Garry Wills

Published simultaneously in Canada by Ambassador Books, Ltd., Toronto

All rights reserved
For information, address the publisher,
George Braziller, Inc.
One Park Avenue, New York 16, N.Y.

Library of Congress Catalog Card Number: 66-15757

First Printing

Printed in the United States of America

DESIGN BY JULIUS PERLMUTTER

55144

ACKNOWLEDGMENTS

I wish to thank Professors Henry T. Rowell of the Johns Hopkins University and Michael C. J. Putnam of Brown University for reading and correcting my introductory remarks. I am deeply grateful for their learned ministrations; and for shortcomings that survived their suggestions and improvements I am alone responsible. I also thank the following for permitting me to publish certain of their translations for the first time—Richard E. Braun (Catullus 45, Martial 9.15), Nicholas Kilmer (Horace Epodes 3, 8), and Thomas Steele (Martial 1.10, 2.3, 2.19, 5.34, 8.27, 8.35, 10.95, 11.44). And I am especially grateful to *Arion* magazine, which has done so much to stimulate translation from the Latin and Greek, for permission to put under hard cover the following translations that first appeared in this young journal—*Pervigilium Veneris* by E. D. Blodgett and H. O. Weber; Propertius 1.1, 1.6, 1.22 and Ausonius *Oratio* 54-7 by Richard E. Braun; Horace Epodes 12 and Odes 1.11, 1.13 by Nicholas Kilmer; Petronius' poem 99 by Tim Reynolds; and Horace Odes 1.10, Catullus 16, and Sulpicius Lupercus Servasius' "Sapphics" by me.

G. W.

The editor and publisher have made every effort to determine and credit the holders of copyrights of the selections in this book. Any errors or omissions may be rectified in future editions. The editor and publisher wish to thank the following for permission to reprint the material included in this anthology:

Geoffrey Bles Ltd.—for selections from *The Letters of Cicero* by L. P. Wilkinson.

E. D. Blodgett and H. O. Weber—for their translation of *Pervigilium Veneris*.

Bobbs-Merrill Co., Inc.—for a translation from *Odi et Amo, The Complete*

Contents

List of Illustrations

9

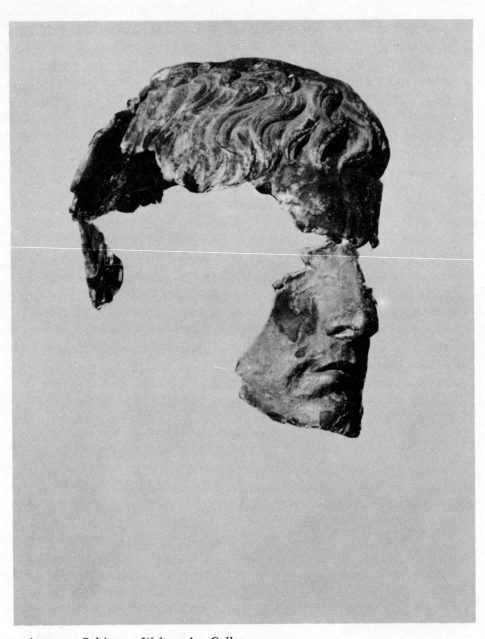

1. Augustus. Baltimore, Walters Art Gallery.

Revive for a moment a broken Coriolanus

Weapons, and their wearer out of Troy
driven to Italy on some
dark plan of things, the toy
(at sea, on land) of gods in anger,
Juno's unassuaged high jealousy;
bruised in all the ways, in war,
gods have of breaking men—

to sink his City's base,
give exiled gods a home:

from this (stuff of my song)
the Latin people trace their birth,
their better men, their walls
to lift up towering Rome.
                    Vergil, *The Song of Aeneas* 1.1-7

INTRODUCTION

Only at nightfall, aethereal rumours
Revive for a moment a broken Coriolanus

Eliot, "What the Thunder Said"

It is customary to contrast the practical Romans with the speculative Greeks—a useful distinction, perhaps, in some areas; not, I think, in their arts. Greek literature is supremely efficient, unencumbered, aimed —a linear undeviating epic, arrowy lyrics, a philosophy that asks and answers to the point. The Roman style is clotted. The outward effort of its drama and epic is impeded by a soliloquizing self-consciousness. Roman satire turns to feed on its own entrails, a watchdog biting no one but the house's occupants. Roman philosophy circles back, always, to a primary ethical doubt whether it is right to philosophize at all. The limbs of Greek sculpture unfold; on Roman statues, arms and legs accumulate. The Homeric epithet, the Pindaric strophe, the Aeschylean chorus were originally conveniences; but in Vergil, Horace, Seneca, the same things are encumbrances, welcomed as such.

Roman art is agglutinative, encrusted; an alien shell is somehow native to it. It is recoiling, reflective, epistolary, congested by its own hourly excretions. Contrast the meditative retorsiveness of Cicero's thought with the ruthlessly efficient way Plato used Socrates as a *persona* through which he could pronounce new truths: the greatest Greek biography, that of Socrates, is simply a convenience for getting things *said*. Up against such inspired opportunism, the Romans seem to bumble. In a sense, they did the "practical" things, like building straight stone-rooted

17

roads, because they were not efficient enough. They could not deal easily with the cosmos, like Plato; so they settled for policing the Mediterranean. The famous boast of Vergil has an odd air of regret about it, a resigned triumphalism:

> Let others better mould the running mass
> Of metals, and inform the breathing brass,
> And soften into flesh a marble face;
> Plead better at the bar; describe the skies—
> Both when the stars descend and when they rise.
> But, Rome, 'tis thine alone with awful sway
> To rule mankind, and make the world obey.

Aeneid 6.847-52 (Dryden)

Rome's greatness seems to have been built on a series of such melancholy conquests. They saved their real admiration for the losers. Vergil has Aeneas leave an *ex voto* at a shrine to celebrate Troy's defeat as if it were a triumph (*Aen.* 3.286-8). This is the Aeneas who is comforted by the thought that there are "for all things, tears; a mind wincing at man's pain" (*Aen.* 1.462). Livy tells us (22.61) that Rome celebrated an inverse triumph for the general who had undergone Rome's severest defeat "yet refused to despair." Caesar won at Pharsalus; but the court poets of Caesar's own heir Augustus glorified one of the men who was defeated, the man of whom Lucan later wrote:

> Let gods shift, always, to the winning side,
> Cato to one (lost) cause, liv'd true and died.

Pharsalia 1.128

When Christians were attacked for drawing the anger of the old gods down on Rome, St. Augustine answered with the rather cheap gibe that the Romans derived their city from conquered gods—those brought out of a flaming Troy by Aeneas—and they should not be surprised if the poor things keep up a losing record (*De Civ. Dei* 1.3). It is a taunt that hides a deep truth: Rome did draw its strength from defeat. Vergil fixed the city's foundations in Aeneas' exile; he reared the ordered arches of Rome over the dark mystery of Palinurus, the human sacrifice, the man who must die if Aeneas is to reach Italy: *Unum pro multis dabitur caput* (*Aen.* 5.815).

18

2. Portrait bust. Rome, Museo Vaticano.

. . . breathes strength in from wounds the iron gives it . . .

Rome's "finest hour"—that time after Cannae when Rome, as Livy tells us, celebrated its own power to endure defeat—is defiantly linked, by Horace, with Rome's Trojan ancestry of disaster. He makes Hannibal, in the course of those endless victories that were powerless to end Rome, lament that

> This people born out of the dead town's fires,
> this other Troy, poising over Tuscan waves
> bringing its gods, sons, sires
> to Italy—
> like tree-sinew splintered at
> where Algidus is darkened under leaves—
> breathes strength in from wounds
> the iron gives it.
>
> *Carmina* 4.4, lines 53-60

Rome's dark, static literature, so fastened upon defeat, lost its appeal in the nineteenth century. That time of progress and optimism put Homer on the central throne of influence that had been occupied by Dante's Vergil. For the first time "classical" art came to mean that of the Greeks, not the Romans. Since then, the revaluation has advanced at such a pace that we can hardly imagine a period when Ovid was the most seminal poet of Europe, when Seneca was the pattern of living drama, when Lucan and Statius were active poetic forces.

To us, it is no wonder that this change took place, only that it was so long coming. Roman literature is not only derivative, but defiantly so; it boasts of its debts. In the earliest literature we have we find things like Ennius' praise of a hero as *multa tenens antiqua*, "a man tenacious of old things." The epitaphs of the first great authors—of Naevius, Ennius, Plautus (p. 244)—sound a knell for the death of the language; and from that time on Latin is largely a dirge for good things departed. Later authors—all but the fastidious Horace—have a nostalgic piety for early ones. Rough lines and phrases of Ennius fill out Vergil's epic—almost as if Milton had worked partially modernized lines from Beowulf into the texture of *Paradise Lost*. There is an astonishing literary conservatism in the Roman poems: all their corridors echo each other. This robs the work of that fresh "primitive" air the romantics loved. The instant, inevitable line is missing; it is all wrought stuff. There is no Roman Archilochus, or Villon, or Burns. On the friezes of the Parthenon, time is frozen—the figures do not breathe until you turn your back. But Roman statues never breathe. It is an airless world.

An airless world—*à huis clos:* a modern world. The Romantic, Victorian, Edwardian approaches to antiquity—the pseudo-Aeschylean Prometheus of Shelley, the Homer of Arnold or of T. E. Shaw, the Shavian Euripides of Verrall and Murray—are interesting, and quaint, and as distant as the nursery. We have become less interested in the bright future than in that creature who warily advances into it—in man; and the Romans explored that creature with a dogged thoroughness. We have returned to the "neoclassical" authors in our literature—to Dryden and Pope, Johnson and Swift—with a realization that their emphasis on reason was not the facile optimism of the Enlightenment. They were desperately in love with intellect out of a realistic sense of man's precarious hold on order. A haunted and sleepless Johnson praised the settled things; a tortured, maddened Swift recommended calm; the London of Pope was also Hogarth's—just as the Rome of Pliny was that of Martial. We now watch Boswell's daily encounter with his own weakness as attentively as the Renaissance humanists pored over Cicero's self-revealing letters. We have a new kind of interest in man; we are bound to return to the Romans.

Ours is a period that Dostoevsky talks to. Then why not Tacitus? Beckett;—why not Seneca? Gide;—why not Martial? Joyce;—why not Petronius? Kierkegaard;—why not Augustine? Niebuhr;—why not Lucretius? We, like the Romans, do not have the lidless gaze that creates great tragedy. It takes an irrecoverable purity, a kind of lightheartedness, to live with the tragic vision. One sees deeper in calm, not muddied, waters. Seneca wrote bombastic fantasies of blood that are oddly unconvincing for one who witnessed a purge as voracious as Stalin's. With all his gracefulness he yearns for gore, asks vainly for apocalypse—like his own Oedipus, who petitions heaven to finish the job it began when he struck his eyes from their sockets:

> Now, by those eye-holes thrust thy hand into the very
> brains . . .

Phoenissae 180 (Thomas Newton)

In these weird plays of "escape," Seneca runs from rivers of real blood to oceans of stage blood. They are "dark comedies," closer to Genet and Beckett than to Sophocles.

Many of the finest Romans seem to have lived with a permanent

3. Alberto Giacometti, *Chariot*. New York, The Museum of Modern Art.

*. . . there is an internal distance between
the person and his office . . .*

prescience of disaster. One finds it in the portrait busts. The haunted face—how well history has sculptured it for us, in the features of Dostoevsky, Joyce, Thomas Mann, Eugene O'Neill, Robert Oppenheimer; and this "modern" face is that of the Roman busts—faces impervious to what lies just before them, masks that proclaim an exceeding inner busyness, one that eats at them. The more lifelike and individual these busts become, the more are they death's heads. Some achieve the subtlety of expression to be found in Donatello's St. George—the face of frightened heroes, simultaneously facing the dragon and their own fear. In his languidly triumphal pose, the Augustus of the Prima Porta (p. 282) seems to be attending to more insistent voices within him while he moves through the political choreography of his office. The very lack of formal tautness in Roman sculpture alienates the portrait-face from its body— as the lonely head on a work of Lehmbruck or Giacometti looks, from far off, down its own elongated limbs. The Roman dutifully lives his public performance, but there is an internal distance between the person and his office.

A condescending attitude toward Roman "practicality" came from the romantic aesthetic at its most narrow, and many popular treatments of Latin poetry are infected with its standards. Mackail longs to hear the horns of elfland faintly blowing in the work of men who were stalked by darker spirits than elves. Garrod, in his *Oxford Book of Latin Verse,* assures us that a fey quality, some stray fire, "often redeems Roman literature from itself." Highet and others seize upon the Celtic background of Catullus and try to turn him into a Yeats. Dido becomes the center of the *Aeneid*—a poem which looks rather lopsided as a result. The dubious history of Lesbia-Clodia is endlessly recomposed, in the vein of Highet's introductory paragraphs on her (which I quote in their entirety):

> And Clodia?
> Ah, Clodia.

These critics reflect the romantic belief that, as soon as one leaves fairyland, one finds nothing but factories. If Catullus is not a Gaelic bard, he is in danger of becoming a Roman Gradgrind. It is a dreary, self-defeating way to approach the Romans—liking them only when they can be caught in un-Roman attitudes (which often have to be invented), searching for an Asian, Spanish, or Gallic strain in Roman literature.

The value of the Romans must be sought precisely in their Roman-ness—in their stiff, self-conscious grip on known things, their fear of the unknown, their dependence on the family, their Italianate love of children, their extraordinary sympathy with the animal world, their guilty admiration of foreign ways, their uneasy assumption of a more sophisticated role in the world, their puritan pride and nobility and hypocrisy, their vast gift for self-revelation. They are a troubled people who can profitably trouble us. We do not need to spin romances around the edge of their history to make it significant for us.

If the Romans have a special relevance for the modern world, that relevance is nowhere more marked than in America. The Romans had their roots in deeply held agrarian principles, but found themselves exercising world power through a cosmopolitan complex; they too felt a nagging sense of betrayal as they saw the farm, the simple ways, the old faiths disappear in a bustle of commercial and military expansion. They were Puritans who, once restraints were shattered, forced themselves toward a dark prurience far from the innocent obscenities of Greece.

Rome defined itself through a series of clashes with older, more sophisticated cultures—with the Etruscans, the Phoenicians, the Greeks, the Egyptians. The Romans cast themselves in the role of simple, virtuous folk destined to smash the brittle glory of the over-civilized. In the person of Cato the Censor, the prime representative of this ideal, they made themselves a divine scourge of the Punic infamy. It is ironic that a later myth would represent the fall of Rome as the disintegration of an empire in need of the barbarians' "fresh blood." It is a myth the Romans would have understood; they had used it in their day. Tacitus, the urban sophisticate, describes the "primitive" Germans with a touch of half-conscious envy.

Romans always had a sharp nostalgia for the fields. Even their worst poets surpass themselves when a landscape is to be described. And all of them associated morality with simplicity, simplicity with the countryside. The city was foul, the country pure. Even those who must live in the city should undergo periodic cleansings in the fields. Nothing could be more distant from the Greeks' love of their political hive with all its buzzing. Socrates seems almost to suffer decompression "bends" when, in the *Phaedrus,* he rises some way toward the air outside Athens. The Agora exercised a centripetal force, the Forum a centrifugal: the Roman was always yearning to sneak away to his villa, or at least to get home, to pull the wondrous walls of color we can still see at Pompeii around himself and his intimates. There is a warmth in the very word *domus* that does not surround the Greek word for house, *oikos*. The difference is still felt in English—the difference between the Latin "domestic" and Greek words for the abstract principles of dwelling together ("economy," "ecumenical").

ii

The great, continuing challenge to Roman identity came from Greece. The Romans seem to have sensed from the outset that their fate depended on the terms of their accommodation to Greek thought. Some now think the best thing Rome could do for the world was to lose its war of nerves with Hellenic culture; according to them, Rome is valuable only as a coarse wrapping and protector for the more precious wares of Greece. This verdict of history was anticipated, and feared, and (I believe) forestalled, by men like Cicero. Rome's task—to maintain identity while learning from Greece—is labored at throughout Vergil's *Aeneid,* which performs a balancing act between the extremes of philhellenism and principled barbarism. Aeneas comes from the world of Hellenic myth and heroism; but he is a Trojan, the victim of Greek slipperiness—of Ulysses' plan, and Epeius' craft, and Sinon's histrionics. And even though Aeneas has learned, with Laocoon, to curse the Greeks and their gifts, he must still be purified of his Homeric past. One by one, he loses friends, followers, his father, his possessions—those Eastern riches he sees sparkling their way down to the sea's floor, *Troia gaza per undas (Aen.* 1:119). He must renounce his entire past in order to build a new world. The mystery of Aeneas is that the Roman can use his Hellenic heritage only after he has renounced Hellas. In Italy itself, Aeneas is initiated into the mysteries of the sacred place where Hercules cleared the earth of a monster and made a shrine—the sacred site of Rome. He finds, there, earlier links with Italy. He fights those who will be his friends and subjects, curing the bellicose disease of high-spiritedness with a necessary "bloodletting." And even then, like Moses, he does not enter the promised land he opens for others. He must marry into an Italian family, become a minor local king, if his descendants are to sway the world from Rome.

The climax of the *Aeneid* comes when much of the spirit of the Italian defender, Turnus, enters into his conqueror; when the defeated man wins. This triumph is adumbrated when Juno, acting as Turnus' representative in heaven, capitulates to Jove, but on her terms—the preservation of Italian ways under the foreigner's rule. She pleads with Jove, above the battle:

> But let the Latins still retain their name,
> Speak the same language which they spoke before,
> Wear the same habits which their grandsires wore.
> Call them not Trojans: perish the renown
> And name of Troy, with that detested town.
> Latium be Latium still; let Alba reign,
> And Rome's immortal majesty remain.

Aeneid 12.823-28 (Dryden)

And Jove agrees:

> From ancient blood, th'Ausonian people sprung,
> Shall keep their name, their habit, and their tongue:
> The Trojans to their customs shall be tied.
> I will, myself, their common rites provide:
> The natives shall command, the foreigners subside.
> All shall be Latium; Troy without a name;
> And her lost sons forget from whence they came.
> From blood so mix'd, a pious race shall flow,
> Equal to gods, excelling all below.

Aeneid 12.834-39 (Dryden)

(There was constant danger that Greek, the world language, the vehicle of administration and commerce throughout the Roman Empire, would displace Latin as the language for ambitious literary and philosophical work. This explains Vergil's great emphasis on the preservation of the native tongue—and the complaints of many Romans that Greek was considered "more refined" than Latin: see Pliny's and Juvenal's remarks on pp. 195-97.)

The lure of Greece was complex. It offered brilliant thought and art and poetry. But the stiffer sort of Roman found it difficult to separate the "atheistic" quietism of the Epicureans and Academics from the ennobling aspects of Greek philosophy. Greek love of beauty seemed to be infected with profligacy and perversion. Things were made worse by the fact that the Greeks with whom the Romans had the greatest natural sympathy—the Dorians of Sparta, the people of that Hercules who had cleansed the site of Rome—were the great spokesmen for aristocratic Greek homosexuality. Rome had no institutional mystique to support and control homosexuality—which made it more appealing than ever to some Romans.

Thus there came to be a heavy intellectual tariff on the importation of things Greek. Cicero could present the Epicurean philosophy in Latin dress, but he had always to pin a helpful Stoic refutation to it. On the other hand, when one wanted to tell a naughty story, one simply made all the bad girls Greek—as Americans once told "French" stories. Plautus' and Terence's plays all have their setting in a Greek "gay Paree." The imagined mistresses of poet after poet have Greek names, which were not only "allowed," but had the convenient liquidity and metrical lilt of the Greek language—girls like Horace's Lalage and Glycera.

Roman resentment of Greece led those who adapted Greek forms to practice a subtly deprecatory manner toward their work. One of the rhetorical devices that proved most useful in disarming their stolid countrymen was the *recusatio:* when opening a lyric poem, or publishing a set of such lyrics, the poet claims that his *real* aspirations are to create a serious work glorifying Rome or the Emperor—but, alas, the author's slender talent buckles under a task so weighty, and he (along with his readers) must settle for this poor second-best. The pretense such a disclaimer involves is often pretty thinly veiled; but it is Ovid who reduces the whole thing to absurdity. In the first poem of his *Amores,* he claims that he keeps *trying* to write heroic hexameters, but Cupid deftly sneaks a foot out of every second line—turning it into the love-metre.

The instincts of a Cato were partially vindicated by the Romans who exposed themselves to Greek ways. The moral, rigid, self-questioning Roman, obsessed with ethics, could not quite "bring it off" when asked to be a detached, gay observer of the universe. He felt that he was posing; often, that he was betraying his own past. The dark strain in Roman literature is often brought to the surface by contact with the Greeks. The compulsive obscenity of those rebelling against puritan standards is not a happy thing. The distance between Aristophanes and Petronius is that between Rabelais and Henry Miller. For Romans, sexual release and sadism often go together (as in the torture scenes of Apuleius); and so do preaching and prurience (in Lucretius and St. Jerome as well as in Apuleius or Juvenal).

4. Portrait bust. Rome, Palazzo Capitolino.

. . . the face of a dyspeptic corporation head
who should have been a village mayor . . .

Another theme also enters Western literature through the Romans—a thing that became very important in Elizabethan drama—the intertwining of the fascinations exercised by power and by sex. The torture of ambition and lust are, for them, aspects of a single darkness over the soul. The renunciation of Dido is a purification of Aeneas' heart; but it is, simultaneously, the loss of a throne, of the walls and city he has longed for in his wanderings. Cleopatra, in the poems of Horace and Vergil, is the symbol of a literal *lust* for power. Horace connects her designs on the Capitol with her perverse revels and her eunuchs—she would unsex men by her domination. Vergil singles out three things in his description of Cleopatra (*Aen.* 8.696-713)—her wild religious rites, her premature despair over the defeat of her favored one, and her suicide. The same three things mark the career of that monstrous woman who tries to block Aeneas' entry into Italy—Amata. Many have noticed the similarities between Turnus and Mark Antony; fewer have adverted to the fact that Turnus' ally against Aeneas-Augustus is a religious, impassioned woman modeled on Cleopatra. This may indicate that her interest in Turnus is not prompted simply by plans for her daughter's future; in fact, the timing of Lavinia's famous blush suggests that her mother's enthusiasm for Turnus deeply troubles her. In more ways than one, Turnus "moves in the shadow" (*Aen.* 11.223) of "Amata," the treacherous object of men's love. This is a sickly shadow, the kind that is cast across the political work of Seneca and Tacitus and over the private agonies of Catullus and Propertius. Sex carried implications of domination or submissiveness, of manliness or effeminacy, of loyalty or rebellion, that call up political analogues to these men. Anticipations of Messalina or Agrippina haunt the *Aeneid,* as their historical presence darkens Seneca's *Medea* and their memory tortures Juvenal. There is a strain of savage misogyny in all Roman political satire (see pp. 348-52).

It is astonishing that the Romans held up so well (and so long) against their many internal enemies. The Colosseum was an uncommonly apt hub for the wheel of Roman empire: like it, Roman culture had a large external simplicity, a labyrinthine internal life, and subterranean passages prowled by animals. Yet tremendous energies were expended to keep the Roman's "split personality" from reaching a point of suicidal fission. The Roman leader was by principle a farmer, by necessity and choice a bureaucrat; his face, on some of the busts that have come down to us, is that of a dyspeptic corporation head who should have been a village mayor. But, each in their own way, Caesar and Augustus, Cicero and Vergil, Horace and Quintilian, tried to heal this inner division. Caesar is the sophisticated but laconic hero, combining the best of Greece and Rome, in the careful self-portrait drawn for us in his histories. Cicero tried to adjust the Roman character to Greek intellectual skills (a far more important task than the invention of Latin words for Greek concepts—the achievement he is most popularly credited with). Augustus tried to unite the city and the countryside, the past and the future, Republic and monarchy, Cato and Caesar. The one thing Horace wanted from politics was that it not impinge upon his attention very much; but Maecenas, that master recruiter of talent for Augustus, was not mistaken in his expenditures on Horace. The poet achieved a new kind of union between critical faculties and political submissiveness —just as he gave an urbanite's subtlety to the old Roman love for the countryside. Quintilian (taken here as a symbol of the other educational theorists of Rome) gave respectability to the insidious foreign arts by convincing people that they could be "practical."

But the great synthesizer of all elements in the Roman genius was Vergil. Maecenas, when he sponsored the young man, came as close as anyone ever has to creating a poet. He did not, of course, call up the talent out of nothing; but he recognized it, channeled it, made it serve the purpose he desired. Or did he? There is a strange ambiguity in the situation. Augustus wanted not so much a laureate as a Minister of Education—one who would teach the people a proper respect for their paternalistic ruler, a ruler who, in what must have been Augustus' favorite line of the *Aeneid,* "spares the submissive and breaks the rebellious" (6.853). But Vergil seems to have conceived his job, at least to some extent, as that of educating the *ruler.* His epic is more a handbook for the prince than for his subjects. Educating the ruler was not a task that Vergil could go about in any obvious way, despite his noble predecessors in this mission. Both Plato and Aristotle had at various times instructed governors; but Hellenic parallels had to be disowned when they were used too openly, and here, as in his use of Homer, Vergil achieves the perfect acclimatization of his Greek exemplars to his Roman audience. It was a delicate game he had to play; and scholars have been arguing ever since whether, when the game was over, Augustus had turned Vergil into a toady, or Vergil had turned Augustus into the philosopher-king. Perhaps the truth is a mixture of the two views. After all, Augustus, like all wise men, probably wanted a teacher, though he could hardly admit it; and Vergil, without being entirely satisfied with

30

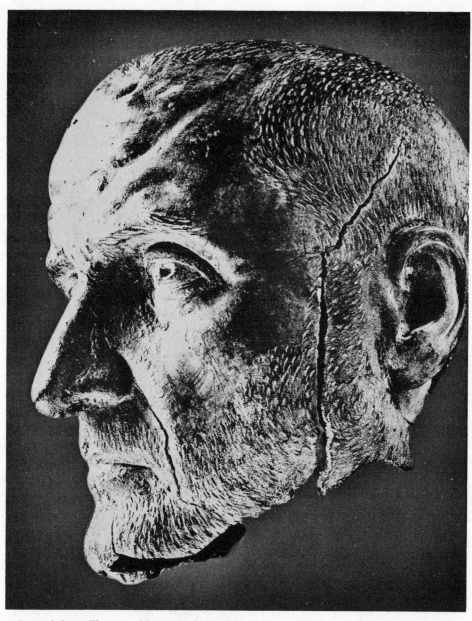

5. Portrait bust. Florence, Museo Archeologico.

. . . masks that proclaim an exceeding inner busyness . . .

the only candidate available, probably wanted a king to serve. In this, as in so many other things, he is the first voice of European chivalry.

The Romans' triumph, then, is not in their external administrative monuments, but in the self-exploration this outer bustle forced upon them. In a famous speech, contrasting the Athenians and the Spartans, Thucydides says that the former move outward, everywhere, with a quicksilvery restlessness, while the latter shrink further within themselves. In these terms, the Romans had the recoiling Spartan temperament, but they were led by history to undertake the Attic tasks of imperial expansion. By combining these thrusts, by moving simultaneously outward and inward, they opened a whole new spectrum of individual consciousness. They turned defeat into a kind of victory—much as Vergil made a fierce loyalty toward the past (*pietas*) summon Aeneas into the hazards of the future; or as Aeneas himself dedicated Greek armor taken in the battle his city had lost. There is much of Rome in that boast of things accomplished by defeated men—*haec de victoribus arma*. It explains why the Romans continue to exercise their hold upon us; why they still conquer, under conquered gods.

iii

I do not intend to give any systematic historical background for these selections; but a warning or two may head off misunderstandings that arise because of anachronistic reading. First of all, the political terminology of the Romans is colored by their history, and cannot be too simply translated into English derivatives. For instance: beneath the systems described as "The Republic" and "The Empire," a far older system perdured, one based on the ethical values of ancient clan law.

The primary unit in Roman politics is the family. Duty toward it, loyalty within it, is the basis of all other loyalty (*pietas*). "Parties" are not formed on a program or ideology, but by some tie between prominent men and their families (*amicitia*), a personal tie often expressed by intermarriage. The controlling families are under a constant pressure to use public achievement, triumphs, spectacles in order to maintain the prestige (*dignitas*) on which are based their social prominence (*gloria*) and their right to give counsel to the state (*auctoritas*). This prominence puts them inside the charmed circle that controls membership in the Senate (the supreme seat of *auctoritas*) and election to the most prestigious office, the consulate. Those outside the charmed circle enter Roman political life by taking up a satellite position (as "clients") toward one or other clannish complex (*factio*). A client gives and earns allegiance (*fides*) from his patrons, and extraordinary talent and services may lift him from the status of a dependent to that of an equal (as happened to the "new man," Cicero). When talent goes unrewarded— as in the case of Juvenal—the personal submission demanded of a "client" can be very galling.

The source of real power—Senate, army, or Emperor—changes in the course of Roman history; but that power is always diffused through the old family channels, or some vestige of them. Several misconceptions are prevented if this is remembered. The Roman insistence on external splendor, Cicero's nervous regard for his precarious *dignitas*, the reduction of all politics to a personal level, the importance of giving public games as a lordly gesture (so clearly marked in Suetonius' records), the family-feud aspect of Roman political life (e.g. the gang wars described in Cicero's *Pro Milone*—a Hatfield-McCoy aspect of life that could lead to city-wide proscriptions), the role of marriages in social life (Sir Ronald Syme notes that Caesar not only knew how to fight well, but how to marry well), the morning ritual of a client's attendance on the person of his leader or leaders—all these are interconnected parts of a political system with deep and lasting roots among the Romans.

Things we think of as private virtues—amity (*amicitia*), a wife's devotion to her husband's career, family loyalty—were political institutions essential to the constitutional workings of Rome. Amity, for instance, was not an affection or internal disposition merely, but a formal alliance with a semicontractual character, a kind of treaty between persons. (When Cicero, in his essay *De Amicitia,* says amity can only be established "among the good," he is setting up a standard of *political* probity: one does not incur the strict political obligations of *amicitia* with a man who is bound to exploit them to the state's detriment.) Things we regard with suspicion or disapprobation—a constant regard for one's social splendor, a "spoils system" of factional self-aggrandizement, a personal submission to the prominent, a political loyalty based on personal ties rather than principles—were the very building blocks of social order in Rome. They cannot be judged in isolation from their matrix.

Since the selections in this book are not given in chronological order,

I shall give a rough sketch of the temporal framework within which the various authors make their appearance.

The early rule of Etruscan kings in Rome acted as a temporary civilizing force which, like the reforming era of the tyrants in Greece, had to be violently rejected if the political process was to continue its development. The role played by an antityrannical myth in the Greek city-states was played by an antimonarchical mystique in Rome—a code that led to the empty legal forms of the Empire, but undoubtedly had a tempering effect on certain Emperors, who pretended to less power than they really had, and sometimes lived down to their pretensions. The Etruscan kings were overthrown around the end of the sixth century B.C., and the "Republic" was launched -the oligarchy, we would probably call it. During the fifth and fourth centuries, Rome's power was extended, by treaty and war, throughout the Italian peninsula. In the third century, Rome pushed out into the Western Mediterranean and battled for supremacy there with Carthage. In the second century, she took control of the Eastern Mediterranean from Greek rulers.

We have some rude scraps of a native literature, but the real beginning of Roman letters comes during the Second Punic War (220-201 B.C.), when triumph, wider trade, intensified contact with the Greek culture of Sicily, and the presence of Greek slaves like Livius Andronicus (who translated Greek works into Latin), led to a fusion of native and Greek forms. Epic and drama were the first forms to be appropriated—Gnaeus *Naevius** (?-201?) and Quintus *Ennius* (239-169) wrote extensively in both forms. Ennius, moreover, accomplished the remodeling of the Latin metrical system to correspond with Greek models.

In the second century, drama had its premature yet final period of vitality among the Romans—especially in the tragedies of Ennius and Lucius Accius (170-80?), the comedies of Titus Maccius *Plautus* (250?-184) and Publius Terentius Afer, or *Terence* (190?-159). The imitation of the Greeks in the theater had its counterpart in the prose written and read by the circle that clustered around the younger Scipio (P. Cornelius Scipio Aemilianus—to whom Cicero sends the imagined vision of pp. 302-10 below) and Gaius Laelius (in whose mouth Cicero put his reflections on amity). Scipio's circle extended patronage to Terence, read and approved original Roman work like the satires of Gaius

---

* I print in italics the most familiar name of those authors represented in this anthology.

34

6. Portrait bust. Munich, Glyptothek.

. . . battered by time, now; but they began battered . . .

Lucilius (180-102), befriended Greeks like the historian Polybius and the philosopher Panaetius, and helped conceive the ideal of a Hellenized Rome—over the opposition of fierce nationalists like Marcus Porcius Cato (234-149), the famous "elder Cato," the Censor. Cicero idealized the Scipionic circle for its combination of Roman and Greek letters, its cultural liberalism and political conservatism—for the group came into conflict with the reforming brothers Tiberius and Gaius Gracchus.

The reforms of the Gracchi (from 133 B.C. on) touched off a century of social strife and civil war which culminated in Caesar's destruction of the Republic and Augustus' foundation of the Empire. This troubled century of terror and purge was a time of literary brilliance. Titus *Lucretius* Carus (94-55) restated the Epicurean philosophy in passionate verse; but the main poetic movement was that of the "New Poets." The Romans' first imitations of Greek had focused on literature of the great periods—Homeric epic, fifth-century tragedy, fourth-century comedy. But in the war-torn Roman first century, the antiheroic attitudes of Alexandria became popular—the profession of polished triviality, that deflation of grandiosity undertaken by the supreme Alexandrian, Callimachus. Some Latin poets had already turned to the later Greek epigram for their models, minor poets of the second century like Valerius *Aedituus* and Quintus Lutatius *Catulus*. But now a group of major poets gave their attention to the Alexandrian forms—epyllion, epigram, love poem. This group included Gaius Helvius Cinna, Furius Bibaculus, and—the major figures—Gaius Licinius Calvus and Gaius Valerius *Catullus* (87?-54?).

Republican' prose of the first century reaches its culmination in the work of Marcus Tullius *Cicero* (106-44), Gaius Julius Caesar (102?-44), and Gaius Sallustius Crispus, or *Sallust* (86-35). A minor genre of the period was the mime, from which we have fragments by Decimus *Laberius* and *Publilius* Syrus.

With the beginning of the reign of Augustus (27 B.C.), we enter the famous "Augustan Age," when Rome celebrated its own history and greatness in the prose of Titus Livius, or *Livy* (59 B.C.-A.D. 17), and in the poetry of Publius Vergilius Maro, or *Vergil* (70-19). The ideals of the "New Poets" were developed in two directions by the Augustans. The "official" poets, who enjoyed the patronage of Maecenas, stretched the Alexandrian sensibilities far enough to reconquer certain heroic forms. In his *Georgics*, Vergil shattered the brittle Theocritean idyll by looking back to Hesiod, and then moved from epyllion back to authentic epic.

36

The other major poet of the circle, Quintus Horatius Flaccus, or *Horace* (65-8), combined the wry self-awareness of the Alexandrians with the lyric energy of the early melic poets—Alcaeus, Sappho, Anacreon.

A different direction was taken by those who, following the example of Catullus, developed Greek love poems into the autobiographical elegy. This group includes Gaius Cornelius Gallus (69-26), the friend of Vergil who died in political disgrace; Albius *Tibullus* (54?-19), the protégé of Messalla and a friend of Horace; Sextus *Propertius* (50?-15?), who was partly associated with the Maecenas poets; and Publius Ovidius Naso, or *Ovid* (43 B.C.-A.D. 18).

With the death of Augustus (A.D. 14) we enter the Christian era and the so-called. Silver Age of Latin. The period of the Julio-Claudian emperors (14-68: Tiberius, Caligula, Claudius, Nero) was not a time for free literary expression. Under Nero, for instance, the satirist Aulus *Persius* Flaccus (34-62) died too young to be executed, but the philosopher-poet Lucius Annaeus *Seneca* (4?-65), the versatile dilettante Gaius *Petronius* (?-66), and Seneca's nephew, the young poet-rival of Nero himself, Marcus Annaeus Lucanus, or *Lucan* (39-65), were all victims of the Emperor. The popular encyclopedist Gaius Plinius Secundus, or *Pliny the Elder* (23?-79) did survive, only to be killed in the eruption of Vesuvius. One of the few untroubled careers of the early Christian era was, appropriately enough, that of the modest fabulist *Phaedrus,* who seems to have published his work during the reigns of Tiberius and Caligula.

The Neronian censorship was somewhat relaxed by the Flavian emperors (69-96: Vespasian, Titus, Domitian), but philosophers, especially the Stoics, were expelled from Italy during their reign. This is the period of the educator Marcus Fabius Quintilianus, the epigrammatist Marcus Valerius Martialis or *Martial* (40?-104?), and the epic poet Publius Papinius *Statius* (50?-95?).

Under the liberalizing influence of Nerva and Trajan (96-117), there were three main authors: the historian Cornelius *Tacitus* (55?-117?), his friend the epistolary civil servant Gaius Plinius Caecilius Secundus, or *Pliny the Younger* (61?-113), and the satirist Decimus Iunius Iuvenalis, or *Juvenal* (60?-131?). In the reign of Hadrian (117-138), the Emperor's secretary, Gaius Suetonius Tranquillus (69?-140?), is the major author. Sometime in the second century, Lucius Apuleius (125?-?) wrote his *Metamorphoses.*

The first Christian writer included in this selection is Quintus Septimius Florens Tertullianus, or *Tertullian* (150?-240?) who begins a distinguished line of Christian authors in Africa. Unless the anonymous *Vigil of Venus* was written earlier, there is nothing to detain us until we reach the fourth century, when Christianity became the established religion under the Emperor Constantine (323-337), and a flourishing Christian literature marks a break with the past and a bridge to the future. The poets represented here are Aurelius *Prudentius* Clemens (348-405) and the hymnist Ambrosius, or *St. Ambrose* (335?-397). The principal prose writers are Eusebius Hieronymus, or *St. Jerome* (348?-420), and Aurelius Augustinus, *St. Augustine* (354-430). Pagan literature is continued in the century by Claudius Claudianus, or *Claudian* (370?-*post* 405). Those who ignore the religious division, or mix their paganism and Christianity, are the gay Christian, Decimus Magnus *Ausonius* (310?-394), and some minor figures like Flavius *Vopiscus* (who preserves a rousing soldiers' song for us) and the author of one memorable poem in sapphics, *Sulpicius Lupercus Servasius*.

At the point where this book's subject begins to merge with the Middle Ages, I include a selection from two authors who lived into the sixth century, Anicius Manlius Severinus *Boethius* (480-524) and Octavianus, or *Octavian*. Though the book must come to an end, Latin literature does not.

iv

A word, finally, on the selections in this book; and on the translations. There is good reason to distrust any anthology. Masterpieces are, by definition, works of distillation; they cannot be further refined without severe loss. Cutting them does not concentrate, but diffuses. Some take this principle and apply it to mean that, though all anthologies are bad, the least objectionable are those that do the least cutting. It is not as simple as that. One gets no idea of the *Aeneid* from twenty short excerpts; but at least he does not *think* he will. Yet some people do think the perusal of, say, three or four complete books of the *Aeneid* is a reasonable substitute for reading the poem. They are not only wrong, but wastefully wrong. After committing their time to such a large chunk of the work, they should get a return on the investment by going on to read the rest, which will enrich and put in its true perspective the part already studied. Reading three books is not reading the *Aeneid*; in fact, it is hard to judge what that *is* doing.

Is there no room for anthologies, then? Not for the normal ones, which take the "field" in chronological order and give a large chunk of each "major author"—a book or two of Lucretius or Caesar, a speech or two of Cicero. At each stage, one does too much and too little. There is no substitute, when studying an author or an artifact, for total exposure, or as near to that as life's hourglass will allow. Better to read one author well and forget the *membra disiecta* of the other twenty or so.

You rightly infer from this that I do not pretend to give, in this book, an adequate picture of any one author or artifact. When I print an excerpt* from, say, Dryden's version of the *Aeneid*, it is not meant to suggest what a masterwork that epic is, what a fine poet Vergil is, what a good translator Dryden is. There may be some indication of all these things, but that is not the final justification for the passage's inclusion. I offer the excerpt, in significant conjunction with other short passages, to throw light on an area of Roman awareness, concern, failure, or achievement. As the title indicates, this is a book about Roman *culture*—the thing Vergil shared with others, not the virtues that were unique in him.

A composite picture of this sort can be built up from scraps and separate *aperçus,* each of which may have a higher use in its original location, as part of a great poem or prose work, without making it unavailable for this subsidiary use. And later study of the individual works is made more interesting and profitable for having considered the artist's points of contact with other Roman thought and work. The late T. R. Glover, a fine scholar, said that Tertullian's close observation of children indicates that he, like Augustine, had a child of his own, since "such observation . . . is not common in Classical authors." Perhaps the vague picture of Vergil's Ascanius, a dashing horseman and hunter who can still be dandled on Dido's knee, blinded Glover to the Romans' deep love of children and their exact observation of them (as in Vergil, *Ecl.* 4.68, Horace, *Ars. P.* 158-60, Cicero *De Fin.* 5.42). Glover's slip shows how useful it can be to sample the Roman authors under topical headings.

The book, then, tries to create a balanced impression of Roman concerns. This is a task of criticism, a legitimate one in itself, even if I fail to do it justice in this case; one not subject to the usual criticism

---

* Omitted passages are indicated either by ellipses or three dots centered on the page.

directed at anthologies. It is not (primarily) a sampling of Roman literature, but of Roman life. You will find in it more of Pliny the Elder than of Tacitus. The maxims of Publilius, which St. Jerome learned in his school days, are negligible as literary efforts; but they tell far more about the ordinary Roman's sensibilities than do Caesar's accounts of Gallic campaigning. Pliny's encyclopedia lays bare the assumptions of an entire age. His nephew's letters express the code of those men who maintained the vast fabric of the Roman Empire—men in love with leisure, and wealthy enough to enjoy it, but with a stern sense of duty to the public order. And the coarser side of Roman taste can be found in Lucan's gory epic, the ancient equivalent of a best-selling historical novel or a Cecil De Mille "spectacular." (This does not mean of course, that I neglect my own or my reader's comfort: although excerpts are chosen for their ability to contribute to the total cultural picture, I try to use passages of some intrinsic interest or beauty as well.)

Partly, of course, sheer accident determines the selections—my shortcomings; the availability of translations; the ability of a passage to speak for itself, without footnotes. All these considerations narrow the material from the outset. Furthermore, I rely on poetry more than on prose, since its concentrated form makes it reveal nuances in a single line that would require long passages in prose. The vicissitudes of history have already done much of our winnowing for us. Caesar, for instance, was a poet and a great orator; but, apart from a poetic fragment, all one can read of him now (and that in some other book, not this) is the artfully inconspicuous propaganda he wrote about his wars. These works are so "objective" that Caesar always speaks of himself, in them, in the third person—not unfavorably. Caesar is historically important, his Latin is clean and efficient and pedagogically useful, so he is usually included in books of this sort. Where he does not belong. Better to read *about* him in Lucan or Suetonius.

Now, the translations. I have not acted on any single principle in choosing translations. Each version must sacrifice some things to gain others; what is lost, what gained, will vary from work to work according to the excellences of the author and the capacity of the translator. Even very sensible general rules must bow to these facts. For instance: the nearest thing to a good universal rule in this matter is that poetry should be translated into some *poetic* form; but R. E. Latham's prose translation of Lucretius is, so far, the best complete version we have. (Dryden only did excerpts.) What I *have* looked for is a correspondence between the author's virtues and the translator's. Ezra Pound often praises Golding's translation of the *Metamorphoses,* which does indeed have a rough-riding vigor. But the better it is in its own line, the farther it departs from the polish and point of the hypersophisticated Ovid. The Elizabethan translations of Seneca's plays are often praised; but their buckety-buckety dialogue has nothing in common with the morbid rhetorical finish of the original. Only in the shorter verses of the choral sections do the Elizabethans approach Seneca's virtuosity.

A perfect matching of virtues is rare. One finds this sympathy more often in works that are not direct translations of the Latin, but are more subtly under its influence. The presence of Cicero is felt more compellingly in the prose of the seventeenth-century masters—Milton and Browne, Jeremy Taylor and John Donne—than in translations of the speeches. Bishop Taylor, especially, can unite opulence with economy as Cicero did:

> All the succession of time, all the changes in nature, all the varieties of light and darkness, the thousand thousands of accidents in the world, and every contingency, to every man and to every creature does preach our funeral sermon, and calls us to look and see how old sexton Time throws up the earth, and digs a grave where we must lay our sins or our sorrows, and sow our bodies till they rise again in a fair or in an intolerable eternity.

Sometimes the echo is more direct. In Donne, for instance:

> And is any rational ant
>   (the wisest philosopher is no more),
> is any roaring lion
>   (the most ambitious and devouring prince is no more),
> is any hive of bees
>   (the wisest councils and parliaments are no more),
> is any of these . . .

Compare that with the opening of Cicero's speech for Archias:

> Si quid est in me ingeni, iudices,
>   (quod sentio quam sit exiguum),
> aut si quae exercitatio dicendi
>   (in qua me non infitior mediocriter esse versatum),

41

> aut si huiusce rei ratio aliqua ab optimarum artium studiis ac
>   disciplina profecta
> (a qua ego nullum confiteor aetatis meae tempus abhoruisse),
> earum rerum omnium . . .

It is not surprising that the only adequate translation of Cicero I have been able to find comes from the seventeenth century. Unfortunately, Sir Charles Sedley did only one speech, and that a minor one (*Pro Marcello*); but it captures the authentic fullness and nervousness, what Cardinal Newman called Cicero's "felicity in the choice and perfection in the collocation of words":

> When the trophies and monuments erected by you shall decline and hasten to a period (for there is no workmanship of art, or effect of industry, which old age does not impair by degrees, and finally demolish), this justice and lenity of yours shall have a quite contrary fortune, and, the more it grows in years, become still the more fresh and flourishing; so that how much soever any length of time may detract from the stateliness of your fabrics shall certainly be added to the height of your commendation . . . It will be matter of astonishment to all future generations when they shall read and hear of the charges you have borne, the provinces you have subdued, and what has been done by you in Germany, in the Ocean, and in Egypt—the perusal and report, I say, of your victories above belief, of all your trophies and triumphs, shall questionless amaze and confound posterity. But unless this imperial city shall, by your authority and contrivance, be immovably pitched upon a solid bottom, your great and formidable name then will only shift and wander about the world, but have no certain abode nor any settled habitation.

Rarely does an author find the translator he deserves. The young Swinburne should have translated the *Pervigilium Veneris,* whose closest English equivalent is the parodos of *Atalanta in Calydon.* Edward Thomas should have translated Vergil's *Georgics,* describing yet transfiguring a real countryside:

> The light wind frets
> And drifts the scum
> Of may-blossom . . .

For the obliterative economy of Martial, one must turn to Hilaire Belloc:

> I said to Heart, "How goes it?" Heart replied:
> "Right as a Ribstone Pippin!" But it lied.
>
> Paunch talks against good liquor to excess,
> And then about his raving Patroness;
> And then he talks about himself. And then
> We turn the conversation on to men.

Cummings should have done some of the Catullus poems—a lapse on his part that Frank O. Copley has tried to repair. Robert Frost was the perfect man to deal with the amenities and astringencies of Horace's letters and satires. Robert Fitzgerald should be hounded by all the foundations in America to attempt the *Aeneid*—a poem to which his talents are even better attuned than to the *Odyssey*.

But we must settle for the versions that *have* been attempted. There is a vast body of work done from the Latin—over the past centuries, far more than from Greek. But in recent years the beam has swung. Greek is well served now—by Fitzgerald's *Odyssey*, Lattimore's Aeschylus, Arrowsmith's Euripides, Douglass Parker's Aristophanes, Bernard Fagles' Bacchylides and Pindar, Guy Davenport's Archilochus and Sappho, by the anonymous translator of *Timothy* and *Titus* in the New English Bible, by Lattimore again in his fine version of *Revelations*. There are promising signs in Latin—Horace Gregory's Ovid, James Michie's Horace (the best-sustained translation of all the odes since Christopher Smart)—but we must, in many cases, seek out the older translations to get some dim idea of the original's vigor. Luckily, we have Dryden.

Purists may well object to the hodgepodge of styles that results from this ransacking of English literature. It is disconcerting to move from Elizabethan to eighteenth-century prosody on the same page. But the method has its advantages, despite (and partly because of) the jolts it gives one: Latin comes to us through the large "translating" effort of the tradition that carried it down to us; both the influence of Latin on history and of history on the preserved Latin *corpus* are vividly brought to mind when we see the ancient texts play across the entire range of our own literature. We cannot detour around our own language to get to the classics; we must journey back *through* it to the sources.

Once one balances the dividends and penalties of this approach, it becomes a matter of interest in itself to see how Latin affected men of different eras. From the Elizabethan age we have the translators of Seneca (in their choral sections), Philemon Holland's chatty informative Pliny, and Christopher Marlowe matching Lucan bombast for bombast.

From the seventeenth century I include translations by Ben Jonson and Richard Lovelace; an excerpt from the Jacobean "Birth of Hercules" (the acting version of Plautus' *Amphitruo*); and much of Sir Richard Fanshawe's *Aeneid* IV. This last version, by the way, shows how difficult it is to erect rules for translators. Ideally, the *Aeneid* should be translated in a verse form that could run through the entire poem, as Vergil's hexameters do. Clearly Fanshawe's Spenserian stanzas would not serve in the more heroic parts of the poem; but they give an appropriately ornate and enclosed atmosphere to the book in which many want to linger (as Aeneas himself wanted to), afraid of the colder winds that blow outside this interlude. The enfolding richness is there in the original, and Fanshawe earns his right to the Spenserians by reproducing it.

Other seventeenth-century translators represented here are Sir Charles Sedley, the Earl of Rochester, the Earl of Roscommon, and—the greatest translator in English history—John Dryden. He can master what he himself called (with a glance at *Tristia* 4.10) "the trifling tenderness of Ovid," yet render, as well, the bruised abusiveness of Juvenal, the slapstick of Plautus, the masochistic preachiness of Lucretius, the arch sincerity of Persius, or the "tactical intertwinedness" of Horace (the last in one of the great poems of our language, "Descended of an ancient line . . ."). His greatest failure, unfortunately, is his most famous Latin effort, his Vergil. Vergil is outside any man's reach (a decade before his complete edition, when he published some samples in *Sylvae,* Dryden wrote "methinks I come like a malefactor, to make a speech upon the gallows, and to warn all other poets, by my sad example, from the sacrilege of translating Virgil"); and Dryden was past his prime when he undertook the task—sixty-two when he began, sixty-six when he finished, three years before his death. (For a discerning treatment of Dryden's Vergil, see Robert Fitzgerald's article in the Autumn 1963 issue of *Arion*; for an inept one, L. Proudfoot's *Dryden's Aeneid and Its Seventeenth-Century Predecessors,* Manchester, 1960.)

The eighteenth century is represented by Addison, Swift, Pope, Johnson, Walpole, by the great scholar Porson in a convivial mood, by Kit Smart, and by W. Guthrie, who has done the best complete translation of Cicero's speeches. The nineteenth century makes the slimmest contribution—Baron Byron and Edgar Poe. But our century is represented by A. E. Housman, Alfred Noyes, Louis Zukovsky, Ezra Pound, Louis MacNeice, Horace Gregory, Robert Fitzgerald, Robert Lowell, and John Updike—a list that lends an air of unreality to the old question "Is Latin a living influence?"

Naturally, each period and each translator made a different set of decisions about the liberty proper to a translator. I have let these stand, along with errors caused by old editions or faulty classical equipment. But I have, with some reluctance, excluded outright "adaptation"— reluctantly because this meant Johnson's Juvenalian reveries were not eligible, nor Shirley's dramatic treatment of Ovid's "Contest of Arms," nor Swift's Hogarthian retelling of the Baucis and Philemon story. The only borderline case I have admitted is the "Birth of Hercules"—comedy must be put in instantly effective form if it is to be played (as anyone knows who has gone to a modern presentation of Plautus). Pound's Propertius is an admitted adaptation (or "homage"), but I have included only some excerpts that stay close to the original.

I have tried to soften, somewhat, the chronological jumble by some modernizing of spelling and punctuation. I have even sneaked a gloss into the text of some older passages, rather than resort to learned apparatus in a book where it does not belong. The English texts thus produced are not scholarly ones. The titles appended to all pieces are also mine.

PART I

The Fields and Their Gods

What we think of as "pastoral"—nostalgia for the land—was created when Vergil moved from the Alexandrian conceits of his Eclogues *to the romantic realism of the* Georgics. *Theocritus' Greek idylls are a sophisticated game; the Hesiodic material is too close to the land to yearn for it—it wrestles with the seasons and the soil. But Vergil, scanning the landscape with an observant eye, is also looking for a lost Eden. He brings night and storm into the idyll. He has a brooding empathy with the landscape and its animals—as in this cawing line followed by a stiff-legged, stalking line:*

Tum cornix plena pluviam vocat improba voce
et sola in sicca secum spatiatur harena.

Georgics 1.388-89

Raucous, contemplating rain, the crow
picks its lonely prints out in the sand.

The Georgics *are Vergil's most intensely Roman work. Rome was a thing apart from the surrounding countryside, forever longing to rejoin it. The city ruled the world, but the country haunted the city. The Romans themselves thought that their best qualities had been brought in from the fields (or, more likely, left there); especially their religion. Its deepest currents ran under cultivated fields, a religion of the hearth and of the furrow.*

Even the gods they borrowed from the Greeks take on a native air after a while: Hermes, in becoming Mercury, becomes something close to Puck (see pp. 84-94). The difference between the two sets of gods was put this way by Gilbert Chesterton:

the Greek polytheism branched and blossomed upwards like the boughs of a tree, while the Italian polytheism ramified downward like the roots. Perhaps it would be truer to say that the former branches lifted themselves lightly, bearing

flowers; while the latter hung down, being heavy with fruit
. . . What strikes us in the Italian cults is their local and
especially their domestic character. We gain the impression
of divinities swarming about the house like flies; clustering
and clinging like bats about the pillars or building like birds
under the eaves . . . It was the god of the corn and not of
the grass, of the cattle and not the wild things of the forest;
in short the cult was literally a culture; as when we speak of
agriculture.

*These clustering deities could become oppressive—as St.
Augustine remarks of the divine mob scene Roman religion
made out of the bridal chamber (p. 96). But even St. Augustine,
in his African church, had a special Roman affection for
the metaphor used by the Christian God: "I am the vine."*

SKIES

[Of Dawn's team]:
wide nostrils
whinnying day.

I gaze there up
through structured
liquidness of air.

Autumn eases summer, then,
the sheering Hiems' edge.

Where the push
of leaning mountain
first picks it out
is Night.

The time for nothing, Night,
held light in its high prison.

What echoes in
night's resonating shield?
　　The Wagon lashes on and on
　　its starry team.

49

White wheel of lights
articulating dark air.

Ennius, *Fragments* (G. W.)

COSMIC SYMPATHIES

And that by certain signs we may presage
Of heats and rains, and wind's impetuous rage,
The sov'reign of the heav'ns has set on high
The moon, to mark the changes of the sky;
When southern blasts should cease, and when the swain
Should near their fold his feeding flocks restrain.
For, ere the rising winds begin to roar,
The working seas advance to wash the shore;
Soft whispers run along the leavy woods,
And mountains whistle to the murm'ring floods.
Ev'n then the doubtful billows scarce abstain
From the toss'd vessel on the troubled main;
When crying cormorants forsake the sea,
And stretching to the covert wing their way;
When sportful coots run skimming o'er the strand;
When watchful herons leave their wat'ry stand,
And mounting upward, with erected flight,
Gain on the skies, and soar above the sight.
And oft, before tempest'ous winds arise,
The seeming stars fall headlong from the skies,
And, shooting thro' the darkness, gild the night
With sweeping glories, and long trails of light;
And chaff with eddy-winds is whirl'd around,
And dancing leaves are lifted from the ground;
And floating feathers on the waters play.

. . .

Wet weather seldom hurts the most unwise;
So plain the signs, such prophets are the skies.
The wary crane foresees it first, and sails

50

Above the storm, and leaves the lowly vales;
The cow looks up, and from afar can find
The change of heav'n, and snuffs it in the wind;
The swallow skims the river's wat'ry face;
The frogs renew the croaks of their loquacious race;
The careful ant her secret cell forsakes,
And drags her eggs along the narrow tracks:
At either horn the rainbow drinks the flood;
Huge flocks of rising rooks forsake their food,
And, crying, seek the shelter of the wood.
Besides, the sev'ral sorts of wat'ry fowls
That swim the seas, or haunt the standing pools,
The swans that sail along the silver flood,
And dive with stretching necks to search their food,
Then lave their backs with sprinkling dews in vain,
And stem the stream to meet the promis'd rain.
The crow with clam'rous cries the show'r demands,
And single stalks along the desert sands.

.   .   .

Not that I think their breasts with heav'nly souls
Inspir'd, as man, who destiny controls;
But with the changeful temper of the skies,
As rains condense, and sunshine rarefies,
So turn the species in their alter'd minds,
Compos'd by calms, and discompos'd by winds.

Vergil, *Georgics* 1.351-69,
373-89, 415-22 (John Dryden)

LOVE DRIVES THE UNIVERSE

I

Mother of Rome, delight of gods and men,
Beloved Venus, who under the fleeting stars
Fillest the freighted sea and earth's ripe fields,

O since through thee alone all forms of life
Are born, and climb into the sun's sweet light,
Goddess, before whose lovely advancing feet
The winds and towering clouds scatter and flee,
And the labouring earth discloses odorous flowers,
And the sea falls into a shining calm,
And the assuaged heavens mellow with light.
For when the spring-like face of day awakes,
And the West Wind, unloosed, flies procreant forth,
Then first the coursing birds, smitten at heart,
Betray, Lady, thy entrance and thy power,
And then the beasts caper in happy pastures
And swim swift floods; so all created things,
Captive to thee, drawn by their own desire,
Stray through the world where'er thy presence leads.
Through all the seas and hills and swelling streams,
Wing-fluttering woods and green, luxuriant plains,
Thou harryest them with lust, that none shall fail
To carry their eternal races on.

Lucretius, *On Reality* 1.1-20
(J. C. Squire)

I I

Tomorrow, tomorrow shall earth's ears be lent to Love's
command.

Fresh from the year's grave
spring comes singing, and hear: like birds
the lovers fly together where the wood, in green
shower, unbinds her hair like rain
fall. Joined in love, the lovers lie
under the green shade of roof and flowering wall,
tomorrow, when each shall sing with Love, love tomorrow.

Remember . . . the eastern sea lay shivering; then
Love leapt from firmament and arching foam,
dark and strutting with two-legged horse
in a rain of love. Tomorrow
let Love dance with the world, love tomorrow.

Look: now Love embosses this dark year with flowers.
Young buds lean to the breast of the westwind
and night, withdrawing, spatters their warm
clusters with dew; shaken from the clear eyes of night,
shivering, one by one each perfect tear falls
and dissolves their lingering shrouds for dawn.
Flushed by Love's blood and Desire's mouth,
color of the sun, of jewels, of flames
which shoot from your warm bed,
oh rose, veiled within your damp shroud,
open yourself to Love's command and
this new morning, naked and untouched, so
as a bride come forth in fiery veil,
burning with Love's seed, all burning, love tomorrow.

Desire at their sides, fresh girls go
to consecrated grove and call of Love.
Unarmed, Desire keeps the holiday
of Love. Go with him, girls, in play
his weapons lie forgotten;
unclothed he will appear, commanded, and unarmed
with arrow, spear, or flame, he seems
so harmless—but watch girls, when Desire plays
unarmed, unclothed, it looks so
charming, and Love calls to all, love tomorrow.

Virgin, Love sends you unbroken girls to ask
your hunting cease, to keep unstained
your wooded sanctuary. Love only asks
if modesty can bend: then that you join her
if it is time. For you may see the three
long nights of dancing celebration, and
laughing crowds push through your sacred wood,
under your green roof, flowers in their hair.
Look: here's wheat and wine. The long night
rings with song. Love reigns in the woods,
Virgin, come or leave us alone, tomorrow,
when Love leads the world, love tomorrow.

Love speaks her laws from high, flowering Hybla,
summons Pleasure to her side. Hybla, dress your sides

53

with flowers to your feet. Pour forth with flowers
whatever one whole year can bring. Turn your face
from naked Lust and come
from the fields, the mountains, and the forests,
from little woods, from springs, from wherever you
may be, to sit by her, the mother of Desire, tomorrow
when Love springs up in the world, love tomorrow.

To the force of fresh-sprung flowers
Love will add a green shade;
tomorrow the elemental air will embrace
the earth, when he, the cloud-born, fathers
the spring's new year, when he, concealed
in rain, flows through the loins of his fond love,
when he, over that great form, fills the earth
with seed and guards its growth.
She, with secret strength, fires the spirit,
governs the mind and flesh for love.
She floods the easy path with flowering seed,
led through sky, through earth, and through the waters.
She orders the world in knowledge of the ways of birth,
tomorrow, when the world is realized in Love, love
       tomorrow.

Through her the Trojans came among the Latins.
Lavinia went in marriage to her son.
Through her the virgin gave way to War.
She joined the Romans with the Sabines; stem
of Ramnes and of Quirites, and great Romulus,
beginning of her line, great Caesar, end.
Tomorrow, all your children, all earth's people, love
       tomorrow.

Look now, the bulls wallow in the yellow grass,
when all, in joy, are joined in love. In the shade
see the rams run with the flock; Love lends the birds
their songs. And now in the marsh the swan calls
his rough cry, and under the shade of a poplar,
the nightingale answers his song with her own song
of love so sweetly, you could not believe she sings
to light the guilt of her barbaric lord.

54

She sings, we are quiet. When shall my spring
come? When will my silence end, when
may I sing as the swallow? My talent is lost in silence,
poetry gives me no second glance. And
those who sit in silence die in silence, tomorrow,
tomorrow, when earth's ears are lent to Love's command, love
     tomorrow.

Anonymous, *Vigil of Venus' Feast*
(E. D. Blodgett and H. O. Weber)

SNOWBOUND

Swift rivers are with sudden ice constrained,
And studded wheels are on its back sustained—
A hostry now for waggons, which before
Tall ships of burden on its bosom bore.
The brazen cauldrons with the frost are flawed;
The garment, stiff with ice, at hearths is thawed;
With axes first they cleave the wine; and thence,
By weight, the solid portions they dispense.
From locks uncombed, and from the frozen beard,
Long icicles depend, and crackling sounds are heard.
Meantime perpetual sleet and driving snow
Obscure the skies, and hang on herds below.
The starving cattle perish in their stalls;
Huge oxen stand inclosed in wintry walls
Of snow congealed; whole herds are buried there
Of mighty stags, and scarce their horns appear.

Vergil, *Georgics* 3.360-70 (John Dryden)

THE SNOW'S SERMON

See high Soracte etched in snow
and, below, the branches whitely wrestled down,
the rivulet's swift–soft splintered into hard–still.
(Brrr! another log, warm us,
another, more logs, Thaliarchus,

55

7. Etruscan wolf, with modern Romulus and Remus. Rome, Museo dei Conservatori.

The city ruled the world; but the countryside haunted the city.

and wine with four summers in it.)

> Can gods bring peace
> upon seas civil-warring with themselves,
> and draw the thin unwavering lines of ash
> or cypress up in unstirred air?
> No reason—(why? shall we see it?)
> —to wait for that.
> Wrest what warmth one can
> from every moment, take youth
> as it passes, join the dance
> before it ends, before you whiten
> into human winter.

The open fields, the city streets,
the assignation made, the night
filled with whispers—take life's spring!
(Where is she hiding?—
follow the trail of laughter
she left as a clue,
be fooled by pretty resistance,
fight the ring from her finger
before she has time to give it to you.)

Horace, *Songs* 1.9 (G. W.)

COUNTRY OVER CITY

I

Once on a time (so runs the fable)
A country mouse, right hospitable,
Receiv'd a town mouse at his board,
Just as a farmer might a lord.
A frugal mouse upon the whole,
Yet lov'd his friend, and had a soul;
Knew what was handsome, and would do 't
(On just occasion) *coute qui coute.*

He brought him bacon (nothing lean),
Pudding that might have pleased a dean,
Cheese such as men in Suffolk make
(But wished it Stilton, for his sake).
Yet to his guest tho' no way sparing,
He ate himself the rind and paring.
Our courtier scarce could touch a bit,
But showed his breeding and his wit:
He did his best to seem to eat,
And cried "I vow you're mighty neat.
But Lord, my friend, this savage scene!
For God's sake, come and live with men.
Consider, mice (like men) must die,
Both small and great, both you and I:
Then spend your life in joy and sport,
(This doctrine, friend, I learnt at court)."

The veriest hermit in the nation
May yield, God knows, to strong temptation.
Away they come, thro' thick and thin,
To a tall house near Lincoln's Inn
('Twas on the night of a debate,
When all their lordships had sat late).

Behold the place, where if a poet
Shined in description, he might show it,
Tell how the moon beam trembling falls
And tips with silver all the walls—
Palladian walls, Venetian doors,
Grotesco roofs, and stucco floors . . .
But let it (in a word) be said:
The moon was up, and men abed,
The napkins white, the carpet red,
The guests withdrawn had left the treat.
And down the mice sat, *tête à tête*.

Our courtier walks from dish to dish,
Tastes for his friend of fowl and fish,
Tells all their names, lays down the law:
"Que ça est bon! Ah goutez ça!
That jelly's rich, this malmsey healing.

Pray dip your whiskers and your tail in."
Was ever such a happy swain?
He stuffs and swills, and stuffs again.
"I'm quite ashamed—'tis mighty rude
To eat so much—but all's so good.
I have a thousand thanks to give—
My lord alone knows how to live."

No sooner said, but from the hall
Rush chaplain, butler, dogs and all:
"A rat, a rat! Clap to the door."
O for the heart of Homer's mice,
Or gods to save them in a trice!
(It *was* by providence, they think,
For your damned stucco has no chink.)

"An 't please your honor," quoth the peasant,
"This same dessert is not so pleasant.
Give me again my hollow tree,
A crust of bread—and liberty."

Horace, *Satires* 2.6, lines 80-117
(Alexander Pope)

II

I will, as briefly as I may,
The sweets of liberty display:

A wolf half famished, chanced to see
A dog, as fat as dog could be
(For one day meeting on the road,
They mutual compliments bestowed):

"Prithee," says Isgrim, faint and weak,
"How came you so well fed and sleek?
I starve, though stronger of the two."

"It will be just as well with you,"
The dog quite cool and frank replied,
"If with my master you'll abide."

"For what?"

59

"Why, merely to attend,
And from night-thieves the door defend."

"I gladly will accept the post.
Why shall I bear with snow and frost,
And all this rough inclement plight,
Rather than have a home at night,
And feed on plenty at my ease?"

"Come then with me."

      The wolf agrees.
But as they went the mark he found
Where the dog's collar had been bound:
"What's this, my friend?"

         "Why, nothing."

            "Nay,

Be more explicit, sir, I pray."

"I'm somewhat fierce and apt to bite,
Therefore they hold me pretty tight,
That in the daytime I may sleep,
And night by night my vigils keep.
At eveningtide they let me out,
And then I freely walk about.
Bread comes without a care of mine;
I from my master's table dine.
The servants throw me many a scrap,
With choice of pot-liquor to lap;
So I've a bellyful, you find."

"But can you go where you've a mind?"

"Not always, to be flat and plain."

"Then, dog, enjoy your post again.
For to remain this servile thing,
Old Isgrim would not be a king."

        Phaedrus, *Fables* 3.6
        (Christopher Smart)

III

You ask me how my farm can pay,
　　Since little it will bear.
It pays me thus—'Tis far away,
　　And you are never there.

　　　　　　　Martial, *Epigrams* 2.38 (J. A. Pott)

FIELD OFFERING

If suppliant palms, upraised at the sacrifice,
Placate the gods, my field-weary Phidyle,
　　At each new moon, if hard-won first-fruits
　　Plead, and the darkening blood between them,

Fear, then, no more that wind out of Africa!
What need hast thou of costlier offerings?
　　Far, far from here, though the axe be waiting,
　　Feeds upon Alba the Pontiff's victim.

Our Lares ask—no gift of thy lowlihead!—
Crown them with sprays of myrtle and rosemary!
　　Their small bright statues, no less kindly,
　　Cherish your hearth and your clustering vineyard.

O guiltless hands, your touch on the altar-stone
Moves all the heavens, though nothing of cost you bring,
　　But crackling salt and sacred wheat-cake,
　　Piously flung to the dying embers.

　　　　　　　Horace, *Songs* 3.23 (Alfred Noyes)

UMBRIA

Forever you ask me who, of what quality, what locality
　　are the holy spirits of my ancestors, Tullus,
　　　in the name of friendship forever.
You know if you know Perusia, the grave of the fatherland,
　　deathplace of Italy in the hard season when Roman
　　　disunion drove the citizens

61

(You foremost grieve me, Tuscan dust, who let my kinsman's
body be dumped without a crumb of your dirt to cover the
 bones).
 You may know that it was Umbria,
at the nearest point, Tullus, impinging upon
the plain below, that begot me. Fertile Umbria, a milky land.

Propertius, *Elegies* 1.22 (Richard E. Braun)

THE TILLED BATTLEGROUND

Then, after length of time, the labouring swains
Who turn the turfs of those unhappy plains,
Shall rusty piles from the ploughed furrows take,
And over empty helmets pass the rake—
Amazed at antique titles on the stones,
And mighty relics of gigantic bones.

Vergil, *Georgics* 1.493-97 (John Dryden)

FARM LABOR: NIGHT SCENE

Some works in dead of night are better done,
Or when the morning dew prevents the sun.
Parched meads and stubble, mow by Phoebe's light,
Which both require the coolness of the night;
For moisture then abounds, and pearly rains
Descend in silence to refresh the plains.
The wife and husband equally conspire
To work by night, and rake the winter fire:
He sharpens torches in the glimmering room;
She shoots the flying shuttle through the loom,
Or boils in kettles must of wine, and skims
With leaves the dregs that overflow the brims,
And till the watchful cock awakes the day,
She sings to drive the tedious hours away.

Vergil, *Georgics* 1.287-96 (John Dryden)

NOCTURNE

Night fell and weary bodies everywhere
Sought rest. The woods and the killing seas were still,
The stars mild in mid-orbit—all nature rested,
The beasts and the colored birds and whatever widely
The lapsing waters hide or the hard earth holds in thicket,
All were enthralled in sleep.

Vergil, *The Song of Aeneas* 4.522-29
(Patric Dickinson)

DEATH AND NIGHT

Angel-inhabitants of heaven, be glad!
Be glad, God's hidden world!
Where the king has conquered,
let the trumpet sound our rescue!
Joy, too, for earth, touched with lightning-brilliances,
limned in the everlasting monarch's light!
Earth, savor your release
from the encircling murkiness.

Paschal night this,
and this the Lamb, whose blood
makes doors of chosen ones inviolable.

This the night
You led our fathers out of Egypt, sons of Israel
who walked with dry feet through the sea.

This the night
whose fiery pillar burned sin's darkness from the world.

This the night
that from the present age's evil and dark sin
brings Christ's faithful back to pardon,
makes them, wherever they are, one holy company.

This the night
in which, death's fetters shattered,
Christ rose from hell in triumph,
gave us rebirth where first birth was but death.

This, Your strange deference over us,
this love without traceable limit,
this liberation of a slave by the ransom of a son,
shows us why Adam had to sin:
that Christ might cancel that sin by his death.
Blessed Fall!—
to bring us such a rescuer!
Indeed a blessed night
which knew the secret time of Christ's return from death.

.   .   .

This is the night
of the scripture:
"Night's light will be daylight . . .
a night to brighten all my happiness."
This night's sanctuary, then,
wards off sin, washes guilt away,
lifts the fallen into innocence, consoles the sad,
dispels hate, settles peace, breaks pride.

St. Ambrose (?), *Blessing
of the Paschal Candle* (G. W.)

EXILED FROM THE LAND

While you, Tityrus, under leaves that riddle light
think through your thin reed a woodland song,
I lose my fatherland, my labored earth;
exiled from fields, while you, slumbrous in shadow,
send modulated "Amaryllis" through the leaves
and hear them whisper her to you again.

.   .   .

Happy who looks out on the land and calls it his
in his old age;
calls it enough, though pastures run too soon
against hard rock, or down
to soft mud's weediness.
Her own familiar grass the pregnant ewe
will ever crop, no strange flocks
will infect her as she strays.
Happy, in old age, you the intimate
of streams, of haunted fountains.
Shade cools you as the Hybla bees renew
their everlasting robbery of the shrub
delineating your land and the next—
whose buzz will billow you in sleep,
as breezes waft your workman's songs
out from the rock where his vines are,
and pigeons you have raised
screech muffledly, while the dove's
soft querulousness fills the air
around her elm.

Vergil, *Eclogues* 1.1-5,
46-58 (G. W.)

THE SHEPHERD'S DEATH

Daphnis is dead. Now, nymphs, weep mournfully,
The hazel trees and rivers saw him die.
Daphnis is dead, and, near, his mother cries
To all the gods, the stars. No shepherd drives
His flock through field or stream. No beast will pass
To drink from icy pool or crop the grass.
Daphnis, the woods and dreaded hills have said
That the fierce lion weeps since you are dead.
You told us Asian tigers draw the god's
Swift chariot. We followed you and trod
The fields in Bacchic dance and wove soft leaves
With wands. As wild vines tangling crown the trees,
Grapes grace the vine, the bull the herd, and corn-

Sheaves glitter in the grass, so you adorned
Your comrades. Fate has seized you. Now the fields
Are empty of the rural gods. Now yields
The furrow, which we sowed with barley seed,
Unfruitful darnel. And the wild oats breed.
Where waving violets and narcissus grew
Are brambly shrubs. Here softly, shepherd, strew
The ground with leaves, the fountain, there, with shade;
He'd like it so.

Vergil, *Eclogues* 5.20-41
(Anne Greet)

TRITON

Then ocean's master called to sea-wreathed Triton
Who at echo of Neptune's voice came from the sea
Like a tower of sea-green beard, sea creatures,
Sea shells, grey waters sliding from his green shoulders
To sound his horn, to wind the gliding rivers
Back to their sources, back to rills and streams.
At Neptune's order Triton lifted up
His curved sea shell, a trumpet at his lips
Which in the underworld of deepest seas
Sounds Triton's music to the distant shores
Behind the morning and the evening suns;
And as his voice was heard through land and ocean
The floods and rivers moved at his command.
Over all earth the shores of lakes appeared
Hillsides and river banks, wet fields and meadow,
As floods receded and quays came into view:
A cliff, then a plateau, a hill, a meadow,
As from a tomb a forest rose and then
One saw trees with lean seaweeds tangled
Among their glittering leaves and wave-tossed boughs.

Ovid, *Transformations* 1.331-47
(Horace Gregory)

66

ARGO, THE HEROIC SHIP

On Pelion's top one time were born the pines
(men say) that sparkling swam the Neptune-waves
to Phasis' floods and confines Aeetean,
when picked young men, oaks of the Argive youth,
the golden fleece of Colchis prayed to steal,
down the salt deeps dared race their nimble craft,
and swept the bright blue sea with piney palms.
for them the goddess of forts on city heights
herself made up the light wind flying car,
and joining a weft of deal to an inbent keel
first taught the unlettered Sea to be a road.
      Soon as her bow slashed through the windy plain,
and wrenched by oars the wave grew white with foam,
up faces rose from out the main's white swirl,
sea-daughters, Nereids, at the portent wond'ring.
that day, if e'er, men saw with mortal eye
the daughters of the deep, the naked nymphs,
breast-high uprising from the hoary swirl.

Catullus, *Songs* 64.1-18 (Frank O. Copley)

THE TREE THAT RODE THE WORLD

This racer of the watery plain
Could once outstrip the fleetest sail
With oary fins to swim the main
Or winged with canvas, fly before the gale.

On Pontus streams she freely rides,
Whom roots once fastened to the shore;
And, turned a tenant of the tides,
Reviews the mountains where she grew before,

Where once she stood a living shade,
And (veiled in clouds) her head did rear,
Her verdant tresses round her played,
Sung to the wind, and danced in open air.

Of old, Cytorus-top she crowned;
And, at his bottom while she moves,
Renews acquaintance with the ground,
Her kindred trees, and her coeval groves.

Here, where she tempted first the tides,
And crept on unexperienced oars;
On bounding billows toss'd she rides,
Secure on surges, as of old on shores—

Whether when, hovering in the sky,
The wandering winds did loosely blow;
Or sweeping from all quarters fly
When Jove abroad on all their wings would go.

At last she left the stormy seas,
But to no gods her vows did make,
Till now her vessel, laid at ease,
Sleeps on the bosom of the gentle lake.

Here her old age its rest obtains,
Secure from all the watery war;
And consecrates its last remains
To thee, bright Castor, and thy brother star.

Catullus, *Songs* 4 (Alexander Pope)

DEATH OF A SAILOR

Ahead of all the master pilot steers;
And, as he leads, the following navy veers.
The steeds of Night had travel'd half the sky,
The drowsy rowers on their benches lie,
When the soft God of Sleep, with easy flight,
Descends, and draws behind a trail of light.
Thou, Palinurus, art his destin'd prey;
To thee alone he takes his fatal way.
Dire dreams to thee, and iron sleep, he bears;
And, lighting on the prow, the form of Phorbas wears.
Then thus the traitor god began his tale:

"The winds, my friend, inspire a pleasing gale;
The ships, without thy care, securely sail.
Now steal an hour of sweet repose; and I
Will take the rudder and thy room supply."
To whom the yawning pilot, half asleep:
"Me dost thou bid to trust the treach'rous deep,
The harlot smiles of her dissembling face,
And to her faith commit the Trojan race?
Shall I believe the Siren South again,
And, oft betray'd, not know the monster main?"
He said: his fasten'd hands the rudder keep,
And, fix'd on heav'n, his eyes repel invading sleep.
The god was wroth, and at his temples threw
A branch in Lethe dipp'd, and drunk with Stygian dew:
The pilot, vanquish'd by the pow'r divine,
Soon clos'd his swimming eyes, and lay supine.
Scarce were his limbs extended at their length,
The god, insulting with superior strength,
Fell heavy on him, plung'd him in the sea,
And, with the stern, the rudder tore away.
Headlong he fell, and, struggling in the main,
Cried out for helping hands, but cried in vain.
The victor daemon mounts obscure in air,
While the ship sails without the pilot's care.
On Neptune's faith the floating fleet relies;
But what the man forsook, the god supplies,
And o'er the dang'rous deep secure the navy flies;
Glides by the Sirens' cliffs, a shelfy coast,
Long infamous for ships and sailors lost,
And white with bones. Th' impetuous ocean roars,
And rocks rebellow from the sounding shores.
The watchful hero felt the knocks, and found
The tossing vessel sail'd on shoaly ground.
Sure of his pilot's loss, he takes himself
The helm, and steers aloof, and shuns the shelf.

Vergil, *The Song of Aeneas*
5.833-68 (John Dryden)

69

8. Dog. Rome, Museo Vaticano.

Nor opening hounds . . .

9. Stag and hound. Rome, Museo Vaticano.

. . . the trembling stag affright.

KINSHIP WITH ANIMALS

"O impious use! to Nature's laws oppos'd,
Where bowels are in other bowels clos'd;
Where, fatten'd by their fellows' fat, they thrive,
Maintain'd by murder, and by death they live.
'T is then for naught that Mother Earth provides
The stores of all she shows, and all she hides,
If men with fleshy morsels must be fed,
And chaw with bloody teeth the breathing bread:
What else is this but to devour our guests,
And barb'rously renew Cyclopean feasts!
We, by destroying life, our life sustain,
And gorge th' ungodly maw with meats obscene.
    "Not so the Golden Age, who fed on fruit,
Nor durst with bloody meals their mouths pollute:
Then birds in airy space might safely move,
And timorous hares on heaths securely rove;
Nor needed fish the guileful hooks to fear,
For all was peaceful, and that peace sincere.
Whoever was the wretch (and curst be he)
That envied first our food's simplicity,
Th' essay of bloody feasts on brutes began,
And after forg'd the sword to murther man.
Had he the sharpen'd steel alone employ'd
On beasts of prey that other beasts destroy'd,
Or man invaded with their fangs and paws,
This had been justified by Nature's laws,
And self-defense; but who did feasts begin
Of flesh, he stretch'd necessity to sin.
To kill man-killers, man has lawful pow'r,
But not th' extended license to devour.

.   .   .

O tyrant! with what justice canst thou hope
The promise of the year, a plenteous crop
When thou destroy'st thy lab'ring steer, who till'd
And plow'd with pains thy else ungrateful field?

72

From his yet reeking neck to draw the yoke,
(That neck with which the surly clods he broke,)
And to the hatchet yield thy husbandman,
Who finish'd autumn, and the spring began!
    "Nor this alone! but, Heav'n itself to bribe,
We to the gods our impious acts ascribe;
First recompense with death their creatures' toil,
Then call the blest above to share the spoil.
The fairest victim must the pow'rs appease;
(So fatal 't is sometimes too much to please!)
A purple fillet his broad brows adorns,
With flow'ry garlands crown'd, and gilded horns.
He hears the murd'rous pray'r the priest prefers,
But understands not, 't is his doom he hears;
Beholds the meal betwixt his temples cast,
(The fruit and product of his labors past;)
And in the water views, perhaps, the knife
Uplifted, to deprive him of his life;
Then, broken up alive, his entrails sees,
Torn out for priests t' inspect the god's decrees.

·   ·   ·

Let plow thy steers; that, when they lose their breath,
To nature, not to thee, they may impute their death.
Let goats for food their loaded udders lend,
And sheep from winter cold thy sides defend;
But neither springes, nets, nor snares employ,
And be no more ingenious to destroy.
Free, as in air, let birds on earth remain,
Nor let insidious glue their wings constrain;
Nor opening hounds the trembling stag affright,
Nor purple feathers intercept his flight;
Nor hooks conceal'd in baits for fish prepare,
Nor lines to heave 'em twinkling up in air.
    "Take not away the life you cannot give;
For all things have an equal right to live.
Kill noxious creatures, where 't is sin to save;
This only just prerogative we have:

But nourish life with vegetable food,
And shun the sacrilegious taste of blood."

> Ovid, *Transformations* 15.87-110,
> 122-37, 470-78 (John Dryden)

THE WORM

I could descant in all candor on the glories of the worm, when I look at its glancing color, its perfect corporal rotundity, its intermeshing of end with middle, middle with end, each contributing something to a thrust toward one-ness in this lowest of things, so that there is no part that does not answer to another part harmoniously. And what of the principle of life effervescing its melodious order through this body?— its rhythmic activation of the whole, its quest for that which serves its life, its triumph over or revulsion from whatever menaces it, its reference of all things to a normative center of self-preservation, bearing a witness more striking than the body's to the creative unity that upholds all things in nature?

> St. Augustine, *The True Religion* 77 (G. W.)

THE BEES

I

As when the Cyclops, at the almighty nod,
New thunder hasten for their angry god,
Subdued in fire the stubborn metal lies;
One brawny smith the puffing bellows plies,
And draws and blows reciprocating air:
Others to quench the hissing mass prepare:
With lifted arms they order every blow,
And chime their sounding hammers in a row:
With laboured anvils Aetna groans below.
Strongly they strike; huge flakes of flame expire;
With tongs they turn the steel, and vex it in the fire—

74

If little things with great we may compare,
Such are the bees, and such their busy care.
Studious of honey each in his degree,
The youthful swain, the grave experienced bee—
That in the field; this, in affairs of state
Employed at home, abides within the gate,
To fortify the combs, to build the wall,
To prop the ruins, lest the fabric fall:
But, late at night, with weary pinions come
The labouring youth, and heavy laden, home.
Plains, meads, and orchards, all the day he plies;
The gleans of yellow thyme distend his thighs:
He spoils the saffron flowers; he sips the blues
Of violets, wilding blooms, and willow dews.

Induced by such examples, some have taught
That bees have portions of ethereal thought—
Endued with particles of heavenly fires;
For God the whole created mass inspires.
Through heaven, and earth, and ocean's depth, he throws
His influence round, and kindles as he goes.
Hence flocks, and herds, and men, and beasts, and fowls,
With breath are quickened, and attract their souls;
Hence take the forms his prescience did ordain,
And into him at length resolve again.
No room is left for death: they mount the sky,
And to their own congenial planets fly.

Vergil, *Georgics* 4.170-83,
219-27 (John Dryden)

II

Father, for this gracious night of pardon
take the evening incense-offer
your hallowed gathering returns to you—
the stately oblation of this wax
wrought from the labor of bees,

brought forward, now, by your priests.
We accept this pillar's preaching
as the bright light fires it in God's honor,
fire dispersed to tapers
yet undiminished at its source
(for it drinks the strength of wax
which the mother bee brought forth
to hold the light upon this precious stand).

St. Ambrose (?), *Blessing
of the Paschal Candle* (G. W.)

STALLION

The colt that for a stallion is design'd
By sure presages shows his generous kind;
Of able body, sound of limb and wind.
Upright he walks, on pasterns firm and straight;
His motions easy; prancing in his gait;
The first to lead the way, to tempt the flood,
To pass the bridge unknown, nor fear the trembling wood;
Dauntless at empty noises; lofty neck'd
Sharp-headed, barrel-bellied, broadly back'd;
Brawny his chest, and deep; his color gray;
For beauty, dappled, or the brightest bay:
Faint white and dun will scarce the rearing pay.
      The fiery courser, when he hears from far
The sprightly trumpets and the shouts of war,
Pricks up his ears; and, trembling with delight,
Shifts place, and paws, and hopes the promis'd fight.
On his right shoulder his thick mane, reclin'd,
Ruffles at speed, and dances in the wind.
His horny hoofs are jetty black and round;
His chine is double; starting, with a bound
He turns the turf, and shakes the solid ground.
Fire from his eyes, clouds from his nostrils flow:
He bears his rider headlong on the foe.
      Such was the steed in Grecian poets fam'd,
Proud Cyllarus, by Spartan Pollux tam'd:

Such coursers bore to fight the god of Thrace;
And such, Achilles, was thy warlike race.
In such a shape, grim Saturn did restrain
His heav'nly limbs, and flow'd with such a mane,
When, half-surpris'd, and fearing to be seen,
The lecher gallop'd from his jealous queen,
Ran up the ridges of the rocks amain,
And with shrill neighings fill'd the neighb'ring plain.
    But, worn with years, when dire diseases come,
Then hide his not ignoble age at home,
In peace t' enjoy his former palms and pains;
And gratefully be kind to his remains.
For, when his blood no youthful spirits move,
He languishes and labors in his love;
And, when the sprightly seed should swiftly come,
Dribbling he drudges, and defrauds the womb:
In vain he burns, like hasty stubble fires,
And in himself his former self requires.

Vergil, Georgics 3.75-100 (John Dryden)

THE MONKEY

In all matters, great and small, we take differences of *degree* and give
them names signifying *opposition.* Thus, because man's frame is more
beautiful than a monkey's, we call the monkey's lesser beauty a non-
beauty, and the thoughtless are tricked into thinking man aesthetically
good and monkeys aesthetically bad. They do not fathom the propriety
of measure in a monkey, the correspondence of left limbs with right, the
nexus of parts, the instinctual defense of itself as a unit, and other things
too lengthy to catalogue. But to establish the point even for those of
slow wits, and to make those who resist truth admit to the truth:—ask
them if rotting will disfigure a monkey. If so, then it can grow less pleasing. But what is erased in this process other than beauty, part of which
will remain as long as there is something of the body left to rot? So if
the body itself is obliterated as its beauty disappears, then it was itself a
good and beautiful thing.

St. Augustine, The Meaning
of the Good 14-15 (G. W.)

77

FIGHTING COCKS

Outside we saw gamecocks sharpening toward a scrap. We had to watch; for what horizon do eyes of love not scan, hoping for a hint of reason's beautiful scheme, which checks and impels all things (whether they realize it or not), a scheme that makes its observer quick to respond wherever it beckons?—for it can flash its signals out of anything, in anything. In, for instance, these cocks: the thrust of their heads toward battle, their lifted crests, their darting attacks, skilled parries; pure animal action without mind, yet how apt, every move; for a higher mind works through them, ordering all things. At the last, the victor's right: the exultant crowing, a body taut with pride of power. And the rites of defeat—limp wings, carriage and croak gone awry; all strangely fitting and, by this consonance with nature's set way, beautiful.

St. Augustine, *On Order* 1.25 (G. W.)

COCK-CROW

Builder eternally of things,
Thou rulest over night and day,
Disposing time in separate times
That Thou mayst lessen weariness;

Now crows the herald of the day,
Watchful throughout the wasting dark,
To walkers in the night a clock
Marking the hours of dark and dawn.

The morning star arises now
To free the obscure firmament;
Now every gang and prowling doom
Forsakes the dark highways of harm.

The sailor now regathers strength,
The channels of the sea grow calm;
And now Peter, the living rock,
Washes his guilt in the last crow.

Then quickly let us rise and go;
The cock stirs up the sleepy-head,

78

And chides again the lie-a-bed;
The cock convicts them who deny.

And to cock-crow our hopes reply;
Thy grace refills our ailing hearts;
The sword of brigandage is hid;
And faith returns where faith had fled.

Jesu, look back on us who fall,
Straighten the conduct of our life;
If Thou lookst back, denials fail,
And guilt is melted in a tear.

Thou Light, illumine with Thy light
Our sleeping lethargy of soul;
Thy name the first our lips shall choose.
Discharging thus our vows to Thee.

St. Ambrose, *Hymn* (J. V. Cunningham)

EAGLE

Have you seen the feathered servant of the lightning,
Made by the king of gods king of his wandering
   Kind for his trusty part
In kidnapping the blond boy Ganymede?—

Young blood and eagle's energy first launch him
Out of the nest to meet a sky of troubles,
   And the spring winds conspire,
Now storms are past, to teach his timid wings

Airy adventures. Soon his great sweep sends him
Plummeting down to terrify the sheepfold,
   Or, rage- and hunger-driven,
He lugs the wrestling serpent in his grip.

Horace, *Songs* 4.4, lines 1-12 (James Michie)

CATS

As for cats, mark I pray you how silent they be, how soft they tread
when they steal upon the silly birds; how secret lie they in espial for the

79

poor little mice to leap upon them. Their own dung and excrements they will rake up and hide in the earth, knowing full well that the smell thereof will betray where they are.

Pliny (the Elder), *The Encyclopedia,*
vol. 10 (Philemon Holland)

SNAKES

As they engender together, they clip and embrace, and so entangled they be and enwrapped one about the other, that a man who saw them, would think they were one serpent with two heads. In the very act of generation, the male thrusteth his head into the mouth of the female; which she (for the pleasure and delectation that she taketh) gnaweth and biteth off.

Pliny (the Elder), *The Encyclopedia,*
vol. 10 (Philemon Holland)

INSPIRATION SEEKS THE FIELDS

Bacchus, where am I? Flushed
With god, to what groves, caves, am I being rushed
Inspired? What rocks shall hear
Me shape a poem setting great Caesar's peer-
less glory with the high
Council of Jove, a new star in the sky?
Some freshly hatched, supreme
Achievement, still unmouthed, shall be my theme.
As the wild reveller,
Sleepless and marvelling, pauses on a spur
To gaze at Thrace, all snow,
The Hebrus and Mount Rhodope's plateau
Tracked by barbarian feet,
I wander in a rapture off the beat-
en path, by brooks, through trees
Where no one goes. God of the Naiades,
God of the bacchanal bands
Who can uproot tall ash-trees with bare hands,

I plan no homespun, slight
Or earthbound song. Welcome, the sweet delight
Of danger! Lord of Wine,
Lead on! I follow, garlanded with vine.

Horace, *Songs* 3.25 (James Michie)

THE COUNTRY FEAST

Hush, all. Our crops, our lands we purify
the way our fathers chose in days gone by.
Come, Bacchus, grapes in bunches on each horn.
Come, Ceres, wreathing round your brow with corn.

The day is holy. Rest, earth. Rest, O plough.
The share's hung up. Now let all labouring cease.
Unstrap the yoke, and at the manger now
let oxen gay with garlands munch in peace.
These hours in happy worship must be spent,
so let no spinner touch the spinning-gear;
and if last night you were incontinent
and fell to Venus, keep away from here.

These powers ask pureness. Clean, your hands, and mine,
to draw the water. Clean, the clothes we wear.
The holy lamb now nears the gleaming shrine,
the files in white with olive in their hair.

We cleanse the farms. We cleanse the farmers too.
Gods of our fathers, drive all ill away.
Preserve our crops from drought and blighting dew,
our slowfoot lambs from pouncing wolves, we pray.

Then the sleek farmer, heaping lumps of wood,
will dream his teeming meadows in the flame,
while the farm's children (pledge the stock is good)
make huts of branches as a festal game.

The liver-markings show my prayers win.
Propitious gods have granted me the sign.
Bring smoked Falernian from the cobwebbed bin.
Undo the Chian jar and pour the wine.

81

Pour out the day with wine. It's holiday.
Be drunk and shameless, happy as you sprawl.
But don't neglect with every drink to say:
Good luck Messalla. Say it, one and all.

The country and the country's gods I praise;
for they refined man's acorn-appetite
and bade him take the slabs of wood and raise
a leafy shelter for the rainy night.
They tamed the bulls, and for the waggon made
the curving wheel. Then savage times were past.
Fruits warmed the air and through the garden-shade
the irrigating waters flowed at last.
Gold grapes were pulped to juice by trampling feet
and sober water mixed with wines that cheer.
The fields bore corn, and through the glow of heat
earth's shock of yellow hair was shorn each year.

Across the meadows gads the bee of spring,
anxious to glut with sweetness every cell.
Then first the rustic, tired with furrowing,
struck up a tune to match the season's spell;
and on his oatpipe, full of food, he tried
to hymn the gods that he had made of wood.
It was a rustic, Bacchus, who first dyed
his body red, and danced the best he could.
To ease his hardship offerings were designed.
His special he-goat memorably bled.
And out of flowers the rustic lad first twined
a garland destined for the Lar's old head.

The country feeds the sheep whose glistening wool
will give a deal of trouble to the girls.
Spin on, you wenches, spin and card and pull.
Your backs are stiff, but still the spindle whirls.
And women weaving in Minerva's toil
sing as the clay-weights swing in clattering looms.
Desire was first engendered of the soil
mid cattle and the mare's unsated wombs.
There first he bent his inexperienced bow,
yet now he never misses once his mark.
These are not beasts he's shooting to lay low,

82

but girls and lads of courage, in the dark.

O chant the adored god. Call on him aloud
to bless your flock, but whisper your own claim;
or shout them both. So merry are the crowd,
the Phrygian pipes, that none will hear your name.
O play and laugh. Now night has yoked her teams,
the bawdy stars are dancing in her wake.
Behind them darkens Sleep, and duskier Dreams
waver and vanish in the stir they make.

Tibullus, *Elegies* 1.10 (Jack Lindsay)

SILENUS

The scudding satyrs ran before their god;
Silenus on his ass did next appear,
And held upon the mane (the god was clear);
The drunken sire pursues, the dames retire;
Sometimes the drunken dames pursue the drunken sire.
At last he topples over on the plain;
The satyrs laugh, and bid him rise again.

Ovid, *Erotic Technique* 1.540-46 (John Dryden)

THE FARM SPRITE

Faunus, fleet-foot lover of flying wood-nymphs,
Turn, on tiptoe; enter my sunlit farmland;
Look, oh gently look on my flock enfolded
    Here, with its firstlings.

Bless, and gently go. On thy boisterous feast-day,
Cyprian wine shall flow, where the chosen victim
Stains the fresh-cut turf, and thine ancient altar
    Smokes with our incense.

Goat and kid shall frisk in the flowering grasses,
Ploughmen dance!—on earth!—while the festal village
Claps its hands in time, and the unyoked oxen
    Rest where the streams flow.

10. Horse. Rome, Museo Vaticano.

Sharp-headed, barrel-bellied, broadly back'd.

There the wolf shall stray, and the flock not fear him,
There, while all the slaves of the land go singing,
Autumn beech-leaves, flying in gold and crimson,
    Fall, at thy feet, Faun.

                    Horace, *Songs* 3.18 (Alfred Noyes)

COME, PUCK

I

Facile Mercury, mercurial
offspring of Atlas, who coached clods
and made them men, with speech,

one-god Western Union for the gods,
infant father of the lyre
improvised from tortoise shell,
deft at laughter and at theft—

Apollo, when he found you had
pickpocketed his cows from him,
blustered till he saw (then laughed)
that you had swiped his bow as well.

And out of Troy at night you stole
with Priam through the Grecian fires
unharmed, with ransom for his son.

You, at the end, lead all
us shadows to eternal rest
with golden wand, you darling of the gods
and of the elves.

                    Horace, *Songs* 1.10 (G. W.)

II

They say he is called Mercury, "one who runs between" (*medius currens*), because words course back and forth among men. The Greeks call him Hermes, from the hermeneutic arts which use speech; he is the

85

patron of business, where bartering goes on in words; the wings on his head and feet symbolize words' swift passage through air; and he is called the herald because words are the ambassadors of thoughts . . .

St. Augustine, *City of God* 7.14 (G. W.)

HUCKSTER'S PRAYER

There is a fountain near the Capene Gate,
Hallowed by Mercury, its clients state.
The loose-clad vendor comes and, duly pure,
Takes water thence in fumigated ewer.
Some bay leaves dipped in this will sprinkle dew
On wares he destines for an owner new;
He sprinkles too with dripping bay his hair
And utters in his trickster's voice a prayer:
"Absolve me from my lies in times gone by;
Absolve me from this day's duplicity;
Whether I called thyself to witness or
By Jove, too high to hear me, falsely swore,
Or against any god with knowledge sinned
Or goddess, may my words be as the wind;
And may the coming day bring scope for lies,
Nor any god regard my perjuries.
Give me but gain and joys that gain confers,
And make it pay to have tricked my customers."

Ovid, *The Calendar* 5.673-90 (L. P. Wilkinson)

MERCURY'S MISCHIEF

One night, while Jove is making love to a woman in the guise of her long-absent husband, he posts Mercury outside the house to intercept any messages from the real husband. The chameleon-god Mercury, adapting himself to his surroundings, assumes the form of Sosia, the absent husband's favorite slave. Naturally, the husband does send a message; and, naturally, he sends the real Sosia to deliver it. As Sosia approaches his

*master's house, by night, he sees a menacing stranger standing
guard over it and swinging a large club . . .*

SOSIA *(aside)*. Who can tell whether, I now wanting a lodging, he be one
of those that will entertain a man of free cost, at the sign of "The
Cudgel"? Or it may be he is some pitiful gentleman that, knowing
my master hath made me watch for the one half of the night, he will
be so good as lay me asleep for the other. I do not like his look. For
the love of god what a sturdy knave it is to see, too!

MERCURY *(aside)*. In good time, Sir! Well, now will I advance my voice a
little, that he may hear me. *(Louder, addressing his club.)* In faith,
gentle cudgel, you have done me service to speak of this month—
much about that time it was when you laid nine asleep altogether.

SOSIA *(aside)*. His cudgel and he are very familiar, as it seems. I pray god
I be not drawn into their acquaintance, too. Let me see, it has laid
nine asleep, as he says, already. 'Tis an odd number, that same nine.
'Tis ten to one an I be not taken up to make it even.

MERCURY *(violently, as arguing with himself)*. I will! I will stay no longer!

SOSIA *(starting back in terror)*. It is even as I said! What the devil shall
I do?

MERCURY *(still aside)*. He shall never 'scape my fingers.

SOSIA *(in hushed puzzlement)*. Whom doth he mean, think ye?

MERCURY *(as if aside)*. Whosoever comes next in my walk, *he* shall have
cudgeling—his belly full!

SOSIA *(reflectively)*. I do not love to eat thus late in the night. He may do
well to bestow his alms on them that be hungry.

MERCURY *(shadow-cudgeling, then, with a sigh of satisfaction)*. Ah, *'tis* a
cudgel for the nonce! 'Tis not a hair lighter than it should be.

SOSIA *(lurking)*. Now he hath weighed it. The next thing he has to do is
to measure it—upon my shoulder.

MERCURY *(tenderly)*. What if I give him but a gentle blow, to cast him in
a slumber?

SOSIA *(with mock relief)*. Then he saves my life! For I want *nothing* but
sleep!

MERCURY *(self-reprovingly)*. But what talk I of this? *My* cudgel, I know,
cannot give a gentle blow. It never touched man yet but it marred
the fashion of his face.

87

SOSIA (*whimpering*). *That's* well! Then belike I am to have a new face. I had even as lief keep my old still, though it be none of the best.

MERCURY (*in exaltation*). Come, my cudgel is wood mad to be at him!

SOSIA (*helpfully*). An it be so mad, would you wood-tame it a little on the walls first, ere it beat my shoulders.

MERCURY (*with a theatrical start*). Is there not a voice come flying to my ears?

SOSIA (*backing off*). Has my voice wings, then? An I had known so much before, I would have clipped them (by my voice's leave).

MERCURY (*searching*). It is some villain sure, that I must be fain to load with blows.

SOSIA (*hysterically*). A good jest! I can scarce go empty, I am so weary. How shall I do, think ye, when I am laden?

MERCURY (*attentive*). Hark! Methinks I hear some saucy fellow talking.

SOSIA (*relieved*). An his name be Saucy, good enough! My name is Sosia.

MERCURY (*eureka-ing*). O, I see him now! Here he comes towards me.

SOSIA (*bracing himself*). I begin to feel myself in a monstrous evil taking. I must needs confess I can scarce tell where I am. As for my lord's message, that's scared out of my head by this time. But yet I will set a good face on't, and speak as well as my heart will give me leave, to make him the more unwilling to meddle with me.

MERCURY (*ending, at last, the long-distance fencing*). Sirrah! Whither walk you there?

SOSIA. Si-Si-Sir, what have you to do, that are a maker of new faces?

MERCURY. Sirrah, tell me in few words, from whence you come, whose you are, and whither you go.

SOSIA. In as few as you would wish, sir: I come from thence, sir, I am my master's man, and am going hither. I think you are answered.

MERCURY. Answered, indeed!—after a fashion. But I will bridle that tongue of yours, an ye answer me no handsomer!

SOSIA. You seem to mistake me, sir. I am no horse, that my tongue should be bridled.

MERCURY. I believe I shall make you a horse—or some such thing (you know my meaning)—yet ere you and I part.

SOSIA (*nervously*). Ha. Ha. He. I dare say you mean an ass, sir!

88

MERCURY. I am glad you are merry, sir. But you will tell (I am sure), for all this, what business you have here.

SOSIA. Nay then, sir, what business have *you* here?

MERCURY. I will not stick to tell you, sir, I am one of the watch appointed here for this night.

SOSIA (*with infinite relief*). 'Tis well done! When enemies are abroad, watch and ward should be kept at home. But i' faith, master watchman, an you be a good fellow, tell them within that one of their family is come.

MERCURY. I know not how you mean, sir, "one of their family." But, an you be not gone the sooner, I fear me *I* shall use you somewhat *too* "familiarly."

SOSIA. Begone, quoth he! Why I tell you, man, here I *dwell* and here I am servant.

MERCURY. And I tell you: Stay but a little longer, I'll make you be carried away as if you were *master*.

SOSIA. How mean you that, sir?

MERCURY. Marry, "with state"—upon men's shoulders. If I but once lift up this cudgel . . .

SOSIA. Do what you will, sir, but I say still and will maintain that I am one of this household.

MERCURY. You will be*gone!*

SOSIA. Will you let one from coming into their own house?

MERCURY. Is this your house?

SOSIA. It is, I will stand to it.

MERCURY. I pray thee, who is thy master, canst thou tell?

SOSIA. Amphitryon, the general of the Theban army, husband to Alcmena.

MERCURY. Amphitryon *thy* master? Tell me then, what's thy name?

SOSIA. I am called at home Sosia, old Davus was my father.

MERCURY. Out upon thee, villain! Comest thou hither with so many lies patched together?

SOSIA. Indeed, my coat may be patched, but I know not what you mean by patching of lies.

MERCURY. Your coat may be faced, too, may it not? Well, for your patching and facing, I will give you a bombasting too, to teach you to speak truly hereafter.

SOSIA. But how an a man will not be bombasted?

MERCURY. But how an a man cannot choose?

(*He beats him.*)

SOSIA. HEI! HEU! HOI! I beseech you, sir!

MERCURY. Darest thou say to me, villain, thou art Sosia when I myself am Sosia?

SOSIA (*dumbfounded, to the audience*). Alas, what shall I do?

MERCURY (*drawing back after the beating*). Nay, this is but a little of the best, to that that is behind. Now, sir, an a man may ask you: Whose are you, I pray you?

SOSIA. Oh, yours, sir, yours! I wear your colors—(*ouch*)—here; none but yours, sir. You have taken me, methinks, into your own hands.

MERCURY. Tell me then, wherefore are you come?

SOSIA. 'Tis plain, sir (I marvel you will ask the question, you see yourself): to be beaten.

MERCURY. I'll beat you better yet, an you answer me not the sooner: Whose man are you, once again?

SOSIA. An I will tell you once again, I am Amphitryon's man, Sosia.

MERCURY. What! Again "Sosia"?

(*He beats him again.*)

SOSIA. Murder! Murder! Some honest Theban come help me!

MERCURY. Your bawling shall not help you. I tell thee yet again, I am Sosia.

SOSIA. An you be not, would you were else taken for me, that you might be as surely cudgeled as Sosia is.

MERCURY. Now! (*Draws back again from the beating.*) Tell me once more: Who is your master?

SOSIA. Even whom you will, sir.

MERCURY. And what might be your name?

SOSIA. Nay, be you my godfather, sir! I pray you, give me what name you will. I think you had best call me Stockfish instead of Sosia, for you seem to take me for no less.

MERCURY. This is you that said even now you were Sosia, you Amphitryon's man?

SOSIA. I confess, sir, my tongue tripped. I would not have said "Sosia," I would have said "So-as-you-say."

MERCURY (*complacently*). I knew he had no servant Sosia but myself. I think thou wert not well in thy wits.

SOSIA (*uneasily*). May a man but speak to you, sir (by your good leave) a word or two of free cost, without paying for it?

MERCURY. Go to, I am content to make truce with thee for a time.

SOSIA. Swear you will not touch me, then.

MERCURY. Trust me of my word, I will not.

SOSIA. And so I may, now I remember me; for hitherto you have kept it with me. But how if you break it now?

MERCURY (*solemnly*). Then let Mercury be Sosia's mortal enemy!

SOSIA. Well, now I may speak what I list! *I* am Amphitryon's man. Sosia.

MERCURY (*raising his cudgel and moving forward*). You *are,* sir?

SOSIA. Sir, you have made truce with me, and are bound by your word! And I speak nothing but truth!

MERCURY. I care not for that.

SOSIA. Nay, use me as you please. I confess you are the better man. Yet I will never deny, while I live, but that I am Sosia, one of the servants of this house.

MERCURY (*lowers his club, astonished at this sudden stubbornness— then, affecting pity*). Out of doubt, I see now thou art not well in thy wits.

SOSIA (*exasperated, carried away by his own bravado*). Good lord, sir! That you will deny that I am my master's Sosia! Did not our ship come this night from the haven? Did not my master send me hither? Do I not stand now before our house? Have I not a lantern in my hands? Have I not been well cudgeled? What should let me, then, to go straight into our house?

MERCURY. *Your* house?

SOSIA. Aye, our house. So I say. Do what you will.

MERCURY. Villain, thou hast lied hitherto in every word thou hast spoken.

For I am that Sosia that went with Amphitryon from hence, that was present at the action, saw the town delivered, and know that my lord killed King Pterelas with his own hands.

SOSIA (*to himself, astonished*). How now? Nay then, I will not believe myself that I am Sosia an he go on thus a little further. (*Out loud.*) But I pray you, sir (an a man may speak without correction), you say you were by at the delivery up of the town. Can you tell a man what present was given Amphitryon by the Teleboeans?

MERCURY. The cup that King Pterelas himself was wont to drink in.

SOSIA (*aside*). He has told it! (*To Mercury.*) But—an you will not be angry for asking, sir—where might this cup be?

MERCURY. 'Tis sealed up in a casket with Amphitryon's own seal.

SOSIA. (Oh infinity!) I beseech you, sir, but the seal?

MERCURY. The sun rising, drawn in an azure coach with four flame-colored horses.

SOSIA (*in bewildered debate with himself*). By Jupiter, he hath put me down by plain arguments! I must be fain to go get me a new name, for anything I see. Yet I cannot imagine where he should learn all this! But now I remember myself, I will ask him one thing he shall never be able to tell me while he lives—that I did alone in the tent when no Christian man was by me. (*Severely, like a schoolmaster.*) Sir, if you be Sosia, when the legions had been a good while in chase of the enemy, what did you alone when you came to your lord's tent? Tell me but that, and I yield forever.

MERCURY. I ran to a hogshead of wine and filled a bottle . . .

SOSIA (*aside*). He is in the way already . . .

MERCURY. . . . then sat me down upon a field-bed by, and drunk it off every drop.

SOSIA (*aside*). True! by the lord, true! Unless he were then in the bottom of the bottle, I cannot guess how the devil he should know it.

MERCURY. Now, sir, have I convinced you by sufficient proofs that I am Sosia?

SOSIA. You say you are, sir.

MERCURY. And have reason to, I think.

SOSIA (*in tears*). But I durst be sworn by Jupiter that I am Sosia.

MERCURY. And I dare swear by Mercury that Jupiter will believe me on my word before he will believe thee on thy oath.

SOSIA. I beseech you, sir, do but tell me who *should* I be, as you think, if I be not Sosia?

MERCURY. Sir, when I leave to be Sosia, you may be he for anything I know. In the meantime, begone presently—or else you know what will follow.

SOSIA (*to himself*). As I live, when I look upon him he is so like me that methinks I see myself in a glass. His hat, his clothes, are like mine—his leg, his foot, his stature; his nose, his lips, his cheeks, his beard; every part of him! What should I say more? If he have as many blows on his shoulders as I have too, there was never two eggs liker one another. And yet methinks, on the other side, when I remember myself, I was never (that I can call to mind) but the same man. I remember my master, I know his house. I am not asleep. I am not drunk. Why then! Should I not be Sosia? I *am* Sosia! And I will go into our house, that I will!

MERCURY (*quietly*). Whither now, sir?

SOSIA (*weakening*). To our house.

MERCURY. Yet again "*our* house"? Get you gone quickly without more words, you had best, or else I'll make your skin of more colors than the walls of your house.

SOSIA (*pleads*). May not I go tell my mistress what my master bade me?

MERCURY. Go tell *your* mistress what you list. As for her that dwells here, she is my mistress; and if you see her today, it shall cost you dearly.

SOSIA. Nay, I'll begone first! 'T has cost me enough already, even if you would bear part of the charges! (*In retreat, mumbling to himself.*) Lord in heaven, what a thing is this? What's become of me, frow ye? When did I lose myself? When was I changed? Did I leave myself yonder, and perhaps forget it? For he hath all the shape I have here, as just as a hair. Well, I will return to my master and let him know of all that has past. If he hath forgotten me too, I will even to the font and unchristen myself again.

Plautus, *Amphitruo* 293-462 (Anonymous Jacobean playwright, from "The Birth of Hercules")

When he returns to his master, Sosia has a hard time describing what prevented him from delivering the message to Alcmena . . .

SOSIA. What would you have, sir? I came thither, but the other-I was there before me—for that there was two I's is as certain as that I have two eyes in this head of mine. This-I, that am here, was weary, the other-I was fresh. This-I was peaceable, and t'other-I was a hectoring bully-I.

AMPHITRYON. And thou expect'st I should believe thee?

SOSIA. No, I am not so unreasonable, for I could never have believed it myself if I had not been well beaten into it. But a cudgel, you know, is a convincing argument in a brawny fist. What shall I say but that I was compelled at last to acknowledge *myself!* I found that *he* was very-*I,* without fraud, cozen, or deceit. Besides, I viewed myself as in a mirror, from head to foot—(he was handsome, of a noble presence, a charming air, loose and free in all his motions)— and saw he was so much I that I should have reason to be better *satisfied* with my own person (if his hands had not been a little of the heaviest).

AMPHITRYON. Once again, to a conclusion! Say you passed by him and entered into the house.

SOSIA. I am a friend to truth, and say no such thing. He defended the door, and I could not enter.

AMPHITRYON. How? Not enter?

SOSIA. Why, how should I enter—unless I were a sprite, to glide by him and shoot myself through locks and bolts and two-inch boards!

AMPHITRYON. O coward! Didst thou not attempt to pass?

SOSIA. Yes, and was repulsed and beaten for my pains.

AMPHITRYON. Who beat thee?

SOSIA. I beat me.

AMPHITRYON. Didst thou beat thyself?

SOSIA. I don't mean I-here. But the absent-me beat me-here-present.

AMPHITRYON. There's no end of this intricate piece of nonsense.

> Plautus, *Amphitruo* 594-620
> (John Dryden, "Amphitryon")

DIVINE BUREAUCRACY

The question is: out of the swarm of gods, which one or ones presided over the empire's spread and maintenance?—(obviously this grand task is not left to the sewer-goddess Cloacina, to the goddess of voluptuary enticement Volupia, to the libertine-goddess Libertina, to the god of baby tantrums Vaticanus, or to the cradle-goddess Cunina). How could this book hold even the names of all the gods to whom they parcel out tasks, one job one god? They do not, for instance, think farming is safely left to a single god, but commit the flatlands to Rurina, the mountain plateaus to Jugatinus, the lower hills to Collatina, the valleys to Vallonia. They cannot even trust a single stalk of corn to a single goddess—to Segetia, say; but must put Seia in charge of it as a seed in the earth, pass it on to Segetia when it pushes aboveground and forms a standing crop, call in Tutilina when it is reaped and stored. Who would have thought that Segetia, a goddess, could not even look over the corn in its entire career from grassy beginning to withered sheaves? But even this is not enough for those who think the more gods the merrier—the better to bring man's poor soul into unholy intercourse with a hive of godlets, and keep it sequestered from the one true God's embrace: they put Proserpina in charge of the budding ears, Nodotus in charge of the stalk's linkages and joinery, Volutina in charge of the sheath that clothes the husk; when the husks split and reveal the ear, Patelana presides; Hostilina (from an old word for "leveling") evens off the field's fringy tops; Flora is there at the flowering, Runcina (from the word for "uproot") at the ploughing-under, and—well, forget the rest; though it does not shame them to give the whole catalogue, it bores me.

I have only given you this sampling to show that they cannot be so brash as to say such gods established, defended, or rescued the Roman Empire. Each is too busy with his own task to undertake any general supervision over the whole! What time has Segetia for the Roman Empire, who is too busy with her stalks to extend her attention even to the trees? When would Cunina learn military arts, who cannot play hooky from her cradles? How should Nodotus join the army, who cannot even raise his eyes, off the stalk-joint he guards, up as high as the sheath? Why, we appoint a single fellow to serve as doorkeeper; and that is enough, since he is only a man. But it takes three gods to watch the door—Forculus for the panels, Cardea for the hinges, and Limentinus for the jamb (poor Forculus could not watch his domain *and* the hinge *and* the jamb).

. . .

When man and woman are joined, the joiner god (Jugatinus) is on hand. So far, so good—but: the bride must be conducted to her domicile (here's god Domiducus); must, once there, be made to remain (goddess Manturna joins in); and what of the rest? Defer to man's sense of shame: let plain old flesh and blood do their lusty work, under a decent veil of modesty. Why this flocking of gods to the bedroom when even the bride-attendants are gone? They are not there to do something hard— like help the bride maintain her virginity; they simply ease the task of taking her virginity away, breaking down any obstacles a maiden's modesty may interpose. For this task the gods and goddesses rally round: Virginiensis, Subigus, matronly Prema, Pertunda, Venus and Priapus. Still, why the crowd? If even the husband needed help with his job, one divine ally should suffice (male or female deity, it does not matter). Why not Venus, for instance, all by herself; whose very name is a boast that through her agency virginity is lost? If men have any self-respect (where gods have none), should not a couple, believing all these divine helpers of both sexes are attending and lending their assistance, grow even more self-conscious—he less ardent, she more shy? Or if Virginiensis has already removed the virgin's clothes, Subigus has slipped her into position, and Prema has pinned her there, what job is left for Pertunda? —let her make a blushing exit; the man can take it from there. Indeed, the act she is named for only he should do. If a god did this deed, the rival husband would call allies to help him save his wife from the heavenly rape (the way new mothers ask for help against Silvanus). As a matter of fact, a spare male *is* in the bedroom—Priapus, on whose immense nasty member the bride (acting on grave matrons' precepts) takes her ceremonial ride.

St. Augustine, *City of God*
4.8, 6.9 (G. W.)

THE FIELDS AND THEIR GODS

A NEW GOD AT THE HEARTH

I

As a mother's flesh mediates solid food to her child (who can eat nothing but the milk produced by her body), so the Lord took on flesh when he came to us, that he might mediate to our childish minds the milk of divine wisdom.

St. Augustine, *First Sermon
on Psalm 30* (G. W.)

II

When "the Word was incarnated and dwelt among us," he compounded, at his nativity, a healing paste to cleanse our heart's eyesight, so we could see his grandeur through the ministry of this earthiness . . . A dust had blown upon man's eye, earth blew up against it and irritated the eye, so it could not look upon the light. The irritation is salved: as earth irritated it, an earthy paste is ordained to heal it. For all pastes and medications are of earth. You were blinded with dust, with dust you are cured; flesh blinded you, flesh cures. The soul became *carnal* by attuning itself to fleshly motions, and the heart became blind; but the Word became *incarnate,* the doctor mixed you this paste. He came to cure with flesh the flesh's fault . . .

St. Augustine, *On St. John's Gospel*
2.16 (G. W.)

III

Man's maker was made man . . . that the bread might be hungry, the fountain thirsty, the way tired by traveling, the truth falsely accused, the judge of the living and dead condemned, justice wrongly judged, wisdom whipped by its students, the grapes gashed with a chaplet of thorns, the foundation suspended on wood, strength weakened, health wounded, life killed.

St. Augustine, *Sermon* 191 (G. W.)

97

SHARING EARTH'S AGE

Happy is he that owns ancestral lands
where all his days from youth to age are cast.
There, where the baby crept, the hobbler stands
and sees, beyond his farm, the years go past.

For no tumultuous miseries he craved;
no unknown waters slaked his wandering thirst;
the seas, for gain or pay, he never braved;
with raucous lawsuits he was never cursed.

His inexperience looks upon the stars
more freely, ignorant of the town nearby.
The changing crops are all his calendars;
apples mean autumn, spring a blossoming sky.

The sun goes down and rises still from earth,
and toil is all the clock that makes his day.
He knew the acorn whence the oak had birth,
and groves are aging with his locks of grey.

Claudian (Jack Lindsay)

PART II

Ages of Man

From bambino *to* vecchio (*if not to* briconne), *the ordinary Italian of the classical world lived his three score and ten much as the modern one does—within the family. He loved the liquidity of his language (p. 107); he had his superstitions (pp. 126-28) and earthy wisdom (pp. 110-12), his garlic (p. 128) and* vino (*p. 123*).

> *Sit Latium . . .*
> *Sit Romana potens Itala virtute propago.*

THE AGES OF MAN

At first, the child, with feet new-trained to walk,
Plays with his mates all day; or, at a nothing
Bursts into rage which, in an instant, turns
To laughter, and still changes every hour.
Then comes the beardless boy, set free from school,
Riding his horse, rejoicing in his hounds,
Who haunts the Campus Martius; soft as wax
If evil moulds him, fretful at the curb
Of wisdom; careless what the morrow brings;
Prodigal of his coin; a sprightly colt,
Swift to desire, and swifter to forego
What yesterday he swore he loved the best.
Then manhood, all for riches now, and friends,
A slave to proud ambition, and ashamed
To think his firm intent could ever change.
Last comes old age, with all its gathering ills,
Still seeking more, and yet afraid to use
Its life-long hoard; sans courage and sans fire;
Full of delays; content with hope deferred;
Testy and grumbling, wishing that the world

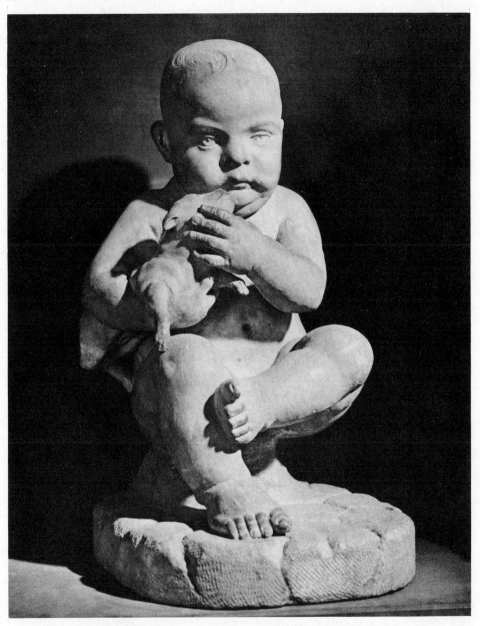

11. Boy and puppy. Rome, Museo dei Conservatori.

. . . children are moved instinctively by the images of virtues whose seeds they have within them . . .

Were once again as when he was a boy.
So, with the flowing tide, much good comes in;
But, when it ebbs, it carries much away;
And so to every age belongs its part;
Youth must not play the dotard; nor the boy
Ape manhood. Nature's law must rule the stage.

Horace, *Dramatic Technique* 158-78 (Alfred Noyes)

INFANCY

I

For new-born babies lie there at first as though they were entirely lifeless, but when they gain a little strength, they use both their minds and their senses, to sit up, use their hands, and recognize their nurses; next they begin to enjoy the company of children of their own age; they like to be with them; they love to play, and they begin to listen to little stories. If they have anything left over, they like to give it to others. They begin to be more inquisitive about what goes on at home, and to be capable of study and learning, and they want to know the names of people they see. In their games with their playmates, if they win, they are beside themselves with joy; if they lose, they are downcast and depressed; all of which is far from accidental.

For Nature apparently has created human faculties for the perception of every virtue, and therefore children are moved instinctively by the images of virtues whose seeds they have within them; for these seeds are the prime elements of nature, and when they grow, virtue begins, as it were, to germinate. For we have been born and made to contain in us the first principles of action: love of our fellow man, liberality, and gratitude. Our souls are adapted for containing wisdom, commonsense, and courage, and rejecting their opposites, so that those sparks, as it were, of the virtues which I have said we see in children are not accidental; from them philosophical reason ought to be kindled, so that we can follow reason as leader as though it were a god, and so come to the goal that Nature has set before us. For at the risk of repetition let me say again that in tender years and in the undeveloped mind can be detected the natural faculty as though through a mist; as the soul progresses and grows stronger, it does indeed recognize that natural faculty, but in such a way that it can progress still further, though it is in itself still incomplete.

Cicero, *Supreme Good and Evil*
5.42-43 (Paul MacKendrick)

II

How to suck, to sleep when soothed, to cry when my body vexed me—this I knew, and no more. Later I began to laugh, first in sleep, then when awake. So at least I am told of myself; and believe, when I look at other babies; though I do not remember. Gradually I began to sense where I was, and wanted to make my wishes clear to any who could satisfy them; but I could not. The wishes were in me; the fulfillers outside, and they had no organ of perception that could reach inside my mind. So I tossed my limbs and voice about, doing what little I could, of any sort, to enact something like my wishes—which turned out very *un*like them. And when my desires were not complied with (either because others did not understand me, or knew better what was good for me), I grew indignant at adults for not serving me, at free men for not being my slaves; and took my revenge on them by crying.

St. Augustine, *Confessions* 1.7-8 (G. W.)

III

There are some who think infants do not dream, since the soul's activities are developed only with the passage of years. They should observe how children flinch, nod, and flash smiles while they sleep; and discern in all these things how easy is the soul's rise to the surface of a body as soft as a child's.

Tertullian, *The Soul* 49.1 (G. W.)

FOR THE CHILD, A NEW WORLD

Muses
Muses of Sicily
Now let us sing a serious song

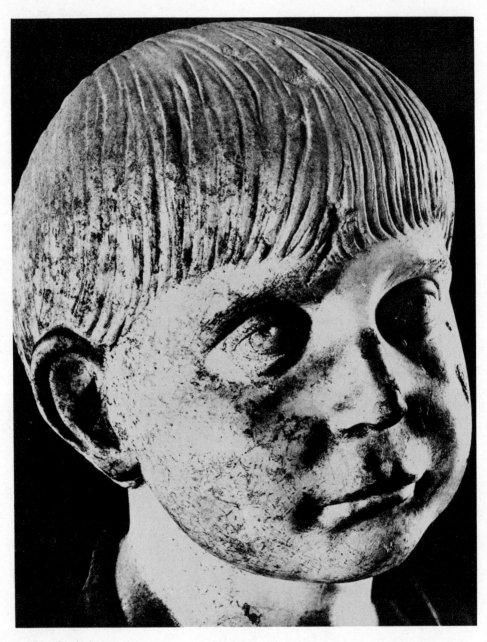

12. Boy. Paris, Louvre.

*. . . how easy is the soul's rise to the
surface of a body as soft as a child's . . .*

There are taller trees than the apple and the crouching
     tamarisk
If we sing of the woods, let our forest be stately

Now the last age is coming
As it was written in the Sibyl's book
The great circle of the centuries begins again
Justice, the Virgin, has returned to earth
With all of Saturn's court
A new line is sent down to us from the skies
And thou, Lucina, must smile
Smile for the birth of the boy, the blessed boy
For whom they will beat their swords into ploughshares
For whom the golden race will rise, the whole world new
Smile, pure Lucina, smile
Thine own Apollo will reign

And thou, Pollio
It is in thy term this glorious age begins
And the great months begin their march
When we shall lose all traces of the old guilt
And the world learn to forget fear
For the boy will become divine
He will see gods and heroes
And will himself be seen by them as god and hero
As he rules over a world of peace
A world made peaceful by his father's wisdom

For thee, little boy, will the earth pour forth gifts
All untilled, give thee gifts
First the wandering ivy and foxglove
Then colocasia and the laughing acanthus
Uncalled the goats will come home with their milk
No longer need the herds fear the lion
Thy cradle itself will bloom with sweet flowers
The serpent will die
The poison plant will wither
Assyrian herbs will spring up everywhere

And when thou art old enough to read of heroes
And of thy father's great deeds
Old enough to understand the meaning of courage

Then will the plain grow yellow with ripe grain
Grapes will grow on brambles
Hard old oaks drip honey

Yet still there must remain some traces of the old guilt
That lust that drives men to taunt the sea with ships
To circle cities with walls
And cut the earth with furrows
There must be another Tiphys
Another Argo carrying picked men
And there must be a war, one final war
With great Achilles storming a last Troy

But when thou hast grown strong and become a man
Then even the trader will leave the sea
His pine ship carry no more wares
And everywhere the land will yield all things that life requires
No longer need the ground endure the harrow
Nor the vine the pruning hook
The farmer can free his oxen from the yoke
Then colored cloths no longer will need lying dyes
For the ram in the field will change his own fleece
To soft purple or saffron yellow
Each grazing lamb will have a scarlet coat

"Onward, O glorious ages, onward"
Thus sang the fatal sisters to their spindles
Chanting together the unalterable Will

Go forward, little boy, to thy great honors
Soon comes thy time
Dear child of gods from whom a Jupiter will come
See how for thee the world nods its huge head
All lands and seas and endless depths of sky
See how the earth rejoices in the age that is to be

O may my life be long enough to let me sing of thee
With strength enough to tell thy deeds
With such a theme not even Thracian Orpheus could
    outsing me
Not Linus either, though Apollo prompted him
Help from Calliope herself could not make Orpheus' song
    the best

And even Pan, with Arcady as judge
Yes Pan, would fall before me when I sang of thee

Learn, little boy, to greet thy mother with a smile
For thee she has endured nine heavy months
Learn, little boy, to smile
For if thou didst not smile
And if thy parents did not smile on thee
No god could ask thee to his table
No goddess to her bed.

Vergil, *Eclogues* 4 (James Laughlin)

SPEECH

You cannot believe, unless you pay close attention, how many devices nature has wrought for us to use in speech. For in the first place an artery stretches from the lungs to the inner part of the mouth, whereby the voice, starting from the mind, is caught up and uttered. Then the tongue is situated in the mouth and fenced about with teeth; it shapes and limits unduly loud sounds, and when it strikes the teeth and other parts of the mouth makes the sound of the voice distinct and clipped; and so we Stoics usually compare the tongue to the pick, the teeth to the strings, the nostrils to the sounding board which echoes to the string in music.

Cicero, *On the Nature of the Gods*
2.149 (Paul MacKendrick)

CHILDREN'S HYMN

We are all virgins here,
boys and girls in a ring.
Diana holds us dear
and in her praise we sing.

Latona's child and Jove's
(a mighty god is he),
you woke in Delos' Groves
under an olive-tree

that you might be the Queen
of lonely gullied hills
and forests thick with green
and brabbling mountain rills.

As Juno does, you aid
the moaning mother's plight—
you Lady of the Shade,
you Moon with bastard light.

The sky is yours to keep.
You let the farmer know
when it is time to reap,
when it is time to sow.

Take any name you will
and lend your ancient grace
unchanging kindly still,
blessing the human race.

Catullus, *Songs* 34 (Jack Lindsay)

PLAYING HOOKY

When I was young, I, like a lazy fool,
Would blear my eyes with oil to stay from school,
Averse from pains, and loath to learn the part
Of Cato, dying with a dauntless heart—
Though much my master that stern virtue prais'd
Which o'er the vanquisher the vanquish'd rais'd,
And my pleas'd father came with pride to see
His boy defend the Roman liberty.
But then *my* study was to cog the dice,
And dext'rously to throw the lucky sice;
To shun ames-ace (that swept my stakes away)
And watch the box, for fear they should convey
False bones, and put upon me in the play;
Careful, besides, the whirling top to whip,
And drive her giddy, till she fell asleep.

Persius, *Satires* 3.44-51 (John Dryden)

13. Boy tormenting goose.
    Rome, Museo Capitolino.

*Bursts into a rage which,
in an instant, turns to laughter
and still changes every hour.*

14. Girl saving dove from snake.
    Rome, Museo Capitolino.

*. . . when courage walks
with apprehensiveness . . .*

POOR REGULUS' ALMANAC

You get what you give.

When courage walks with apprehension,
the way is safe.

With women, it's one of two:
love or hate. No third.

Treat your friend's faults kindly,
and they're yours.

The lover knows "will"
but no "no."

The only honest woman
is the openly dishonest one.

Love, a joy to the young,
a joke on the old.

Peril strikes precisely
where it is ignored.

The good woman wields her power
by yielding it.

The frightened man dies
every day.

Today's "tomorrow" is as lost
as yesterday.

The man is invincible
who vanquishes himself.

Today must go to school
to yesterday.

Ponder in the plural,
decide in the singular.

Honor is honored
even by robbers.

"Thrift" is misery dignified.

The timorous lord
is his own butler's slave.

The man without a country
is a corpse without a grave.

Even one hair
casts its shadow.

Ends pass judgment
on beginnings.

Luck is a mother
who spoils her children.

Who loses honor
never had it.

Your enemy is hiding—
in your heart.

The lowly cannot fall
far.

Congratulations—
catastrophe.

A quick judge judges
(and commits) a crime.

Doubting is halfway
toward knowing.

Far beam?—
from deep fire.

The woman often married
must not fit the bill.

Hate has hidden teeth.

Her salt tear
spices the past.

Keeping gets more
than getting.

One escapes risk
through risk.

Where there's fire,
there's smoke.

Need does not obey laws,
it makes them.

Who ignores traps?—
not those who set them.

Both inevitable:
death and love.

Crowds hide crimes.

The bride's office
supplants the whore's.

Steal his honor,
yours is lost.

It is wealth alone
that rules the world.

Slow punishment is fast-
er than any crime.

Cure for this pain?—
that one.

Absent power, exerted,
is present.

All can,
some won't.

No antidote
for a thunderbolt.

The sage is a fool
who knows how to keep silent.

Publilius, *Maxims from the Mimes* (G. W.)

TRIBUTE TO A TEACHER

Knock on my heart; for thou hast skill to find
If it sound solid, or be fill'd with wind;

And, through the veil of words, thou view'st the naked mind.
For this a hundred voices I desire,
To tell what an hundred tongues would tire,
Yet never could be worthily express'd—
How deeply thou art seated in my breast.
When first my childish robe resign'd the charge,
And left me unconfin'd to live at large;
When now my golden bulla (hung on high
To household gods) declar'd me past a boy,
And my white shield proclaim'd my liberty—
When, with my wild companions, I could roll
From street to street, and sin without control—
Just at that age, when manhood set me free,
I then depos'd myself, and left the reins to thee.
On thy wise bosom I repos'd my head,
And by my better Socrates was bred.
Then thy straight rule set virtue in my sight,
The crooked line reforming by the right.
My reason took the bent of thy command,
Was form'd and polish'd by thy skilful hand.
Long summer days thy precepts I rehearse,
And winter nights were short in our converse;
One was our labor, one was our repose,
One frugal supper did our studies close.

Persius, *Satires* 5.22-44 (John Dryden)

COLLEGE DAYS

Cicero, like every father, had to worry about his son's morals and his own money when young Marcus went to Athens for his "university" training: Please suggest to young Marcus, but only if you think it's reasonable, that he should keep the expenses of his trip and his residence at Athens within the sum due for rent from my property in the Argiletum and on the Avantine Hill. He would have been well content with that if he had stayed in Rome and rented a house . . . There is certainly no need of a carriage and horses at Athens . . .

Cicero, *Letter to Atticus, March 28, 45 B.C.*

113

After these familiar worries over the student's desire for a car, come even more familiar worries over grades: Now, my dear Atticus, do help me out. I am anxious, as soon as I have done all that Brutus requires of me, to run over to Greece. It is very important for Marcus, or rather myself, and indeed for both of us, that I should look in on him at his studies. For do you think the letter you sent me from his tutor Leonides contains much cause for satisfaction? I shall never be satisfied with any report on him which qualifies praise with "if he keeps it up." That suggests anxiety, not confidence. Again, I instructed another of his teachers, Herodes, to write me detailed reports, but so far he has not sent a word. I'm afraid he may have had nothing to tell me which he thought I should be glad to hear.

Letter to Atticus, April 24, 44 B.C.

After a rare letter home: Post from young Marcus at last, and what do you think? A letter written in brocaded phrases, which in itself indicates some progress. And besides, his reports from the others are splendid. Leonides, it is true, still says "so far"; but Herodes' is "excellent" without qualification. Ah well! This is a matter on which I'm quite glad to have dust thrown in my eyes, and content to be credulous.

Letter to Atticus, June 11, 44 B.C.
from Cicero, *Letters* (L. P. Wilkinson)

GREEN BUDS

Why, like a doe, Chloe,
shy from me—why pant
over untravellable peaks
toward your antlered mother,
heart netted in thin shadows, hesitant
at every whisper?

It is only spring
ripening tremulously
around (and in) you
in stirred branch and bud,
only the slither along limbs
of liquid green lizardy life
that makes you shiver.

You are no lion's prey (nor I a lion),
no longer the mother deer's thing;
it is man who stalks you;
woman. Turn to him.

Horace, *Songs* 1.23 (G. W.)

LOVERS' OMENS

Acme in his arms, Septimius calls her "Mine.
If I don't love you hopelessly
and am not ready constantly
to lose as much more hope as may be,
in Libya and singed India
let me come up alone against a green-eyed lion."

Love, at this avowal,
now from their left, as before from the right,
sneezes His approval.

Tipping her face back lightly, her mouth is red as wine,
she kisses his drunken "peepers"
and names him Life and calls him Hers.
"Let's serve Lord Love beyond all others,
by as far more as burns His fire
bigger and bitterly in the poor, weak pith of me."

Love, at this avowal,
from the left as before, now from their right
sneezes His approval.

Now the two set out, for good hope has been divined;
trusting and loved, poor and loving,
the pair of souls in common holding.
Septimius prefers her keeping
to Syrias and Britannias;
Acme in him alone gains both solace and passion.

Who knows other people
richer in blessings? Who has had a sight
of a love more hopeful?

Catullus, *Songs* 45 (Richard E. Braun)

115

HYMN TO HYMEN

come from your hill, from Helicon,
come from your home, Urania's child
off to her husband steal the bride,
maid to her man, o wedding-god,
    O Hymen Hymenaeus

bind on your brow a flowered crown
of marjoram, the sweet-perfumed
put on the scarlet veil, be glad
glad as you come on snowy foot
    wearing the saffron sandal

come join us on our merry day
sing us the festal wedding-song
in little bell-tones high and clear
give us the beat to dance, lift up
    and swing the pine-torch blazing

here's Vinia, bride to Manlius,
(like Venus Idalian, on that day
she came before the Phrygian judge)
good virgin she, and good the signs
    that mark her day of marriage

call her a flower, call her bright
as any Asian myrtle-branch
that hamadryad elfin maids
plant in the garden where they play
    and nourish with the dew-drops

hither, then, Hymen, turn your steps
come, leave the land of Thespia,
the rock Aonian, and the cave
curtained by waters cool, where flow
    the streams of Aganippe.

summon the lady to house and home
for husband new her want awake

116

15. Young lady. Rome, Museo Nazionale.

. . . by stealth adopt unmeditated grace . . .

her heart with love bind all about
as ivy roving clings and folds
    the tree-trunk in its branches

and you too join us, pure and chaste
maids of honor (for you there comes
a day like this): take up the beat,
sing "Hymenaeus Hymen, O,
    O Hymen Hymenaeus"

gladden his heart when he shall hear
our prayer, for to the task he loves
we bid him turn and come this way,
the guide of holy wedded love,
    the yoke of pure affection.

what god is more besought in prayer
by lovers loving and beloved?
to whom do men more honor pay
in heaven? O Hymen, wedding-god
    O Hymen Hymenaeus

"bless me and mine!" in quavering tones
some ancient prays; "for thee we loose
the virgin's knot," our maidens cry;
fearful of you but eager too
    the bridegroom waits your coming

into a young man's bold hot hands
the fragile bloom of a budding maid
you surrender, though still she clings
to mother's arms, O wedding-god,
    O Hymen Hymenaeus.

without your blessing, love may take
no smallest profit that the world
would count as lawful, but it may
with your consent: who to this god
    would dare declare him equal?

without your blessing there's no house
can bring forth children, there's no sire

can hope for offspring, but they can
with your consent: who to this god
    would dare declare him equal?

the land that knew naught of your rites
could never bring forth guardians
to watch its boundaries, but it could
with your consent: who to this god
    would dare declare him equal?

        Catullus, *Songs* 61.1-75 (Frank O. Copley)

CONSUMMATION

look, bride: the house! your husband's house!
how rich and powerful it is
say but the word, 'twill be your slave
(O Hymen Hymenaeus O
    O Hymen Hymenaeus)

until the day when old age comes
and palsy makes your hoary head
nod "yes" to all, to everything
O Hymen Hymenaeus O
    O Hymen Hymenaeus

lift up (good luck! don't stumble here!)
across the threshold your golden feet
pass through the shining doorway smooth
O Hymen Hymenaeus O
    O Hymen Hymenaeus

see there! within the house he lies,
your husband, on his Tyrian couch
waiting and watching all for you
O Hymen Hymenaeus O
    O Hymen Hymenaeus

for him no lower than for you
flickers within his heart of hearts
the flame, but deeper down it lies

O Hymen Hymenaeus O
    O Hymen Hymenaeus

let go the lovely rounded arm
of our sweet maid, young acolyte
up to the bride-bed let her come
O Hymen Hymenaeus O
    O Hymen Hymenaeus

and you, good matrons, whom your men
have loved so well for years and years,
come, lay our sweet maid in her bed
O Hymen Hymenaeus O
    O Hymen Hymenaeus

now, husband, come: it is your time
your wife lies in the bridal room
see how there shines upon her face
the white bloom of the maiden-flower
    the red glow of the poppy

but, husband, by the powers above,
you're no less handsome than your bride
our Lady Venus never thought
to scorn you—but the hour is late
    come on now, don't be lagging

ah, there you are! you haven't lagged
for long. may Holy Venus shed
a blessing on you, since your want
is honest want, and since your love
    is unconcealed and lawful.

who'd count the sands of Africa?
who'd number all the twinkling stars?
a man would sooner reckon up
their totals than he'd know the tale
    of times you'll sport together.

sport as you will, and may you soon
be blessed with children: it's not right
that any name as old as yours
should fail of children: let it be
    of offspring ever fertile

a tiny Torquatus I'd like to see
safe in his mother's circling arms
hold out his darling baby hands
and give to his father that first fleet smile
 with little lips half-parted

may he reflect his father's face:
a Manlius beyond all doubt
known on the spot by everyone;
and, for his mother, may he show
 her virtue by his features

and may he prove his mother's son
in goodness that will gain him praise
just as men called Telemachus
"the Good" and in his goodness saw
 Penelope, his mother

come, maids of honor, close the door
we've had our fun. Husband and wife,
we wish you every happiness
may health and youth and love and life
 bring you delights unending.

Catullus, *Songs* 61.156-235 (Frank O. Copley)

PREGNANCY

Is it not true, women, that you feel the child within you stir with a life not your own, and by its squirming your organs are shaken, your sides ripple, your womb's whole circuit throbs as the burden in you shifts its center here-there-and-everywhere? And you are happy over these movements, comforted by the certainty that the child is already alive and active; so that if its restlessness falls off, you are afraid. The child inside you even hears noises, starting at sharp new ones. You, meanwhile, deny yourself delicacies, even grow to dislike them, for its sake. You and the child share vicissitudes of health; your very bruises are appropriated by it, each in a place corresponding to yours.

Tertullian, *The Soul* 25.3 (G. W.)

AWAY FROM HOME

Spring breathes warmth back on us
and winter's shrieking
mutes to whisper of Zephyrs
our exile ending
where heat deepens and drenches
the trees and pastures.

Through Asiatic cities
that shine on water
my mind already trembles
and starts to travel,
my feet are tugged and restless
in that direction.

Au revoir to my fellows
in homesickness,
eccentrically held
with me in exile—
scattered now to each
man's truest center.

Catullus, *Songs* 46 (G. W.)

BACK HOME

My lovely not-quite-island, Sirmio,
bright eye of Italy, best land
Neptune washes anywhere
in ocean or in inland water-form, at last
I see you (though I cannot trust
my eyes, that fooled me with your sight
when all they really saw was—Thrace).

Nothing washes troubles
from the mind like rest
in the familiar house,
sleep under one's own roof—
the real reward for labors
that took me from you.

Reacquaint me, Sirmio,
with your subtle loveliness.
And you, Lago di Garda,
in a sparkle of your waters
thrust up laughter
along the shore.

Catullus, *Songs* 31 (G. W.)

IN ANY LAND, ONE'S HOME IS—WINE

Others can praise in their verse Mytilene, Rhodes and its
    glories
  Great Ephesus, high-walled twin-harboured Corinth,
Bacchus's home town Thebes, or Delphi, haunt of Apollo,
  Or Tempe up in Thessaly. Some poets
Concentrate all their lives on a long-drawn epic extolling
  Virgin Athene's city, plucking sprigs of
Olive from Attica's history, wreaths to adorn their foreheads;
  And some, to honour Juno's reputation,
Celebrate Argos, country for horses, and rich Mycenae.
  But, as for me, neither the sturdy Spartan
Hills nor the the low lush fields of Larissa can knock at the
    heart as
  My Tibur does, the Sibyl's blooming grotto,
Anio's fine cascade, Tiburnus' grove and the orchards
  Whose rivulets weave a dance of irrigation.
Winds from the south blow clear; they sweep clouds out of a
    dark sky
  And never breed long rains: remember, Plancus,
Good wine does just that for the wise man—chases away all
  The stresses and distresses of existence.
Hold to this truth in the camp, hemmed round by the glitter-
    ing standards,
  And, when you come home soon to Tibur's leafy
Privacy, keep it in mind. When Teucer was sent into exile
  From Salamis by his father, undismayed he
Set on his wine-flushed brow, they say, brave garlands of
    poplar

And cried to his dispirited companions:
"Fortune will prove more kind than a parent. Wherever she
    takes us,
Thither, my friends and comrades, we shall follow.
Teucer shall lead and his star shall preside. No cause for
    despair, then.
Phoebus, who never lies, has pledged a second
Salamis, rival in name, to arise in a new-found country.
You who have stayed by me through worse disasters,
Heroes, come, drink deep, let wine extinguish our sorrows.
We take the huge sea on again tomorrow."

Horace, *Songs* 1.7 (James Michie)

MARITAL BLISS

I

You wish to marry Priscus, Paula?
   Very wise of you!
Priscus, though, declines, you tell me?
   He's wise, too.

Martial, *Epigrams* 9.10 (Paul Nixon)

II

You're so alike, you're matched for life:
A nitwit man, his nitwit wife.
   (I wonder then why it should be
   That such a pair cannot agree?)

Martial, *Epigrams* 8.35 (Thomas Steele)

III

Hubby handed back your baby?
Paramour returned him?

Are they hinting to you, maybe:
"Find the one who earned him"?

> Martial, *Epigrams* 10.95 (Thomas Steele)

IV

Aper pierced his wife's heart with an arrow—
   While fooling, they rule.
The wife, as it happened, was wealthy.
   He knows how to fool.

> Martial, *Epigrams* 10.16 (Paul Nixon)

V

Caesinia still, they say, is guiltless found
Of every vice, by her own lord renown'd:
And well she may, she brought ten thousand pound.
She brought him wherewithal to be (call'd) chaste;
His tongue is tied in golden fetters fast:
He sighs, adores, and courts her every hour;
Who would not do as much for such a dower?
She writes love letters to the youth in grace;
Nay, tips the wink before the cuckold's face;
And might do more; her portion makes it good;
 Wealth has the privilege of widowhood.

VI

   She duly, once a month, renews her face;
Meantime, it lies in daub, and hid in grease:
Those are the husband's nights; she craves her due,
He takes fat kisses, and is stuck in glue.
But, to the lov'd adult'rer when she steers,
Fresh from the bath, in brightness she appears:
For him the rich Arabia sweats her gum,
And precious oils from distant Indies come,
How haggardly soe'er she looks at home.
Th' eclipse then vanishes; and all her face
Is open'd, and restor'd to ev'ry grace;

The crust remov'd, her cheeks, as smooth as silk,
Are polish'd with a wash of asses' milk;
And should she to the farthest North be sent,
A train of these attend her banishment.
But, hadst thou seen her plaister'd up before,
'T was so unlike a face, it seem'd a sore.

VII

Her head, alone, will twenty dressers ask.
Psecas, the chief, with breast and shoulders bare,
Trembling, considers every sacred hair;
If any straggler from his rank be found,
A pinch must for the mortal sin compound.
Psecas is not in fault; but, in the glass,
The dame's offended at her own ill face.
That maid is banish'd; and another girl,
More dextrous, manages the comb and curl;
The rest are summon'd on a point so nice;
And first, the grave old woman gives advice.
The next is call'd, and so the turn goes round,
As each for age, or wisdom, is renown'd:
Such counsel, such delib'rate care they take,
As if her life and honor lay at stake:
With curls on curls, they build her head before,
And mount it with a formidable tow'r.
A giantess she seems; but, look behind,
And then she dwindles to the pigmy kind.
Duck-legg'd, short-waisted, such a dwarf she is,
That she must rise on tiptoes for a kiss.

Juvenal, *Satires* 6.136-41, 461-73,
490-507 (John Dryden)

A HANDY BOOK OF HOME REMEDIES

The hair of young boy-children which is first clipped off, is held to be
a singular remedy for to assuage the painful fits of the gout, if the same
be tied fast about the foot that is grieved: and generally their hair, so
long as they be under fourteen years of age, easeth the said anguish, if

it be applied unto the place. Likewise, the hair of a man's head cureth the biting of a mad dog, if it be laid to the place with vinegar: it healeth also the wounds in the head, applied with oil or wine. But if it were plucked from his head whiles he hangeth upon the gallows, then it is sovereign for the quartan ague: but we may choose whether we believe it or no. Certainly the hair of the head burnt to ashes, is known to be very good for a cancerous ulcer. If a woman take the first tooth that a young child cast, set it in a bracelet, and so wear it continually about her wrist, it will preserve her from the pains and grievances of her matrice & natural parts. Tie the great toe and that which is next unto it together, you shall see how it will allay any risings and tumours in the share. Bind gently the two middle fingers of the right hand, with a linen thread, mark of what force this remedy is to repress the rheum falling into the eyes, and how it will keep them from being bleared. If all be true that is commonly said, the stone that one hath voided and thrust out of the body, easeth all others that be pained with the stone, if the same be kept tied fast to the share: also it doth mitigate the grief of the liver; and procureth speedy deliverance to women in travail with child. *Franius* affirmeth moreover, that in all these cases it would do the better, if one were cut for it, and that it were taken forth of the bladder by way of incision. If a woman be near her time and looks every day to fall to labour and cry out, let the man come by whom she is with child, and after he hath ungirt himself, gird her about the middle with his own girdle, and unloose the same again, saying withal this charm, *I tied the knot, and I will undo it again,* and therewith go his ways, she shall soon after fall to her business and have more speedy deliverance.

. . .

As for the toothache, it is a common speech, that if one bite off a piece of some tree that hath been blasted, or smitten with lightning, provided always that he hold his hands behind him at his back in so doing, the said morsel or piece of wood will take away the toothache if it be laid unto the tooth. Some there be who give direction to take the perfume of a man's tooth burning in the fire, for to ease the toothache of a man; and sembably of a woman's tooth to help women in the same case. Others you shall have, that prescribe to draw one of the eye-teeth, called in Latin canini, out of the head of man or woman lying dead and not yet interred, and to wear the same against the toothache. It is a common speech, that the earth found in or about a man or woman's skull, is a singular depilatory, and fetcheth away the hair of the eyebrows. As for the grass or weed that groweth therein (if any such may be found) it causeth the teeth to fall out of the head with chewing only.

.   .   .

What moveth us to wish health and say, God help, or bless, when one sneezeth? for even Tiberius Caesar, who otherwise was known for a grim sir, and the most unsociable and melancholy man in the world, required in that manner to be salved and wished well unto, whenever he sneezed, though he were mounted in his chariot.

Pliny (the Elder), *The Encyclopedia*,
vol. 28 (Philemon Holland)

ITALIAN COOKING

Who busts his Daddy's guggle with the grip
Of hands unholy, feed (than hemlock more
Disastrous), garlic. Lord, what rock-ribbed guts
Farmers must have! Venom gnaws at my heart.
Snake in the grass for salad, with his blood
To do me dirt? Or has Canidia drib-
bled in my dish? Handsomer far than all
The other Argonauts, Jason, Medea
Gawked after. Him she anointed with this
So he could yoke and drag unbroken bulls.
She garlicked gifts, revenging on his whore,
And machinaed by dragon through the clouds.
There's nothing worse—not little Dogstar's tinkle
On thirsty Apulia, nor the cloak
That shouldered bubbling flame through Hercules.
Maecenas, if you feel again like giving
Me the hotgut, I pray that every time
You go for a girl's mouth you get a fist,
And she lie pokerbacked at the bed's edge.

Horace, *Intermittent Metres* 3
(Nicholas Kilmer)

BILLS

I

What's this draft whistling through your house?—
    no East wind dank;
an *over*draft is blowing coldly
    from the bank.

Catullus, *Songs* 26 (G. W.)

II

You don't owe a cent, not a cent,
Sestus,
we say.
(For he owes who is able,
Sestus,
to pay).

Martial, *Epigrams* 2.3 (Thomas Steele)

III

So please the gods, soon at my home
as well as anywhere at Rome,
Fabullus, you will nobly dine—
if you will bring good food along,
a pretty wench, some wit, some wine,
and every kind of jest and song.
Then you'll dine well.
                    For things get worse.
I've only cobwebs in my purse.
But I can promise you at least
Love's Essence to adorn our feast,
for Venus and her Cupids lent
my girl their richest beauty-scent.
One sniff, and you'll forget your woes,
praying to be entirely nose.

Catullus, *Songs* 13 (Jack Lindsay)

129

TO HIS WIFE

Love, let us live as we have lived, nor lose
 The little names that were the first night's grace,
And never come the day that sees us old,
 I still your lad, and you my little lass.
Let me be older than old Nestor's years,
 And you the Sibyl, if we heed it not.
What should we know, we two, of ripe old age?
 We'll have its richness, and the years forgot.

Ausonius, *Epigrams* 40 (Helen Waddell)

FOR A DEAD WIFE

 if anything when words are heard no more
 can gratefully by the grave yet be received
 from this our—
 (Calvus, shall I call it Grief,
 this Missing-something
 of a bygone day
 painting afresh the years of youth and love
 this Tear
 we shed for friendships long since lost)—
 surely her death untimely brings less pain
 to your Quintilia than it wakes her joy
 in knowledge of the love you bear for her.

Catullus, *Songs* 96 (Frank O. Copley)

DEAD WIFE TO HER HUSBAND

Paullus, your grief weighs down the earth above me.
It is useless, love; no prayer moves these black gates.
Once we come to this kingdom, we are captives—
the walls of hell are adamant as the Fates.
Though Pluto may hear your pleading here in the darkness,
the Styx will drink your tears and show no sign.

16. Portrait bust. Paris, Louvre.

I set a decent pattern in these halls;
Days had a quiet rhythm . . .

Prayers move the gods; these doors clang shut on shadows
when Charon has taken the toll, as he took mine.
This is the meaning of those wailing trumpets
when fire consumed the couch where my body lay.
Nothing could save me—not our love, our marriage,
ancestral glory, our children who mourn today:
they could not keep Cornelia from her dying.
What am I now but dust that a hand could hold?
Black doom and shallow pools of stagnant water
and the streams I walk through, silent and icy-cold,
you know I come here innocent and unready.
God of the darkness, grant me your dark grace!
Or, if Aeacus sit with his urn beside him,
let him find by lot what punishment I must face.
Let Minos and Rhadamanthus and the Furies
join him as judges. Tell the court, "Be still."
Let the stone roll back, and the wheel stop for an hour,
and the dusty lips of Tantalus drink their fill.
For one day, Cerberus, do not attack your victims,
while the chain hangs slack and quiet from the bar.
If I speak falsehood, send me to join the Danaids
and carry water, like them, in a leaking jar.
Does ancient lineage gain its recognition?
Africa's conquest was my father's boast;
my mother's family was no less distinguished—
each name upholds our house like a solid post.
I was born to this, and when the wreath of marriage
caught up my hair, and I was a woman grown,
it was your bed, my Paullus, that I came to
and now have left. The carving on the stone
says, SHE WED BUT ONCE. O fathers long respected,
victors in Africa, be my defense . . .
and Perseus, proud of great Achilles' kinship
and his who broke through hell's bleak battlements:
I asked no favors when Paullus was made censor;
no evil found its way within our walls.
I do not think I have disgraced my fathers;
I set a decent pattern in these halls.
Days had a quiet rhythm; no scandal touched us

132

from the wedding torch to the torch beside my bier.
A certain integrity is proof of breeding:
the love of virtue should not be born of fear.
Whoever the judge, whatever the lot fate gives me,
no woman needs to blush who sits at my side—
not Cybele's priestess, Claudia, pulling to safety
the boat with the holy image, caught in the tide;
not the Vestal who swore by her robe she would rekindle
the fire they said she had left, and the ash blazed flame;
and most of all not you, my mother, Scribonia—
all but the way of my death you would have the same.
Your grief and the grief of Rome ennoble my spirit;
the tears of Caesar protect my soul in hell.
He mourns for me, half-sister to his daughter—
among men's tears, a god may weep as well.
For my children I wore the mother's robe of honor;
it was no empty house I left behind.
Lepidus, Paullus, still you bring me comfort:
you closed my eyes when death had made them blind.
Twice in the curule chair I have seen my brother;
they cheered him as consul the day before I died.
And you, my daughter, ideal of your censor-father,
choose one husband and live content at his side:
our clan will rest on the children that you give it.
Secure in their promise, I board the boat and rejoice.
Mine is the final triumph of any woman,
that her spirit earn the praise of a living voice.
Paullus, I leave you as pledge of my love our children:
guard them; this care still burns in my dead heart.
Their hands seek yours; their arms lie round your shoulders.
You must take a father's and now a mother's part.
When you kiss their tear-streaked faces, add my kisses.
The house, the whole house, darling, needs your care.
Weep for me—but I beg, let no one see you,
the children least of all guess your despair.
Long haunted nights—how many of them wait you,
with dreams to break the heart and trick the eye.
O when you speak in secret to my phantom,
say every word as though I would reply.

And if our bed in the atrium grows too lonely,
so that a new wife comes to take my place—
dear sons, make her feel welcome; praise her virtues,
proving your own, and do it with good grace.
Mention me rarely. It may rouse her anger
if she and I are constantly compared,
and to her detriment. If he seeks no solace
save days remembered from the life we shared—
as he grows older, let him not be lonely;
sorrows lie heavy enough upon him now.
I would add to yours the years that fate took from me:
love him I love, whose body age will bow.
It is well with me: I wore no robes of mourning;
you come to my tomb, my dear ones, all of you.
I plead no more. Witnesses, rise from sorrow;
a welcoming earth will grant my life its due.

My fathers live in light; the gods reward them.
If I deserve such grace, then bear me toward them.

Propertius, *Elegies* 4.11 (Constance Carrier)

CONSOLATION TO PARENTS

And so Death took him. Yet be comforted:
Above this sea of sorrow lift thy head.
Death—or his shadow—look, is over all;
What but an alternating funeral
The long procession of the nights and days?
The starry heavens fail, the solid earth
Fails and its fashion. Why, beholding this,
Why with our wail o'er sad mortality
Mourn we for men, mere men, that fade and fall?
Battle or shipwreck, love or lunacy,
Some warp o' the will, some taint o' the blood, some touch
Of winter's icy breath, the Dog-star's rage
Relentless, on the dank and ghostly mists
Of Autumn—any or all of these suffice
To die by. In the fee and fear of Fate

Lives all that is. We one by one depart
Into the silence—one by one. The Judge
Shakes the vast urn: the lot leaps forth: we die.
    But *he* is happy, and you mourn in vain.
He has outsoared the envy of gods and men,
False fortune and the dark and treacherous way,
—Scatheless: he never lived to pray for death,
Nor sinned—to fear her, nor deserved to die.
We that survive him, weak and full of woes,
Live ever with a fearful eye on Death—
The how and when of dying: 'Death' the thunder,
'Death' the wild lightning speaks to us.
                              In vain,—
Atedius hearkens not to words of mine.
Yet shall he hearken to the dead: be done,
Sweet lad he loved, be done with Death, and come,
Leaving the dark Tartarean halls, come hither;
Come, for thou canst: 'tis not to Charon given,
Nor yet to Cerberus, to keep in thrall
The innocent soul: come to thy father, soothe
His sorrow, dry his eyes, and day and night
A living voice be with him—look upon him,
Tell him thou art not dead (thy sister mourns,
Comfort her, comfort as a brother can)
And win thy parents back to thee again.

                Statius, *Stuff* 2.1, lines 207-34 (H. W. Garrod)

FOR EROTION

To you, dear parents, I remand
this dead girl gone, my lost delight;
in the darkness take her hand,
guide her past the triple bite:

    She's only six—(or would have been
    if death had waited six more days).

Ageless ones, let her play there;
listen to her lisp my name.

135

She was a little thing to bear:
Remember, Earth, and be the same.

Martial, *Epigrams* 5.34 (Thomas Steele)

TO A DEAD BROTHER

My odyssey of men and towns and seas
has brought me, brother, to these obsequies
too late, where only ashes wait for me
too early blanched, the dumb stuff left of you.

You and the Death that took you hear no plea
but ancient rites, where only tears are new—
to give the formal greeting as you go,
to mean "Farewell" and say "One last hello."

Catullus, *Songs* 101 (G. W.)

REGRETS

My first half century was done
With long ago, the year that's just begun
The fifty-seventh I've enjoyed the rolling sun.

The end is near and near the day
The god long since assigned for my decay—
What useful thing have I contrived in so long stay!

My childhood was a tearful time
Under the smacking ferule; then the prime
Toga brought me to lies and vice and even crime!

Then wanton lust and wild excess
Befouled my youth—alas, I now confess
In sorrow and shame—with filth and mire of worthlessness!

Contention next gave instruments
To my vexed soul and often my intense
Evil desire to conquer bred harsh consequence.

Twice in administering the law
I held the reins over proud towns and saw
The good given their rights, the evil struck with awe.

My gracious Prince at length relieved
My army service and myself received
As his close helper: nearly regal rank achieved!

So life flew by; my hair, grown white
Unnoticed, flashed old age—for I had quite
Forgot under what consul I first saw the light.

The snow flakes on my head disclose
How often since the sun's brought round the snows,
How often to meadows freed from frost returned the rose.

Prudentius, *Hymns* (Asa M. Hughes)

RETIREMENT SECURITY

Four teeth, sweet Aelia, you had:
One cough took two.
Cough two: three, four.

Rejoice, dear Aelia, be glad!
Coughs infinite
Can take no more.

Martial, *Epigrams* 2.19 (Thomas Steele)

THE LEGACY-HUNTERS

I

He gives you gifts and calls you sage
(they're useless gifts and he's a bore);
it seems that he respects your age
(he wishes you to age no more).

II

Gemellus hunts Manilla's hand;
his courting her few understand:
  In such a dog, what can he see?
  —It must be that she has T.B.

III

You're well-born, rich, and childless too.
Is friendship meant for such as you?
  Your childhood pals were pals for free;
  your new friends want a legacy.

Martial, *Epigrams* 8.27, 1.10, 11.44
(Thomas Steele)

IV

I see Dolabella has been left a ninth of Livia's estate on condition he
changes his name. Good essay-question in social ethics: "Should a young
noble change his name in order to benefit under a lady's will?" We shall
be able to answer it with more scientific accuracy when we know how
much a ninth amounts to.

Cicero, *Letter to Atticus* (L. P. Wilkinson)

TROJAN EPITAPHS

Amphimachus and Nastes
  both men Nomion's sons:
A little dust and shadow,
  who were heroes, once.

Troy lies here,
  where Hector's ashes are:
Men and walls—
  a town in one small jar.

Words for Priam's empty grave:
Greeks tore my body, no man gave
me burial. My shade did fly

where Hector in a jar does lie—
in it, Troy and Asia see
and all the little left of me.

Ausonius, *Epitaphs* 17, 14, 23 (G. W.)

AGES OF MAN

"Time was, when we were sow'd, and just began,
From some few fruitful drops, the promise of a man.
Then Nature's hand (fermented as it was)
Molded to shape the soft, coagulated mass;
And when the little man was fully form'd,
The breathless embryo with a spirit warm'd;
But when the mother's throes began to come,
The creature, pent within the narrow room,
Breaks his blind prison, pushing to repair
His stifled breath and draw the living air;
Cast on the margin of the world he lies,
A helpless babe, but by instinct he cries.
He next essays to walk, but, downward press'd,
On four feet imitates his brother beast:
By slow degrees he gathers from the ground
His legs, and to the rolling chair is bound;
Then walks alone; a horseman now become,
He rides a stick, and travels round the room.
In time he vaunts among his youthful peers,
Strong-bon'd, and strung with nerves, in pride of years.
He runs with mettle his first merry stage;
Maintains the next, abated of his rage,
But manages his strength, and spares his age.
Heavy the third and stiff, he sinks apace,
And, tho' 't is downhill all, but creeps along the race.
Now sapless on the verge of death he stands,
Contemplating his former feet and hands;
And, Milo-like, his slacken'd sinews sees,
And wither'd arms, once fit to cope with Hercules,
Unable now to shake, much less to tear, the trees.
    "So Helen wept, when her too faithful glass

17. Old man. Paris, Louvre.

Now sapless on the verge of death he stands,
Contemplating his former feet and hands.

Reflected to her eyes the ruins of her face,
Wond'ring what charms her ravishers could spy,
To force her twice, or ev'n but once enjoy!
   "Thy teeth, devouring Time, thin, envious Age,
On things below still exercise your rage:
With venom'd grinders you corrupt your meat,
And then, at ling'ring meals, the morsels eat."

Ovid, *Transformations* 15.216-36 (John Dryden)

PART III

Love's Crucible

The Romans had to admit their literary indebtedness to Greece in most areas. In two fields, however, they could lay claim to real originality: in satire, and in the love-elegy. From Mimnermus to the late epigrams of the Anthology, the Greek poets treat love as an impersonal force; if they are tortured by it, they observe their own symptoms with a clinical detachment. But the Roman elegists treat love as an engagement of the total person with another person. *Their elegiacs turn epigram into autobiography. The autobiographical form is there, whether the content is fictitious or based on fact: a real need is served by the melodious Latin mistresses—the Lycoris of Gallus, Lesbia of Catullus, Nemesis of Tibullus, Cynthia of Propertius, Corinna of Ovid. The elusive mistress initiates a psychological cold war that tests man's hidden resources. It is only half a joke when these poets talk of love as their field of trial and combat. The war fever even leads them out to the farthest reaches of the romantic code:* dulce et decorum est pro domina mori.

DEEP IN

I was in love
like a bug in a pail.

Laberius, Mime *The Virgin* (G. W.)

PET BIRD

My love's little bird,
teased by her finger-tips
sharpened to quick bites
when the mood is on her

144

to play (as I know she can)
her cares away—

I wish my sad heart
could be eased
by your levity.

Catullus, *Songs* 2 (G. W.)

A FUNERAL

All Venuses and Cupids,
all Love's high society,
compose yourselves for sorrow
pre-Raphaelitically:

The corpse is on the bier (poor bird).

Its mistress is mine,
but she loved it best—
above herself.
It was a charmer, like a child
forever at her breast
(darting here, true, or there,
but chattering always back to her).

Now it takes the dark subumbrous way
from whose bourne no bird returns.
An evil fate for you, you Fates,
who masticate whatever's beautiful!
You took beauty, the bird,
which was bad enough.
But worst of all you
irritated her eye
with a tear.

Catullus, *Songs* 3 (G. W.)

PLAYTHINGS

Hard fate humbles the girl,
she's lost her pet—

145

not Lesbia's trained sparrow
sung by that softy Catullus; nor yet

Ianthis' dark dove wafted
by Stella's words into a world of jet.

Her loveliness is darkened
by a weightier loss of joy:

death took her not-yet-twenty
dear boy

and his not-yet-polysyllable-length
sweet toy.

Martial, *Epigrams* 7.14 (G. W.)

CHARMER

Paint a whitelimbed girl for me
Such as love himself might fashion;
So that nothing hidden be,
Paint her with a lover's passion.
Through her silken garments show
All her body's rosy wonder—
Love will set your sense aglow,
Longing tear your heart asunder.
Call it, when your work you scan,
"Portrait of a wretched man."

Octavian, *Song* (Howard Mumford Jones)

S.O.S. TO VENUS

Angel of Love, high-thronëd in Cnidos
Regent of Paphos, no more repine:
Leave thy loved Cyprus; too long denied us
Visit our soberly-censëd shrine.

Haste, and thine Imp, the fiery-hearted,
Follow, and Hermes; and with thee haste

146

The Nymphs and Graces with robe disparted
And, save thou chasten him, Youth too chaste.

Horace, *Songs* 1.30 (H. W. Garrod)

MAGIC NAME

Utter Morality, the Chaste Mind
(take my advice for it, Fuscus)
needs no bristling guard
of Moorish spears,
no heavy pack
of poisoned arrows—

though boiled by Syrtian sands,
cold-shouldered by the Caucasus,
or dreamy-eyed by fairyland Hydaspes.

Example? I!—alone
in Sabine forests, met a WOLF
while single-mindedly singing to Lalage
(that's the charm) absent-minded
to all else; wended unharmed
my unarmed way by him

—though he was fierce! Worse
than bellicose Apulia feeds
across its acorny wide fields,
wiry as dry Numidia
(whose nipples *only* lions draw)
ever nursed.

So I don't worry: put me out
in a marsh never visited by leaves of spring
(that visit other places annually),
where fogs choke air and land.

Or: where sun rides down
singeing-close upon the plains,
I'm o.k. I sing her name for safety,
Lalage the charmer, my own gentle
wolf-disarmer, who laughs like her name.

Horace, *Songs* 1.22 (G. W.)

147

18. Sicilian girls. Sicily, Piazza Armerina.

. . . warm rain around us as the fountains flow—
then see me brighten at your nakedness . . .

MAGIC WALK

If she but move or look, her step, her face
By stealth adopt unmeditated grace.

Tibullus, *Songs* 3.8, lines 7-8 (Horace Walpole)

LESBIA

Quintia's claims I grant
one by one—white, willowy, tall,
these beauties accumulate in her;
but do not fuse. There are
no scintillations through
those unelectric limbs.

The sum collects, and then coheres
in Lesbia, with all the best of all the others
all her own.

Catullus, *Songs* 86 (G. W.)

THE RING

Hear me, O ring:
my pretty girl shall wear you on her finger!
yourself a Zero—
but your true value is the giver's love.
Go as my gift
to bring my lady pleasure,
circle her finger fair as she fits me
between her thighs when we are deep in love.
Twice lucky ring!
(Strange that a man should envy his own gift!
and yet I know how passionately, how sweetly
she'll stroke and tend it.)
Or rather, I would be that ring, transformed
by Circe's witchcraft or Protean arts
to grace her hand.

149

And now my love, my dear, open your tunic—
your hand to guide me where my touch discovers
your waiting breasts—and then, by lover's magic,
I'll escape your finger
and slip down to the haven of my delight.
(I'd help her seal love letters
in hopes her lips would meet me with a kiss.)
Nor would I let you
imprison me with jewels in a dark casket—
my gentle charms would make you fail to drop me.

Wear me each morning as we bathe together,
warm rain around us
as the fountains flow—
then see me brighten at your nakedness,
and though a ring,
I'll serve you like a man!
Why dwell on fantasies? My gift shall tell her
I'll love but her forever—
                          go, little ring!

                    Ovid, *Love Affairs* 2.15 (Horace Gregory)

SORRY, NO VISA

In this era, Tullus, and in your company,
I have no fear of learning an unknown ocean
(leaving on Adriatic salt or the Aegean).
We could mount the mountains of the utmost north together
and saunter beyond the domes of Ethiopia.
But blenching, blushing, beseeching, she plaits
me around with words and again I remain.

Whole night after night she argues, argues: heat, heat, heat.
Forlorn, and God-forsaken, and there are no Gods;
denying she is mine, or was sometime, or will
be next; she makes the customary menaces to me
(to master in anger from mistress in distress).
I can't hold out an hour: Damn the man
who could be that indifferently in love.

Are knowledge of Athens' sophistications
and a glance at costly Asian antiques
worth so much to me when their price is Cynthia
devising curses against me as my launch withdraws?
and she marks her face, her hands gone crazy, and says
her kisses will belong to the wind that comes against me,
and nothing is harder to bear than betrayal.

Try to surpass your uncle's honored reign.
Restore their ancient rights (forgotten by now)
to our allies. You are the man. Your youth never
has lain negligent for the yen of love: Your love
always has been the business of the nation's wars.
Never may the Boy God bring upon you labors like mine,
nor the universe of particulars my tears know.

Allow me meanwhile, whose luck has always been to lie
beaten, to offer my soul finally to sinful
idleness. Many have been the men who were glad
to die in the extremity of length of love: May I too,
when loam houses me, be listed in that company.
Born unfit for action (even citation)
Fate has impressed me into Love's Service.

You, whether where plush Ionia extends, whether
where Pactólus tints Lydian ploughlands moist-dark,
Whether you pedal on those lands or paddle over
the deep, you will have your share in a welcome New Regime.
If in that future an hour not unpermissive
of reminiscence comes to you, Tullus,
you will know, if I live, under what hard star.

Propertius, *Elegies* 1.6 (Richard E. Braun)

"SEDUCTION" IN "THE COLLEGE OUTLINE SERIES"

Let us consider (if any of us hasn't)
Seduction as a Science.
Here is a tome on the subject;
now be lovers by the book.

Science angles sails into the wind,
    lifts and drops oars on a rationale;
science weights and steers chariots;
    why not find *love*'s Basic Laws?
Not every Sunday horseman or sailor
    can take over for a Halsey or Arcaro!
So with love's finer points, in which
    call me Master of the Hunt,
    or Captain Blithe.

Love is wild, all right, and tricky,
    but only a lad—impressionable.
Even Achilles went meekly to the woodshed
    when he was being schooled by Chiron;
the warrior who frightened all his foes
    (and, come to think of it, his friends)
    was awed by this weak old man,
and the rough hands that mastered Hector
    first fumbled inanely on the lyre;
so why may I not put Dan Cupid,
    another fighting lad,
    under headmaster's discipline?

Ovid, *Erotic Technique* 1.1-18 (G. W.)

ADVICE TO THE MEN

Women have hearts so various and strange,
One learns a thousand ways of making love.
No stretch of land is best for every harvest:
Here vines are grown, and over there, rich olives,
And still another, marvelous in wheat.
The heart takes on disguises out of air,
As many shapes as this wide world contains;
Wise lovers wear a mask for each occasion:
Like Proteus, one is volatile as water,
Or is a lion, or deep-rooted tree,
And then a wild-haired boar. Fish may be caught
In many different ways: some with a spear,

Others with hooks, and many are hauled in
Dragged to the boat in huge cave-bellied nets.
No one technique serves women of all ages:
The full-grown deer is not a careless doe—
She looks before she leaps, the trap unsprung.
Don't boast of learning to dim-witted females;
Or show off wit to shy, suburban matrons
You'll make them feel inferior and stupid—
Some women often fear an honest lover,
Yet always feel at ease with clever liars.

.   .   .

Don't ask a woman's age, or try to guess
Who ruled the state the hour that she was born:
These questions come from gray-faced bureaucrats,
Especially so if she is not too young,
If her first flowers are cut and first white hairs
Torn from her head, or artfully concealed.
These later years are rich, O restless lovers!
These fields yield fruit and you must sow them straightly
While you are quick and strong. Too soon, too soon,
Crook'd-back Old Age walks in on silent feet.
Bend to your oars, or plough the rugged earth,
Or use your fists in tight and bloody battle,
Or mount the girls to make them ask for more—
A warlike test of all your manly powers.
For women know their trade extremely well;
And years of practice make their practice perfect:
Time's loss is turned to gain—their artfulness
Shows never a sign of age—it seems eternal.
However you wish to tune them to your pleasure,
They'll answer in a thousand girlish ways—
No picture paints the methods they employ,
Women have more inventiveness than art.
Women who take you scarcely need temptation:
They love the give and take and yet once more
In bed joined with a man—yet men and women
Should take an equal measure of delight.

I hate to compromise, to take half-kisses—
That's why I lack a yearning for young boys.
I also hate the girl who goes halfway,
Who when she yields thinks that she's spinning wool.
Never mix housework with my joys of love:
I loathe a woman who finds love her duty;
I want to hear her murmuring delights,
Her wordless cries, and "Hold me, stay awhile";
To see her drunk with love, her eyes enraptured,
Or see her drowsy, waiting to be waked,
Yet holding off the moment when she yields.

After a woman passes thirty-five,
Her gifts are ripe, for Nature has endowed her
With skills unknown to girls of seventeen.
Let the impatient drink the new-made wine;
I'll take deep draughts from rich and well-stocked cellars.
Only the full-grown plane tree tempers heat
And shields us from the furies of Apollo—
And fresh-sprung reeds tear at our naked feet.
Would you take Hermione 'stead of Helen?
Is Gorge better looking than her mother?
If you desire beauties at their best,
Seasoned and ripe, and show yourself a man,
Your victories are those of love in glory.
You need not fear to win your just rewards.

Look at that broad sophisticated bed
Where willing lovers lie. Stand guard, my Muse,
Behind the closing door; you need not help them:
They'll speak well for themselves—their hands, their fingers,
Will search out places where Love plants his arrows—
So Hector's hands pleased his Andromache,
Adroit in bed as they were skilled at war—
And so the great Achilles' as he fondled
Slave Briseis when he dropped, weary with fighting,
In her soft bed—his very hands stained red
With Trojan blood. (Was this your pleasure, Briseis,
To know his hand between your yielding thighs?
The naughty girl was happier than ever.)

O love's delight must not be reached too soon,
But warmed by fond delays. When you have touched
That place where women love to be consoled,
Don't be ashamed to stroke it as she wills,
Her eyes as bright as sunlight on clear waters.
Then she'll begin to murmur her soft cries,
Sigh gently, and find words that answer joy.
Don't fill your sail too high, and leave her waiting,
Nor let her speed ahead, keep pace together;
The full delight complete: then man and woman
Spent with their love, drop from each other's arms.
The slow pace is the best when you are free
To play and kiss and then begin again:
No fears to haunt the secret work of love.
But when both time and place are not your own,
All speed ahead, and spur her flanks to motion
As galloping horses racing to desire.

Ovid, *Erotic Technique* 1.753-68, 2.663-733
(Horace Gregory)

ADVICE TO THE GIRLS

Don't load your earrings with crude stones of flashing colors—
That polycolored Indians wear for show—
The kind of jewel that's snatched from greenish waters;
Nor weight your dress with gilded ornaments,
Or lace of gold—such signs of lavishness
In golden nets to trap us, hurt our eyes.
We're captured by an artful elegance.
And don't neglect your hair: one touch of art
'll change your disarray to matchless beauty.
Nor is one style the best for all fair creatures—
Each girl should find her own and gaze devoutly
At what she sees in her own looking glass!
Her face is oval: straightly parted hair
(No ornaments at all) becomes her best—
This fashion was the choice of Laodamia.
Her face is round: then she should show her ears
And knot her hair up high upon her head.

155

One girl should let her hair drop to both shoulders—
The way Apollo looked when lost in music
And his deft fingers stroked the golden lyre.
Another girl should wear a braided crown
Such as Diana wore when she was dressed
Short-skirted for the hunt, waking the terror
Of beasts who ran before her.

                    This young beauty
Should let her hair fall loose—while yet another
Should wind her hair close to her shapely head;
One girl should wear a glittering tortoise shell,
Another, comb her hair in waterfalls.
Count all the acorns of the thick-boughed oak,
Count all the bees that swarm in Sicily,
Count all the savage beasts in Alpine forests,
Yet more than these are ways to dress your hair,
And each new day invents another fashion.
Wild wind-blown styles are often most attractive,
As though the girl had just stepped out of bed,
(And yet she came fresh from a beauty parlor)—
Art often imitates the casual air.
The careless style was famous with Iole
(Who looked disheveled in a fallen city)
Whose air charmed Hercules. He said, "God help me;
This is the girl I love!" So Ariadne
In her distress looked wild and Bacchus raised her
Into his chariot to mount the skies,
While all the happy Satyrs danced and cheered!

Nature is kind to all of you, my dears,
She hints at many ways to hide your flaws.
Though Time strips all of us—hair falls away
As leaves before the wind. A woman tints
Her thin and fading crown with golden washes,
Her hair is more glorious than ever.
Or she can walk out in a Transformation,
Piled high in golden braids upon her head,
And no one thinks the less of her for that!
Even in the Circus, on a crowded morning,

Where marble Hercules and the Nine Muses
Watch everything we do, the ladies buy
New curls or anything their heads desire.

What shall I say of clothes and how to dress?
Gold lace is not my style, nor heavy colors;
I speak for lighter colors and few clothes,
The inexpensive dress that walks the street.
Don't go insane with diamonds and silks
Or try to wear a fortune on your back!
On days when South Wind brings no threat of rain
Look at the cloudless colors of the sky,
Wear these for love, or light, gold-tinted gray,
The color of the Ram (who, so I've heard,
Saved Helle and Phrixus from their shrewd stepmother).
Or soft blue-grays as thin as glancing waves.
(I've dreamt that water nymphs were dressed like that.)
Or take the color that resembles saffron,
Transparent as the dew Aurora wears,
The kind of dress she fancies when she mounts
Bridle and bit on her dawn-breaking horses,
Or soft pale greens like the Paphian myrtle,
Or violet like the brilliant amethyst,
Or white-rose-belted-in-cream, or dazzling whiteness
Seen in the flight of cranes from northern Thrace.
(Nor, Amaryllis, are your colors gone:
The almond tints, and brave bright chestnut browns,
Or natural shades in honey-colored wools.)
Then choose your colors as you'd pluck gay flowers,
As variable as those earth wears in Spring
(Slow Winter dwindles as pink buds appear).
From many colors as these to tint your dresses,
And many more, then take your choice, my dears,
To suit yourselves. Each girl should know her colors!
Smoke-gray is wonderful for white-skinned girls
(Briseis was captured in a dark gray cloak);
And dark-skinned girls look marvelous in white
(White was the costume Andromeda wore

So well the Gods grew envious of her beauty
And doomed the island that was once her home).

. . .

Each girl should know the pleasures of her body
And how to use them when she falls in love:
Your beauties guide your style: a pretty face
Always looks best if girls lie on their backs—
But if your back looks better, hide your face;
Then show your pretty buttocks to your lover.
When Milanion mounted Atalanta,
He raised her lovely legs upon his shoulders;
If you have legs like hers, then get your lover
To do the same for you. A little girl
Should mount her friend and ride him like a pony.
But when a girl's as tall as Hector's wife,
She never rides on top to make him please her.
A woman whose long flanks invite attention
Should turn half-kneeling on the open bed,
Bend back her head and then receive her lover.
But if her thighs look young and her breasts perfect,
She should instruct her lover to stand up,
To mount her as she lies across the sheets.
Nor is it wrong then to let down your hair
Showing the raptures of a Phylleian mother
Her head sunk back in flowing locks around her.
If childbirth shows deep lines above your thighs
Then turn about, and like swift Parthian horses,
Take the delight that quickens your behind.
I know a thousand ways of making love:
One that is easy, never makes you weary,
Is resting half-reclined on your right side—
Of course there're many more. But of these arts
Not even Phoebus' oracles at Delphi,
Nor Ammon with horns sprouting from his head
Could give you more than what my Muse foretells.
These arts my lifework; if my long career
At making love means anything at all,
I speak the truth—my poems proof of it.

A woman when she gives herself to love
Should feel the deepest raptures of her being,
Should be love's act herself and melt away
To join her lover's exquisite delight.
Then she should make sweet sounds and little noises
And name the places that her lover touches.
Even if Nature fails you with half measures
Of what your joy should be, deceive your lover;
Make all the little noises that enchant him—
(O poor unhappy girl if her sweet cunt—
That place where men and women find their haven—
Should not respond to love, pretend it does).
Don't let him think you're lying: spread your legs;
Or moan and sigh and lure him with your eyes.
Look, naughty girl, that place is waiting, ready—
It speaks a secret language, all its own.
And if a woman gets her fill of glory
When she makes love and takes joy in her lover,
She's half-indifferent when she asks for money.
A few words more: as you make love, my dear,
Don't open every window in your room;
A woman's body is enhanced by shadows.

Ovid, *Erotic Technique* 3.129-92,
771-808 (Horace Gregory)

HEART'S DISGUISES

Lesbia forever on me rails,
To talk of me she never fails.
Now, hang me, but for all her art,
I find that I have gained her heart.

My proof is this: I plainly see
The case is just the same with me;
I curse her every hour sincerely,
Yet, hang me, but I love her dearly.

Catullus, *Songs* 92
(Jonathan Swift)

THE ADVANTAGES OF ARTISTRY

Doing, a filthy pleasure is, and short;
And done, we straight repent us of the sport:
Let us not then rush blindly on unto it,
Like lustful beasts, that only know to do it:
For lust will languish, and that heat decay.
But thus, thus, keeping endless holiday,
Let us together closely lie and kiss,
There is no labour, nor no shame in this;
This hath pleas'd, doth please, and long will please; never
Can this decay, but is beginning ever.

Petronius, *Songs* 101 (Ben Jonson)

QUALIFICATIONS

Here's the mistress that I choose.
Careless brawls she won't refuse,
And bawdy words she'll often use;
Lovely, lively, loose in act,
She'll smack and let herself be smacked,
And smacked will snuggle to a kiss.
But if she's not at all like this
And lives a chastely straitened life—
I tremble: she will be my wife.

Ausonius, *Epigrams* 88 (Jack Lindsay)

TAVERN REVELATION

Fie, friends! were glasses made for fighting,
And not your hearts and heads to lighten?
Quit, quit (for shame!) the savage passion,
Nor fall in such a mighty passion.

"Pistols and balls for six!" What sport!
How distant from "Fresh lights and port!"
Get rid of this ungodly rancor,
And bring your elbows to an anchor.

Why, though your stuff is plaguey heady,
I'll try to hold one bumper steady,
Let Ned but say what wench's eyes
Gave him the wound of which he dies.

You won't? Then damme if I drink!
A proper question this to blink!
Come, come; for whomsoe'er you feel
Those pains, you always sin genteel.

And were your girl the dirtiest drab
(You know I never was a blab)—
Out with it! (Whisper soft and low)—
WHAT! IS IT SHE? The filthy frow!

You've got a roaring sea to tame,
Boy (worthy of a better flame)!

What Lapland witch, what cunning man,
Can free you from this harridan?
Saint George himself, who slew the dragon,
Would idly waste his strength this hag on.

Horace, *Songs* 1.27 (Richard Porson)

THE CABARET GIRL

O Syrian dancing-girl with the filleted hair,
who taught you to swing your flanks with that shiver and
    shake?
She's dancing drunk in the tavern's smoky air,
lewd wench, to the clicketing sound the castanets make.

Why stay in the dusty heat where everything withers?
Come here, lie down, and be drunk awhile, you fool.
Look! tankards, cups, bowls, roses, flutes, and zithers,
and a trellis-arbour shadowed by reeds and cool.

In a cave full of music, like Pan's own cave, you can stretch—
the kind of piping you hear neath the open sky.
Thin wine just drawn from a pitchy cask they'll fetch,
and, brabbling and murmuring, water goes swiftly by.

19. Sicilian girls, detail. Sicily, Piazza Armerina.

. . . as a beach ball sails from man to man . . .

Look! there are wreaths from crocus and violets wrought,
gold melilot mixed with the rose's crimson hue.
From the virgin stream of Acheloïs are brought
lilies in willow-baskets—and all for you.

Look! little cheeses drying in baskets of rush,
and plums that come to their sweetness in autumn weather;
chestnuts, and apples with red that is pleasantly lush.
Look! fine Ceres and Love and Bacchus together.

Look! reddened blackberries, grapes in placid clusters,
sea-green cucumbers hanging from tendrils of shade.
Look! the arbour-god—with his willow-hook he blusters,
but even his terrible middle won't make us afraid.

Hither O wanderer. The little ass sweats, and he faints.
The dear little ass is Vesta's own darling. So spare.
The crickets are splitting the thickets with shrilling com-
      plaints,
the lizard is lurking cool in a bramble-lair.

Be wise and drench out the heat with wine in a glass
or a crystal-cup, if that's how you like your wine.
Lie tired in the vine-shade and let the summer hours pass,
and round your nodding head let the roses twine.

Yes, reap the kisses from someone mouth-open, kindly.
Death to the fellow whose questioning eyebrows frowned!
Why keep your wreaths for the ashes huddled blindly?
See your life and not your tombstone with roses crowned.

To hell with the future! Bring wine and the dice-box here.
"I'm coming, so kiss," says Death, and pinches my ear.

The Cabaret Girl, attributed to Vergil
(Jack Lindsay)

GENERAL PRACTITIONER

Twirled, as a beachball sails
from man to man—hand out,

she is there: to nod, kiss, caress,
wink, dart a hand,
nudge a foot.

"Oh look at my ring!"
(her lips pout silent
discourse across the room).

"Come hither, we'll sing!"
(but thither her hand
semaphores flirtation).

Naevius, *The Girl From Tarentum* (G. W.)

SPECIALIZATION

Men flock to Thais
from North and South;
yet she's a virgin—
all but her mouth.

Martial, *Epigrams* 4.84 (G. W.)

FINANCIAL REPORT

Without large sums you're never laid?
True enough; but sums *you* paid.

Martial, *Epigrams* 11.62 (G. W.)

CLODIA

*Caelius, a wild young ally of Cicero, had become one of the
many ex-lovers of Clodia, the notorious aristocrat identified by
many scholars as Catullus' "Lesbia." Clodia was the sister—
according to rumor, the lover as well—of Clodius, who had
brought about Cicero's exile. Clodia seems to have preferred
destroying those who left her, and she tried to accomplish*

this in Caelius' case by bringing suit against him for stealing from her and conspiring with her servants to poison her. Cicero exonerates his friend in this speech, scores against his old enemy Clodius, and enjoys the strange role in which Clodia's prosecuting lawyers had cast her in their speeches— as a defender of public morals. He especially enjoys the story that Caelius had a rendezvous with his poison-peddler at the public baths—one of the places where gossip said Clodia plied her extensive trade and hobby:

I have observed, my lords, that you have with great attention heard my friend Lucius Herennius, and though in a great measure you were enchanted by his wit and manner of expression, yet have I sometimes been afraid that this sly subtle method of introducing a charge might, gradually and insensibly, at last insinuate itself into your belief. For he talked a great deal about luxury; a great deal about lust; a great deal about the vices of youth, and about their manners; and the same gentleman who, in all other lights of life, is gentle and an agreeable master of that mild humanity which wins the affections of mankind, was on this occasion as testy as an old uncle, a censor, or a schoolmaster. He rated Marcus Caelius more than ever a parent did a son, and gave him a long lecture upon intemperance and incontinency.

. . .

It is true, I have both seen and heard of a great number in this city who, having not only gently slipped, and (as we say) "dipped their finger-ends" into this manner of life, but plunged their whole youth into pleasures, have sometimes emerged; have, as the saying is, husbanded what they had, and at last proved great and eminent men. For everybody admits that some scope is to be given to young men, and that the effusion of the youthful passions is directed by nature herself. If by their eruption no life is endangered, no house demolished, then are they generally thought to be gentle and venial.

But to me, from the *common* stain of youth you seemed to endeavor to fix some charge upon *Caelius*. Therefore all that deep silence with which your speech was heard proceeded from the reflections we were led into upon the general immorality of the age. But it is easy to bring a charge against luxury. It would employ me till night should I endeavor to go through all that may be said on that head; a declamation on

165

debaucheries, adulteries, wantonness and expences were endless. Though you had not in your eye any particular person, yet vice in general is a subject that would admit of a grave and copious argument. But, my lords, your wisdom will direct you not to wander from the particular charge; nor, when the prosecutor shall stimulate your severity and gravity and point it against crimes, against vices, against immoralities and against the times, will you discharge your indignation upon a man who is brought to your bar and who, not by his own crimes but the vices of many, is now liable to an imputation by him unmerited.

Therefore dare I not venture to return that answer to your severity which it deserves, (for I meant to be an advocate, and to plead for some indulgence to the sallies of youth). This, I say, I dare not venture upon, nor urge the privilege of green years. I disclaim the plea, which to all others is admitted of. All I beg is: if there lies against this age a general charge (which I own to be heavy), that neither the crimes of others, nor the vices of the times and age, may operate to the prejudice of my client. At the same time, while I beg for this, I do not refuse to answer pointedly to all the crimes that are charged upon him in particular.

There are two charges, one relating to gold, the other to poison, urged against the same person. It is said that gold was borrowed from Clodia, and poison prepared to dispatch her. Everything else urged is not criminal but scandalous, and more properly the subject of a scolding bout than a public trial. To call adulterer, whoremaster, pimp, is to rail not to accuse. For such charges there is not so much as a foundation where you can fix them; they are opprobrious terms rashly poured out, without any grounds, by a passionate accuser.

I have the source, I have the author, I have the precise principle and rise of all these calumnies in my eye. There was a necessity for gold?— he borrowed it of Clodia; he borrowed it without any evidence, and he had it as long as he pleased. Here I can perceive a strong presumption of a certain prodigious intimacy. He had a mind to kill the same lady?—he looked out for poison; he applied to all he could, he prepared it, he fixed on the place, he brought it. Here again I can discern the most inveterate hatred, with a most cruel quarrel broken out. In this whole affair, my lords, we have to do with Clodia, a woman not only noble but notorious—of whom *I* shall say nothing (except so far as I am obliged for the vindication of my client).

But, Gnaeus Domitius, your distinguished penetration informs you that our business lies with her only. If she *denies* that she lent gold to Caelius, if she does not affirm that he prepared poison for her, we are guilty of slander by our mentioning the mother of a family in a manner that is inconsistent with the decency, which the sanctity of matrons requires; but were that lady out of the question, there neither would be a crime of which my client could be convicted, nor any money to carry on the prosecution. So what ought we who are his advocates to do but repel those who attack us? This indeed I would do with great keenness, did there not subsist animosities betwixt me and that lady's husband—I mean her brother (I still fall into that mistake). Now I will act coolly, nor advance a step farther than my duty and the interest of my client oblige me; for I have always thought it unbecoming me to harbor any resentment against a woman, especially a lady who has the character of extending her good nature to all the world rather than of showing her spite to any particular person.

But first let me ask her whether she chooses that I should treat her in a serious solemn old-fashioned, or in a gentle complaisant gallant manner. If she chooses the sour manner and fashion, then must I raise some of the hoary gentlemen from the shades—not such a frilly-faced gentleman as she is fond of, but those bristle-beards which we see in old images and statues, one who will bang my lady, and speak for me if she should scold me into silence. Let some such in her own family start up: There! The blind old gentleman, the most proper that can be! (for his not being capable to see her will save him a great deal of grief).

Supposing now he were to start up, such would be his behavior, and such his language: "Woman, what have you to do with Caelius—with a stripling, with a stranger? Why were you so intimate with him as to lend him money; or why such a foe as to dread his poison? Have you not seen your father? Have you not seen that your uncle, your grandfather, your great-grandfather, and his father—all were consuls? Are you insensible that you were married to Quintus Metellus, a brave nobleman and a worthy patriot, who no sooner left the threshold of his own house than he rose superior to almost all his countrymen in merit, in glory and dignity? When you, yourself of noble descent, by him were married into an illustrious family, why was Caelius so much your intimate? Was he your cousin, your relation, or the bosom friend of your husband? He was none of these. What could be the reason but lust, hoodwinked lust? If you are unmoved at seeing the *manly* images of our family, ought not my daughter, ought not the example of that Quinta Clodia, to have invited you into a competition for the female glory of domestic virtue?

167

Ought not Clodia the Vestal Virgin, who, embracing her triumphant father, prevented his being torn from his car by a spiteful tribune of the people? Why are you infected more with the vices of a brother than with the virtues of a father and a grandfather, which have devolved from me upon the females as well as the males of my family? Did I tear my country from the thoughts of a peace with Pyrrhus that you should daily enter into intrigues of obscene amours? Did I bring in the water that supplies this city that you might use it to your incestuous purposes? Did I lay a road that it might serve as a parade for you and your train of gallants?"

But what am I doing, my lords! I have introduced so grave a character that I am afraid he may suddenly turn to the other side and, with his censorial severity, begin to school Caelius. (But I shall speak of that presently, and in such a manner, my lords, that I hope to vindicate the morals of Marcus Caelius to the severest inquisitors.) But you, madam —(for now I speak to you not in a borrowed, but my own character)— if you dream of proving your actions, your words, your forgeries, your machinations, your arguments, there is a necessity of your accounting for and laying forth all this excessive intimacy, this excessive friendship, this excessive familiarity. While our accusers talk so freely of intrigues, amours, adulteries, the baths, banquets, collations, songs, concerts and pleasure-boats, they at the same time own that they have their instructions from you. But since you were so blindly, so wilfully, so unaccountably obstinate as to be brought into the Forum and before this court, you must either disown and disprove all *they* have advanced, or confess there is no credit to be given either to your accusation or to your evidence.

But if you would have me accost you in a more polite manner, I will treat you thus: I will remove that grim, that almost savage old fellow, I will pitch upon one of these gentlemen present—your younger brother rather than any, who is quite a master in this kind of politeness, who has a mighty liking for you, and from a strange natural fearfulness (and haunted, I suppose, by some phantoms in the dark) lies every night with you, like a little master with his sister (which, come to think of it, he is).

Suppose then that *he* thus accosts you: "Why, my sister, in this flurry? Why this distraction of mind? Why shriek out and make such ado about a trifle? You have gazed upon your handsome young neighbor, his delicate complexion, his graceful shape; his face and eyes have smitten you. You wish to see him often. Sometimes a woman of quality appears in the same gardens? All your riches cannot fix in your arms the young gentleman, though he is not yet emancipated from an old grasping father? He spurns, he spits at, he undervalues your presents?— Go somewhere else! You have gardens near the Tiber, and have taken great care to fit up an apartment near where all our young gentlemen bathe. From thence you may read their proposals. Why do you tease one who loathes you?"

. . .

I speak nothing of this lady. But if there is one of a character different from hers, who has been a common prostitute, who has always lived in an avowed lewdness with some one or other, who orders her gardens, houses and baths to be thrown open to a promiscuous traffic in every impurity; who even *maintains* young men, whose purse makes amends for the sparing allowances of close-fisted fathers; if she is wanton in widowhood, insolent in airs, profuse in wealth, and if her lusts should lead her into expenditure on the kept ones, can I think a man an adulterer who shall make some free addresses to such a lady?

. . .

But is that neighborhood Caelius affected no ways rank? Does the world whisper, do the waters of Baiae murmur, nothing? Yes, they do not murmur only, they roar out—that the lewdness of a certain woman is so barefaced that she has not now recourse to solitude, to darkness and the blind haunts of criminal intercourse, but openly avows the most scandalous practices before all the world and in broad day.

But if any man thinks that even simple fornication is to be denied to youth, I own he is very severe, I dare not contradict him. But I will venture to say that by such an assertion he condemns not only the licentiousness of this age, but even the customs and indulgences of our ancestors. For when was it not practised? When found fault with? When not tolerated? In short, when was there a time in which a thing allowable was disallowed?

Here will I fix the nature of the case (I shall name no lady—but leave that to your own conjectures): if a single woman should set her doors open to the lusts of the world, and openly profess herself of the order of whores, and drive a trade in making entertainments for mere

169

strangers; if she shall practise this in the city, in her gardens, and amidst the numerous company at Baiae; in short, if she should behave in such a manner that by her gesture, nay by her dress and equipage, and not only by her eyes sparkling, or her tongue tipped with lust, but by hugs, by kisses on the water, in the pleasure-boat and at the banquet she appears not practised only, but insolent in lewdness;—if, I say, a young gentleman shall be along with such a woman, give me leave to ask you, Herennius, whether you would consider him as an adulterer, or a gallant? as designing to storm her virtue, or to satiate her venery?

· · ·

Clodia, let not what I have said be applied to you. But, as the prosecutors pretend that they have the impeachment of this affair from you and that they are to prove the fact by your evidence, I demand of you yourself whether, *if* there lives a woman of such character as I have just now described (mighty unlike indeed to you, but a professed, an avowed prostitute), you would look upon a young gentleman who should have an affair with her as an abandoned profligate wretch? If you are not the woman I have drawn (I should hope not), what can they object to Caelius? But if they should admit that you are she, why should we dread a charge that you laugh off? Give us therefore liberty and scope to make our defence; for either your chastity will clear Caelius from the imputation of doing anything flagrant, or your impudence will be a strong plea in his (and other gentlemen's) favor.

But as I seem now to have weathered the shelves and shallows of my speech, the rest of my voyage appears to be smooth and calm. Caelius is charged with two of the most flagitious crimes against the same lady— with gold, which he is said to have borrowed from Clodia; and with poison, by which he was to kill her. He, according to the prosecution, borrowed the money that he might give it to the slaves of Lucius Lucceius, by whom he was to murder Dio the Alexandrian (who then lived with Lucceius). Heavy is the charge, either to waylay ambassadors, or to tamper with slaves to murder their master's guest. This was a design full of guilt.

In this charge give me leave to ask whether Caelius did, or did not, acquaint Clodia with his purpose in borrowing the money? If he did not tell her, why did she give it him? If she did, she was intentionally equally criminal with him. What! Did you dare to take gold out of your shrine? Did you plunder that plundering Venus of yours of its ornaments? Especially as you knew to what a detestable purpose that gold was to be applied?—to the murder of an envoy, to fasten an eternal stain of infamy upon Lucius Lucceius, a man of the greatest sanctity and integrity. Sure your generous soul ought not to have been accessary, your hospitable roof subservient, nor your charitable Venus assisting, to so detestable a crime!

Balbus tells us that Clodia was in the dark, and that Caelius had told her he borrowed the gold to dress himself for the plays. If he was so intimate with Clodia as you pretend (since you give us so many instances of his lewdness), sure he would have told her what he designed to do with the gold. If he was not so intimate with her, she would not have supplied him with it. Therefore, extravagant woman, if Caelius told you true, you were conscious to the crime which the gold you gave was to perpetrate; if he did not tell you, then you did not give it.

.   .   .

But still it is not said whence this poison came, and how it was prepared. They tell us that it was entrusted to Publius Licinius, a virtuous modest young man and the friend of Caelius; that an appointment was made with the slaves that they should come to the Senian bath; that Licinius was likewise to come thither and deliver to them the box with the poison. Here I first ask: What purpose could it serve to carry it to the appointed place? Why did not these slaves come to the house of Caelius? If so great intimacy, so great an intercourse subsisted betwixt Caelius and Clodia, what suspicion could it have raised for the lady's slave to be seen at his house? But if aversion began now to get the better, their intimacy was at an *end,* and the breach proclaimed:—*this,* this was the source of all this mighty concern, of all this "guilt," and of all these "crimes."

"Nay," says our antagonist, "when the slaves discovered to the lady the affair and the criminal practices of Caelius, from the abundance of her cunning she ordered them to promise him everything. But that she might have plain proofs of the poison when delivered by Licinius, *she* ordered the Senian bath to be the place appointed, that she might send some friends thither to lie in ambush, that when Licinius should come in order to deliver the poison, they might rush out and seize him."

I think, my lords, there is a very easy method of confuting all these

171

allegations. Why should she pitch upon the public baths, where I doubt that there is any convenient place where gentlemen fully dressed may be hid? If they were placed in the entrance of the bath, they must be seen; but if they were to thrust themselves into the inner part, that must be very incommodious for persons who had on shoes and upper garments. They might not even have been admitted (unless perhaps that powerful lady had been sharing *her* bath-house fees with the keeper, and wheedled herself into his good graces). And indeed I have been full of suspense to know who these good men and true are, who are said to give the evidence to demonstrate the seizing of this poison; for as yet none of them are named. I do not doubt but they are men of great weight—first, as they are intimate with such a lady; secondly, since they had undertaken to squeeze themselves into a bath (a favor that, no matter what influence she has, she never could have obtained but from men of the strictest honor and the most consummate dignity).

But why do I talk of the dignity of such witnesses? You have a proof of their valor and fidelity. They lurked in a bathhouse;—admirable witnesses indeed! Then they rushed out all of a sudden;—very grave fellows upon my word! For thus they have cooked up their story: he held the box in his hand, he made an essay to give it away; but, before he could do it, these noble nameless witnesses of a sudden started out. But as Licinius was stretching his hand out to deliver the box, the surprise which these gentlemen's sudden appearance gave him made him run away. Great is the power of truth, which of herself easily prevails against all the abilities, the cunning, the industry of mankind, and against all the plots of confederated malice!

But all this idle tale of that female dabbler in old poetical chimaeras, how loose, how improbable, how inextricably perplexed is it! For how could so many men (for they could not be few, both that the seizing Licinius might be done with ease, and that the thing might be proved by a cloud of witnesses) suffer Licinius to slip out of their hands? Where was the difficulty of taking him, when he drew back in delivering the box, more than if he had delivered it? For they were placed there to lay hold on Licinius that he might be taken in the act, either with the poison about him, or after he had delivered it. This was all the woman aimed at, this was all which they whom she employed had to do. Nor indeed can I imagine why you should say that they jumped out too rashly and too hastily—this was the one thing required of them; for this purpose were they placed there, that the poison, the plot, in short the villainy of the whole contrivance might appear to a demonstration. Could they have rushed out at a better time than when Licinius came in, than while he held the box of poison in his hand? For had he actually delivered it to the slaves, the lady's friends would have instantly started out of the bath and seized Licinius, he would then have protested on his honor and denied that he had delivered that box, and, if he had, how could they have convicted him? Would they have said they saw him? In the first place, they must then run the risk of being themselves convicted of a very heinous crime; then, they must have affirmed that they saw what, from the place where they were hid, it was impossible they could see. It follows therefore that they revealed themselves at the very instant when Licinius came, when he produced the box, when he stretched out his hand, when he delivered the poison. This, then, was the unraveling not of a play, but of a farce—in which, when there is no meaning, a fellow slips out of their hands, the castanets rattle, and the curtain is drawn.

Let me therefore ask why the lady's troops suffered Licinius, while he was wavering, uncertain, retreating, endeavoring to make off, to escape out of their hands. Why did they not seize him? Why did they not prove to the strongest conviction, by his own confession, to the eyes of the world and upon the very face of the thing itself, a crime so heinous in its nature? Were they afraid—so many against one; the strong against the feeble; the brisk against the dispirited—that they could not get the better?

There is no connection in the thing. Not a single circumstance supports the allegation, nor could the crime ever be brought to a test. This whole case rests not on arguments, or presumptions, or those circumstances by which the truth is usually cleared up, but on the evidence of witnesses, such witnesses, my lords, as I wait for without the least apprehension—nay, with some degree of satisfaction; my imagination longs to see the neat young gentlemen, the gallants of a rich noble lady, those heroes posted by their she-commander in ambush, holding the bathhouse-garrison!

Let me ask then how, or in what manner, they were concealed? Sure it must be a cavity!—a Trojan horse which admitted and concealed such a number of invincible heroes raised to fight a lady's quarrel. I will oblige them to declare why so many and so brave fellows did not either as he was standing seize, or as he was flying pursue—*one* person, unattended and (as you perceive him there) unable to resist. This, take my word, they can never be able to account for—*if* they shall appear in this court. I will give them leave to be as facetious and as witty as they please (nay, to be even eloquent) over their cups; but the practice at the bar and at the board is different. The arguments used before a bench are not the same with those on a couch; judges make a different appearance from rioters; and, in short, the light of the sun is of another nature than that of lamps.

But if they take my advice, they will play another game, they will make other court, they will display their talents in other business. Let their finery make a figure in that lady's train. Let them outspend everybody else. Let them loiter, let them lie, let them dance attendance;—but let them *not* attack the life and fortune of an innocent man! . . .

Cicero, from *Defence of Caelius* (W. Guthrie)

VANITY, FAIR!

Beautiful
(as you say)
your face is—
beauty your
tongue paints—and
erases.

Martial, *Epigrams* 1.64 (G. W.)

DANGEROUS SEAS

Somewhere in roses
him, young and slim and, urgent
under overarching rock,
perfume-sea-sprayed him

you master, Pyrrha, easily
as your contrived inevitable curls.
Inevitably he will cry
on stars that slip, sea and sky
that crash uncontrollable.

Yes he enjoys you now, idyllically

20. Portrait of a lady. Rome, Palazzo Capitolino.

With curls on curls, they build her head before,
And mount it with a formidable tow'r,
A giantess she seems; but, look behind,
And then she dwindles to the pigmy kind.

idiotically, with no sea-legs for a sea
like yours, once troubled;
believes skies never cloud, waves pitch,
you have no weather-changes in you.

I have sailed those waters, know what storms
hit them.
The spot is marked, and sacred: I made shore
barely, and battered,
and turned my face toward land.

Horace, *Songs* 1.5 (G. W.)

RECORD

"You before any,
even Zeus,
should I wed any"
was her word—

a woman's word,
write it down!
In water.

Catullus, *Songs* 70 (G. W.)

THE ELUSIVE LOVER

now please, if it isn't too much trouble
show me where you're hiding out
I looked for you in Little Park
I looked in all the bookstores
I looked in Father Jupiter's holy temple
    I went down Pompey's portico
    and grabbed onto every dame
    (at least the ones that looked fairly good-natured)
    . . . . and I kept saying to 'em
    "tell me if Jimmy's here, you tramps!"
    one of 'em yanks back her dress and says
    "Chemise? look, eet's 'ere, joost ondair

my peenk teets
bot eet nids bettair man as you
to gat eet!"
aren't you being awfully snooty, friend?
come on, tell us where you're going to be
give, boy, give, let us in on it, tell the world
those babes with the bosoms really got you?
if you keep your tongue shut up in your mouth
you'll lose half the fun of having a dame
talk it up, boy! Venus likes palaver
well, o.k., lock up your lip if you want to
must be Real Love with you this time

Catullus, *Songs* 55 (Frank O. Copley)

WAR—AND PEACE

She had so often cheated me, I thought
I'd shift my camp myself with change of bed.
Phyllis near Dian on the Aventine
is dull when sober: drunk, she's gay enough;
and Teia from Tarpeia's Grove: when wine
has warmed her charms, no single man's enough.
I thought I'd call them in and soothe the night,
I'd try a change of kisses. Yes, I'd dare.
One couch was set in soft and shadowy light.
How were we placed? I stretched between the pair.

From summer-cups of glass my Lygdamus
poured out the rich wines grown on Lesbian ground.
Nile sent the piper. Phyllis danced for us
with castanets, with roses scattering round.
The dwarf with gnarling body played to me,
his stubby fingers twirled the flute unheeded.
The well-filled lamps were blinking drowsily,
the table squatly on its legs receded.
I diced. Though loud the dicing-boxes rang,
the *Dog* and not the *Venus* still was thrown.
They aired their breasts, unseen. Unheard, they sang.

At the Lanuvian Gates I stood, alone.

The hinges grated suddenly outside.
I heard a murmuring voice invade my lair.
O, Cynthia flung the panels open wide,
lovely with wrath, with wild and lovely hair.
My wine-loose lips went pallid and I aged.
Down from my fingers fell the cup and cracked.
She flamed, and all the woman in her raged.
I thought I saw a city being sacked.

She scratched at Phyllis' face and made her weep
while Teia shouted out, "Help, fire and murder!"
The skurrying lights awoke the square from sleep;
madly she screamed: for streets the people heard her.
The girls, with tresses torn, crept disarrayed
to find the nearest pub with shuttered door.
Cynthia stood glorying mid the wreck she'd made,
then came and slapt my wicked face once more.
My throat she branded, biting till I bled,
but chiefly at my sinful eyes she aimed;
and when she tired of beating at my head,
she lugged out Lygdamus who lay ashamed
beneath the couch. In vain he clasped my knees.
Poor slave, I too was humbled in defeat.
I raised my palms. At last she heard my pleas,
although she scarcely let me touch her feet.

She said, "If truly now for peace you've prayed,
you'll follow out the laws that I declare.
You must not lounge in Pompey's Colonnade
or watch the shows that crowd the wicked square,
cricking your neck to see the upper-row,
or lift a litter's hangings for a word.
But Lygdamus, the cause of all, must go.
Shackle his legs and sell him. Have you heard?"

I answered, "Yes, my dear, my lesson's learned."
She smiled to see me grown so well behaved.
Then, everywhere the girls had touched, she burned
some sulphur, and the doors she cleansed and laved.
"Bring us new lamps with different oil," she bade.

She sprinkled sulphur thrice upon my head.
She called for change of sheets, and fresh were laid:
we ventured on a second marriage-bed.

Propertius, *Elegies* 4.8, lines 27-88 (Jack Lindsay)

HELLO TO ARMS

All lovers stand erect as men of war:
Cupid has headquarters,
his troops around him—
believe me, Greeks, each lover is a soldier.
When war comes into fashion,
so does Venus!
Old men are feeble soldiers, fuddling lovers;
what the top sergeant looks for in a fighter,
girls look for in a man—
action at night.

          The sentry keeps
his captain's tent in view—
the lover's sleepless eye, his sweetheart's door.
The trooper never fails
his marching orders—
however far a woman takes a journey,
her lover follows her to ends of earth:
he climbs glass mountains,
he wades great rivers
that spread around him in a flood of rain.
And where the mountaintops
are glazed with snow,
he strides through storms, or if he's out at sea,
he battles rough winds through
an eastern tempest.
Nor does he speak of hardship anywhere,
but steers his course by gazing at the stars.
Who other than a lover
or a soldier
braves dark, frostbitten nights through hail and snow?
One matches wits

with wary enemies:
the other keeps an eye on clever rivals.
One mans the siege
against a rock-walled city:
the other entrance to a strong-willed girl.
One climbs through bedroom windows to show valor,
the other forces city gates ajar.
The best attack is:
take them while they're sleeping—
your sword in hand against a naked foe.
That's how Odysseus and Diomedes
came against Rhesus on the Trojan plain,
stole his white horses,
and left him dead upon the conquered field.
So lovers take advantage of the night:
while husbands sleep, their swords are driven home.
Whether he's a soldier,
or an unwanted lover,
the breakthrough is his duty and reward.

Sometimes Mars sways the battle left and right,
and victory's in doubt,
and it's well known that Venus often wavers:
sometimes the loser
rises from defeat
to conquer those who say they'll never fall.
Though some fools say
love has no "fighting spirit,"
love always proves its genius at white heat:
when Briseis was stolen from his side
the great Achilles
was a pillar of flame—
the Trojans had to fight as best they could!
From his wife's arms Hector went hot to war—
she fixed his headgear as he strode away.
And Agamemnon,
greatest of commanders,
stood dazzled at the sight of bright Cassandra
who like a Maenad shook her floating hair.
And Mars in mounting Venus was caught naked

in Vulcan's net
where both went on display—
while their performance was the talk of heaven!

Till recently I spent my time at ease
in country quiet,
in this green shade I dreamed and wrote my verses . . .
then fire caught me . . . for the loveliest girl
waked me to strategy.
I am no coward!
Action at night shall always be my glory.
If you would keep your sword up—
and your spirit—then fall in love!

Ovid, *Love Affairs* 1.9 (Horace Gregory)

NIGHT DUTY

Lady, an elevant is more your speed.
Why are you send-me-gifting, or these letters?
I'm not your hard boy, nor is my nose stopped.
One sense I have, and clearly: I can sniff
A polypussy or a reeking goat
In armpits thickly matted, keener than dogs
Search the sow's hidey hole.

                           She humps herself
With (ertlessly) prick, to reach her rabbi-
titty. The seathing body sweatly stinks
And drools off her complexion wetly: chalk
And crap of crocodiles. She rips orgasmic
The sheets and tumbling mattress hardly up.
Then with tough words she slaps my limpid worker:
"You're not so soft with Minnie as with me.
You spit tri-nightly Minnie, but you're slug
Abed along of me. Let Lizzie die,
And slowly, who sent me this oxey moron,
Hardly ebullient, after my old Bert
From Coney Island hopped to hire hills.
His ligameant something, and stiffer stood

Than deeply trees in rooted deeply mounds.
Sheep woolly skins were dunked and dunked again,
And for whose coming? Nobody's but yours;
So no-one else's party boy would look
Beloveder to his than you to me.
O, I'm so unfulfilled, bucause *eheu fugis*
Like ewe scared of wolves, or hinds of loions."

Horace, *Intermittent Metres* 12 (Nicholas Kilmer)

GETTING ON

I

Your conduct, naughty Chloris, is
Not just exactly Horace's
   Ideal of a lady
   At the shady
     Time of life;
You mustn't throw your soul away
On foolishness, like Pholoë—
   Her days are folly-laden—
   She's a maiden,
     You're a wife.

Your daughter, with propriety,
May look for male society,
   Do one thing and another
   In which mother
     Shouldn't mix;
But revels Bacchanalian
Are—or should be—quite alien
   To you a married person,
   Something worse'n
     Forty-six!

Yes, Chloris, you cut up too much,
You love the dance and cup too much,

Your years are quickly flitting—
To your knitting
Right about!
Forget the incidental things
That keep you from parental things—
The World, the Flesh, the Devil,
On the level,
Cut 'em out!

Horace, *Songs* 3.15 (Franklin Pierce Adams)

II

Ribald romeos less and less berattle
Your shut window with impulsive pebbles.
Sleep—who cares?—the clock around. The door hugs
Firmly its framework
Which once, oh how promptly it popped open
Easy hinges. And so rarely heard now:
"Night after night I'm dying for you, darling,
And you—you just lie there."
Turnabout. For insolent old lechers
You will weep soon on the lonely curbing,
While, above, the dark of the moon excites the
Wind from the mountain.
Then, deep down, searing desire (libido
That deranges, too, old rutting horses)
In your riddled abdomen is raging
Not without heartache
That the young boys take their solace rather
In the greener ivy, the green myrtle;
And such old winter-bitten sticks and stems they
Figure the hell with.

Horace, *Songs* 1.25 (John Frederick Nims)

PLIGHT

LOST: One heart, strayed—
in the vicinity of Theotimus?

183

(it has escaped control before
and been recovered there;

the owner, who might lose *himself,*
cannot explore that snare)

REWARD: If return is made—
or don't you ever intend to, Venus?

Catulus, *Epigrams* (G. W.)

INTO THE NIGHT

Who needs a torch?—our love will light us.
Rain or wind can souse a torch,
While love will flicker on and scorch.
Touch fire to fire, to dis-ignite us.

Aedituus, *Epigrams* (G. W.)

INSPIRATION

Yet you ask on what account I write so many love-lyrics
And whence this soft book comes into my mouth.
Neither Calliope nor Apollo sung these things into my ear,
My genius is no more than a girl.

If she with ivory fingers drive a tune through the lyre,
We look at the process.
How easy the moving fingers; if hair is mussed on her forehead,
If she goes in a gleam of Cos, in a slither of dyed stuff,
There is a volume in the matter; if her eyelids sink into sleep,
There are new jobs for the author,
And if she plays with me with her shirt off,
We shall construct many Iliads.
And whatever she does or says
We shall spin long yarns out of nothing.

Propertius, *Elegies* 2.1, lines 1-16
(Ezra Pound)

UNEQUAL MATCH

In the beginning Cynthia
received me—pitiful, immaculate—
as neophyte, into her eyes. Then, hurling
sight, light, my steadfast pride down, Love trod my head
and taught me to despise your honest
daughters and to live without a plan.
A year of fever has followed unrelieved.
Driven by ruthless Love, I know
the other Gods have turned my enemies.

Milanion, by shunning nothing, -
struggled to break rigorous Atalanta:
he strayed through caverns of Maiden Mountain
confronting hairy predators; and cudgelled by
the Woodland One in Arcady
lay wounded, howling to the rocks;
this way he caught and brought her home: curses
and favors prevailed with Love. But weird
new Love, with novel methods, visits me.

Magi of blood and fire who trick
the moon down, convert my Lady to my
disease. Magi who guide the rivers and rule
the stars, I trust in your litanies. Friends, physicians,
friends who summon sunken bodies
back, discover my unsound heart
a remedy; for, for the freedom merely
to speak out my fury, I would
withstand the cutting and stern cautery.

Over the last lands, past the final
sea, send me, send me where no female knows.
You stay, whom Love obeys; remain in paired
security. My nights are strenuous and harsh
with love. Incessantly the God
of love fills me with emptiness.
I warn you: avoid this sickness. Keep her
whose love you are the expert of,
or recall my words too late in grief like mine.

Propertius, *Elegies* 1.1 (Richard E. Braun)

185

DEATH IN THE LINE OF DUTY

Midnight, and a letter comes to me from our
  mistress:
    Telling me to come to Tibur, *At* once!!
"Bright tips reach up from twin towers,
    Anienan spring water falls into flat-spread pools."
What *is* to be done about it?
  Shall I entrust myself to entangled shadows,
Where bold hands may do violence to my person?

Yet if I postpone my obedience
              because of this respectable terror
I shall be prey to lamentations worse than a nocturnal
    assailant.
And I shall be in the wrong,
              and it will last a twelve-month,
For her hands have no kindness me-ward,

Nor is there anyone to whom lovers are not sacred at
  midnight
  And in the Via Sciro.
If any man would be a lover
              he may walk on the Scythian coast,
No barbarism would go to the extent of doing him harm,
The moon will carry his candle,
              the stars will point out the stumbles,
Cupid will carry lighted torches before him
              and keep mad dogs off his ankles.
Thus all roads are perfectly safe
                    and at any hour;
Who so indecorous as to shed the pure gore of a suitor?!
  Cypris is his cicerone.

What if undertakers follow my track,
                    such a death is worth dying.
She would bring frankincense and wreaths to my tomb,
  She would sit like an ornament on my pyre.

Gods' aid, let not my bones lie in a public location
    with crowds too assiduous in their crossing of it;

For thus are tombs of lovers most desecrated.

May a woody and sequestered place cover me with its foliage
Or may I inter beneath the hummock
          of some as yet uncatalogued sand;
At any rate I shall not have my epitaph in a high road.

          Propertius, *Elegies* 3.16 (Ezra Pound)

LIEBESTOD

My lips apart
The lip I sip
And fragrant breath
Of my sweetheart,
Till nigh to death
My poor soul leaps
From inmost deeps
And tries to force
A way across

And if a minute's more delay
Should make us in our kissing stay,
The poor thing would be all away
And I—a dead man I should be;
For then my darling I should fill,
So living still
Though not in me.

          Anonymous, in Aulus Gellius,
        Attic Nights 19.11 (Stephen Gaselee)

TORTURE

He seems a God to me, or (God willing)
    more than godly, this man
who sits across from you and watches you,
    who hears you laughing sweetly.

It seems to me that now by watching you

187

I am less than mortal,
for my faculties tear loose, I lose even
   every man's dominion:

my tongue slumbers and slender fires slide
   throughout me; those ears ring
of their own accord while the eyes perversely
   peer in inward darkness.

Leisure is a terrible thing, I say.
   Boredom means disorder
and desire. Idleness has broken kings,
   men say, and wealthy nations.

        Catullus, *Songs* 51 (Richard E. Braun)

HAUNTED BY CYNTHIA

A ghost is someone: death has left a hole
For the lead-coloured soul to beat the fire:
   Cynthia leaves her dirty pyre
   And seems to coil herself and roll
      Under my canopy,
Love's stale and public playground, where I lie
And fill the run-down empire of my bed.
I see the street, her potter's field, is red
And lively with the ashes of the dead;

She no longer sparkles off in smoke:
It is the body carted to the gate
   Last Friday, when the sizzling grate
   Left its charred furrows on her smock
      And ate into her hip.
A black nail dangles from a finger tip
And Lethe oozes from her nether lip.
Her thumb-bones rattle on her brittle hands,
As Cynthia stamps and hisses and demands:

Sextus, has sleep already washed away
Your manhood? You forget the window-sill
   My sliding wore to slivers? Day

Would break before the Seven Hills
    Saw Cynthia retreat
And climb your shoulders to the knotted sheet.
You shouldered me and galloped on bare feet
To lay me by the crossroads. Have no fear:
Notus, who snatched your promise, has no ear.

But why did no one call in my deaf ear?
Your calling would have gained me one more day.
    Sextus, although you ran away
    You might have called and stopped my bier
      A second by your door.
No tears drenched a black toga for your whore
When broken tilestones bruised her face before
The Capitol. Would it have strained your purse
To scatter ten cheap roses on my hearse?

The State will make Pompilia's Chloris burn:
I knew her secret when I kissed the skull
    Of Pluto in the tainted bowl.
    Let Nomas burn her books and turn
      Her poisons into gold;
The finger-prints upon the potsherd told
Her love. You let a slut, whose body sold
To Thracians, liquefy my golden bust
In the coarse flame that crinkled me to dust.

If Chloris' bed has left you with your head,
Lover, I think you'll answer my arrears:
    My nurse is getting on in years,
    See that she gets a little bread—
      She never clutched your purse;
See that my little humpback hears no curse
From her close-fisted friend. But burn the verse
You bellowed half a life time in my name:
Why should you feed me to the fires of fame?

I will not hound you, much as you have earned
It, Sextus: I shall reign in your four books—
    I swear this by the Hag who looks
    Into my heart where it was burned:
      Propertius, I kept faith;

If not, may serpents suck my ghost to death
And spit it with their forked and killing breath
Into the Styx where Agamemnon's wife
Founders in the green circles of her life.

Beat the sycophant ivy from my urn,
That twists its binding shoots about my bones
   Where apple-sweetened Anio drones
   Through orchards that will never burn
      While honest Herakles,
My patron, watches. Anio, you will please
Me if you whisper upon sliding knees:
"Propertius, Cynthia is here:
She shakes her blossoms when my waters clear."

You cannot turn your back upon a dream,
For phantoms have their reasons when they come:
   We wander midnights: then the numb
   Ghost wades from the Lethaean stream:
      Even the foolish dog
Stops its hell-raising mouth and casts its clog;
At cock-crow Charon checks us in his log.
Others can have you, Sextus; I alone
Hold: and I grind your manhood bone on bone.

Propertius, *Elegies* 4.7 (Robert Lowell)

PART IV

The Lure of the East

These strong Egyptian fetters I must break.

Antony and Cleopatra 1.2 (120)

East of Italy lay Greece, Asia Minor, Egypt—the exotic (so the Romans told themselves), the enervatingly decadent, the wealthy. On each count Rome disapproved of the Orient; and because of each it was irresistibly drawn there. Cleopatra is a monster, but she can transmute Maecenas' propaganda into a cloaked Horatian tribute (p. 198). Rome never did break its Oriental fetters; eventually, they formed a kind of armor— the kind that cuts the man who wears it.

One Greek taste shared by the Romans may seem particularly odd to us—the art of the well-turned insult. One of the first lyric poets of Greece, Archilochus, took the ritual vaunts raised before and after the Homeric duels and turned them into nonheroic billingsgate. His witty fusion of ira *and* ars *fascinated all antiquity, and made Horace write:*

Archilochus made anger keep its head,
And killed men metronomically dead.

Dramatic Technique 79

The whole point of this art is the combination of nicest form and vulgarest abuse. Some think of the neoclassical epigram as dry and refined, icy and far from earth. But Pope had gone to school to Martial and Juvenal, Horace and Catullus; and theirs is the school of Archilochus, an Augean school.

192

GREEKS

I

I haste to tell thee, nor shall shame oppose,
What confidents our wealthy Romans chose;
And whom I most abhor: to speak my mind,
I hate, in Rome, a Grecian town to find:
To see the scum of Greece transplanted here,
Receiv'd like gods, is what I cannot bear.
Nor Greeks alone, but Syrians here abound;
Obscene Orontes, diving under ground,
Conveys his wealth to Tiber's hungry shores,
And fattens Italy with foreign whores:
Hither their crooked harps and customs come;
All find receipt in hospitable Rome.
The barbarous harlots crowd the public place:
Go, fools, and purchase an unclean embrace;
The painted miter court, and the more painted face.
Old Romulus, and Father Mars, look down!
Your herdsman primitive, your homely clown
Is turn'd a beau in a loose tawdry gown.
His once unkemb'd and horrid locks, behold
Stilling sweet oil: his neck inchain'd with gold;
Aping the foreigners, in ev'ry dress,
Which, bought at greater cost, becomes him less.
Meantime they wisely leave their native land;
From Sicyon, Samos, and from Alaband,
And Amydon, to Rome they swarm in shoals:
So sweet and easy is the gain from fools.
Poor refugees at first, they purchase here;
And, soon as denizen'd, they domineer;
Grow to the great a flatt'ring servile rout:
Work themselves inward, and their patrons out:
Quick-witted, brazen-fac'd, with fluent tongues,
Patient of labors, and dissembling wrongs.
Riddle me this, and guess him if you can,
Who bears a nation in a single man?

193

A cook, a conjurer, a rhetorician,
A painter, pedant, a geometrician,
A dancer on the ropes, and a physician.
All things the hungry Greek exactly knows:
And bid him go to heav'n, to heav'n he goes:
In short, no Scythian, Moor, or Thracian born,
But in that town which arms and arts adorn.
Shall he be plac'd above me at the board,
In purple cloth'd, and lolling like a lord?
Shall he before me sign, whom t'other day
A small-craft vessel hither did convey;
Where, stow'd with prunes, and rotten figs, he lay?
How little is the privilege become
Of being born a citizen of Rome!
The Greeks get all by fulsome flatteries;
A most peculiar stroke they have at lies.
They make a wit of their insipid friend;
His blobber lips, and beetle brows commend;
His long crane neck, and narrow shoulders praise—
You'd think they were describing Hercules.
A creaking voice for a clear treble goes;
Tho' harsher than a cock that treads and crows.
We can as grossly praise; but, to our grief,
No flatt'ry but from Grecians gains belief.
Besides these qualities, we must agree
They mimic better on the stage than we:
The wife, the whore, the shepherdess they play,
In such a free, and such a graceful way,
That we believe a very woman shown,
And fancy something underneath the gown.
But not Antiochus, nor Stratocles,
Our ears and ravish'd eyes can only please:
The nation is compos'd of such as these.
All Greece is one comedian: laugh, and they
Return it louder than an ass can bray:
Grieve, and they grieve; if you weep silently,
There seems a silent echo in your eye:
They cannot mourn like you; but they can cry.
Call for a fire, their winter clothes they take:

Begin but you to shiver, and they shake:
In frost and snow, if you complain of heat,
They rub th' unsweating brow, and swear they sweat.
We live not on the square with such as these;
Such are our betters who can better please;
Who day and night are like a looking-glass,
Still ready to reflect their patron's face;
The panegyric hand, and lifted eye,
Prepar'd for some new piece of flattery.
Ev'n nastiness occasions will afford;
They praise a belching, or well-pissing lord.
Besides, there's nothing sacred, nothing free
From bold attempts of their rank lechery.
Thro' the whole family their labors run;
The daughter is debauch'd, the wife is won:
Nor scapes the bridegroom, or the blooming son.
If none they find for their lewd purpose fit,
They with the walls and very floors commit.
They search the secrets of the house, and so
Are worship'd there, and fear'd for what they know.

Juvenal, *Satires* 3.58-113 (John Dryden)

I I

We never knew this vain expense before
Th' effeminated Grecians brought it o'er:
New toys and trifles from their Athens come,
And dates and pepper have unsinew'd Rome.

Persius, *Satires* 6.37-39 (John Dryden)

GREEK DOCTORS

And here by the way, one word will I speak to the honour of our
Romans for their singular wisdom and providence, namely, that howso-
ever they are grown to good proof and be accomplished in all other arts
and professions of the Greeks, yet their gravity hitherto hath been such,
as they would not give themselves to the practice of this only science.
And notwithstanding the exceeding wealth that accrueth by physic, yet

very few or none of our natural Roman citizens have meddled therewith. And those also that have betaken themselves unto it, presently have forsaken their native language and gone to the Greek tongue. For this opinion verily there is of this art, that if the professors thereof handle it in their vulgar and mother tongue, or otherwise in any other than Greek, all the authority, grace and credit thereof is lost, even with those that be altogether unlearned and know not so much as the Greek alphabet. See the nature and foolish property of our countrymen, to have less confidence and trust in those things which concern their life and death, if they be intelligible and delivered to their capacity; than in others, which they understand never a whit! And hereupon verily it is come to pass, that the art of physic hath this peculiar gift and privilege alone, that whosoever professeth himself a physician is straightways believed, say what he will: and yet to speak a truth, there are no lies dearer sold or more dangerous than those which proceed out of a physician's mouth.

Pliny (the Elder), *The Encyclopedia*, vol. 29
(Philemon Holland)

FEMALE INTELLECTUALS

Some faults, tho' small, intolerable grow;
For what so nauseous and affected too,
As those that think they due perfection want,
Who have not learnt to lisp the Grecian cant?
In Greece, their whole accomplishments they seek;
Their fashion, breeding, language, must be Greek:
But, raw in all that does to Rome belong,
They scorn to cultivate their mother tongue.
In Greek they flatter, all their fears they speak,
Tell all their secrets; nay, they scold in Greek:
Ev'n in the feat of love, they use that tongue.
Such affectations may become the young;
But thou, old hag, of threescore years and three,
Is shewing of thy parts in Greek for thee?
Ζωὴ καὶ ψυχή! All those tender words
The momentary trembling bliss affords,
The kind soft murmurs of the private sheets,
Are bawdy, while thou speak'st in public streets.

196

Those words have fingers; and their force is such,
They raise the dead, and mount him with a touch:
But all provocatives from thee are vain;
No blandishment the slacken'd nerve can strain.

.   .   .

But of all plagues, the greatest is untold;
The book-learn'd wife, in Greek and Latin bold:
The critic-dame, who at her table sits,
Homer and Virgil quotes, and weighs their wits;
And pities Dido's agonizing fits.
She has so far th' ascendant of the board,
The prating pedant puts not in one word:
The man of law is non-plus'd in his suit;
Nay, every other female tongue is mute.
Hammers and beating anvils, you would swear,
And Vulcan with his whole militia there.
Tabors and trumpets cease; for she alone
Is able to redeem the lab'ring Moon.
Ev'n wit's a burthen, when it talks too long;
But she, who has no continence of tongue,
Should walk in breeches, and should wear a beard,
And mix among the philosophic herd.
O what a midnight curse has he, whose side
Is pester'd with a mood and figure bride!
Let mine, ye gods, (if such must be my fate,)
No logic learn, nor history translate;
But rather be a quiet, humble fool:
I hate a wife to whom I go to school.

Juvenal, *Satires* 6.184-99, 434-56 (John Dryden)

ASIAN LUXURY

Persian pomps, boy, ever I renounce them—
Scoff o' the plaited coronet's refulgence;
Seek not in fruitless vigilance the rose-tree's
    Tardier offspring.

21. Greek scene from Pompeii. Naples, Museo Nazionale.

. . . wrap their wondrous walls of color around them . . .

Mere honest myrtle, that alone is order'd,
Me the mere myrtle decorates, as also
Thee the prompt waiter to a jolly toper
    Hous'd in an arbour.

           Horace, *Songs* 1.38 (Christopher Smart)

CLEOPATRA'S DEFEAT

Wine at last! and light
ripple of feet on earth
and a sacred meal
of men with gods!

Till now, the deep wine
of our ancestors
we had not earned;
we had not turned her back
as she breathed graveyard
sickliness across the Capitol,
woman womanizing her foul men,
the bacchic princess drunk on luck
and parched for more.

She sobered up
at Actium
where her ship barely
fluttered free,
a swift dove swifter followed
by the eagle-ship, with winging oars, of Caesar
out of Italy; a rabbit hunted
through Thessalian snows,
he the hunter, with chains for the beast he sought—

    Yet this thing grew
    toward death; did not
    womanly cower in some cove
    or flinch at steel.

    Her calm face surveyed
    her kingdom ruined;

she took the rough resistant venomed thing,
drank darkness through her veins.

Braced to this by harsher things—
that we would lead her into Rome a slave—
she went unhumbled into death, a queen.

Horace, *Songs* 1.37 (G. W.)

SPARTAN GIRLS

The Spartan wrestlers and their rules amaze me—
but, more, the school in which their women train,
where they may exercise their naked bodies
on the same ground on which those wrestlers strain,
and where the swift ball tricks the hand stretched for it
and the hooked rod guides the hoop's rolling flight.
That dusty figure at the goal's a woman;
a woman's in this rough-and-tumble fight!
Another binds her eager hands for boxing;
a fourth girl whirls the discus overhead,
or, with the hoarfrost on her hair, goes racing
after her father's hounds, where they have sped;
puts a horse through his paces, slings a sword on
her white thigh, or a helmet on her head,
fierce as the Amazonian warriors bathing
barebreasted in Thermodon's river bed,
like Helen, when with Castor and with Pollux
she carried arms (so the report persists)
nor blushed before her brothers, one the horseman
and one the champion who fought with fists.
This is that Sparta that indulges lovers,
where couples hand-in-hand in public walk,
no girl goes guarded, no one rants of honor,
none dreads a husband's wrath or threatening talk.
All unannounced, there you may state your business
with neither deputy nor long delay;
a lover's not beguiled by nonessentials,
his dear does not arrange her hair all day.
But here where Cynthia walks are people, people—

I cannot even reach her through that crowd.
I don't know what to wear or how to hail her.
The path I tread what doubts and darkness shroud!

Rome, learn from Sparta's healthy point of view.
Yield! Give us further cause to honor you!

Propertius, *Elegies* 3.14 (Constance Carrier)

NARCISSUS

　　Deep in the forest
Was a pool, well-deep and silver-clear, where
Never a shepherd came, nor goats, nor cattle;
Nor leaf, nor beast, nor bird fell to its surface.
Nourished by water, grass grew thick around it,
And over it dark trees had kept the sun
From ever shedding warmth upon the place.
Here spent Narcissus, weary of the hunt
And sick with heat, fell to the grass, charmed by
The bright well and its greenery. He bent
To drink, to dissipate his thirst, yet as he
Drank another thirst rose up: enraptured
Beauty caught his eyes that trapped him;
He loved the image that he thought was shadow,
And looked amazed at what he saw—his face.
Fixed, bending over it, he could not speak,
Himself as though cut from Parian marble.
Flat on the grass he lay to look deep, deeper
Into two stars that were his eyes, at hair
Divine as Bacchus' hair, as bright Apollo's,
At boyish beauty of ivory neck and shoulder,
At face, flushed as red flowers among white,
Enchanted by the charms which were his own.
Himself the worshipped and the worshipper,
He sought himself and was pursued, wooed, fired
By his own heat of love. Again, again
He tried to kiss the image in the well;
Again, again his arms embraced the silver

22. Cuirass on statue of Augustus. Rome, Museo Vaticano.

. . . an alien shell is somehow native to them . . .

Elusive waters where his image shone;
And he burned for it while the gliding error
Betrayed his eyes. O foolish innocent!
Why try to grasp at shadows in their flight?
What he had tried to hold resided nowhere,
For had he turned away, it fell to nothing:
His love was cursed. Only the glancing mirror
Of reflections filled his eyes, a body
That had no being of its own, a shade
That came, stayed, left with him—if he could leave it.

Neither desire of food or sleep could lure
Him from the well, but flat upon the grasses
There he lay, fixed by the mirage of his eyes
To look until sight failed. And then, half turning,
Raised arms to dark trees over him and cried,
"O trees, O forest, has anyone been cursed
With love like mine? O you who know the ways
Of many lovers in your shaded groves,
Was there at any time in that long past,
The centuries you knew, one who is spent,
Wasted like this? I am entranced, enchanted
By what I see, yet it eludes me, error
Or hope becomes the thing I love; and now
With every hour increases sorrow; nor sea,
Nor plain, nor city walls, nor mountain ranges
Keeps us apart. Only this veil of water.
So thin the veil we almost touch each other,
Then come to me no matter who you are,
O lovely boy, why do you glide from me,
Where do you vanish when I come to meet you?
My youth, my beauty cannot be denied,
For girls have loved me and your tempting glances
Tell me of friendship in your eyes. Even as
I reach, your arms almost embrace me, and as
I smile, you smile again at me; weeping
I've seen great tears flow down your face; I bend
My head toward you, you nod at me, and I
Believe that from the movement of your lips
(Though nothing's heard) you seem to answer me.

Look! I am he; I've loved within the shadow
Of what I am, and in that love I burn,
I light the flames and feel their fires within;
Then what am I to do? Am I the lover
Or beloved? Then why make love? Since I
Am what I long for, then my riches are
So great they make me poor. O may I fall
Away from my own body—and this is odd
From any lover's lips—I would my love
Would go away from me. And now love drains
My life, look! I am dying at life's prime.
Nor have I fear of death which ends my trials,
Yet wish my lover had a longer life,
If not, we two shall perish in one breath."

He spoke and half mad faced the self-made image.
Tears stirred the pool to waves, the wavering features
Dimmed in darkest waters. As he saw them flicker
He cried, "Where are you going? Stay with me;
O cruelest lover come, nor leave me here;
It may be fate for me to look at love
And yet not touch it, but in that deep gaze
Increase unhappy love to misery."
Then in his agony he tore his dress
And beat his naked breast with his pale hands.
As apples ripen, some parts white, some red,
As growing grapes take on a purple shade,
Narcissus' breast put on these darkening colours;
And when he saw them—for the pool had cleared—
He could endure no more, but as wax turns
To liquid in mild heat, as autumn frost
Changes to dew at morning, so did Narcissus
Wear away with love, drained, fading in the heat
Of secret fires.

.   .   .

At this he placed his head deep in cool grasses
While death shut fast the eyes that shone with light
At their own lustre. As he crossed the narrows

Of darkest hell he saw the floating image
Of his lost shade within the Stygian waters.

Ovid, *Transformations* 3.407-90, 502-5
(Horace Gregory)

COMPARATIVE MYTHOLOGY

This is she who was hymned by Grecian poets adept in ancient lore. They pictured her a goddess, driving a chariot drawn by a yoke of lions. By this they signified that the whole mighty mass hangs in airy space: for earth cannot rest on earth. They harnessed wild beasts, because the fiercest of children cannot but be softened and subdued by the duty owed to parents. Upon her head they set a battlemented crown, because earth in select spots is fortified and bears the weight of cities. Decked with this emblem even now the image of the Holy Mother is borne about the world in solemn state. Various nations hail her with time-honoured ceremony as our Lady of Ida. To bear her company they appoint a Phrygian retinue, because they claim that crops were first created within the bounds of Phrygia and spread thence throughout the earth. They give her eunuchs as attendant priests, to signify that those who have defied their mother's will and shown ingratitude to their father must be counted unworthy to bring forth living children into the sunlit world. A thunder of drums attends her, tight-stretched and pounded by palms, and a clash of hollow cymbals; hoarse-throated horns bray their deep warning, and the pierced flute thrills every heart with Phrygian strains. Weapons are carried before her, symbolic of rabid frenzy, to chasten the thankless and profane hearts of the rabble with dread of her divinity. So, when first she is escorted into some great city and mutely enriches mortals with wordless benediction, they strew her path all along the route with a lavish largesse of copper and silver and shadow the Mother and her retinue with a snow of roses. Next an armed band, whom the Greeks call Phrygian Curetes, joust together and join in rhythmic dances, merry with blood and nodding their heads to set their terrifying crests aflutter. They call to mind those Curetes of Dicté, who once on a time in Crete, as the story goes, drowned the wailing of the infant Jove by dancing with swift feet, an armed band of boys around a boy, and rhythmically clashing bronze on bronze, lest Saturn should seize and crush him in his jaws and deal his mother's heart a wound that would not heal. That perhaps is why they attend in arms upon the Great Mother. Or else they signify that the goddess bids men be ready to defend their native earth staunchly by force of arms and resolve to shield their parents and do them credit.

Lucretius, *On Reality* 2.600-43 (R. E. Latham)

GREEK SCIENCE

I

PHILOSOPHY VICTORIOUS

When human life lay grovelling in all men's sight, crushed to the earth under the dead weight of superstition whose grim features loured menacingly upon mortals from the four quarters of the sky, a man of Greece was first to raise mortal eyes in defiance, first to stand erect and brave the challenge. Fables of the gods did not crush him, nor the lightning flash and the growling menace of the sky. Rather, they quickened his manhood, so that he, first of all men, longed to smash the constraining locks of nature's doors. The vital vigour of his mind prevailed. He ventured far out beyond the flaming ramparts of the world and voyaged in mind throughout infinity. Returning victorious, he proclaimed to us what can be and what cannot: how a limit is fixed to the power of everything and an immovable frontier post. Therefore superstition in its turn lies crushed beneath his feet, and we by his triumph are lifted level with the skies.

Lucretius, *On Reality* 1.62-79 (R. E. Latham)

II

EVOLUTION

Within the weed-grown swamps left by the flood
The animal kingdoms of the earth appeared.
The seeds of earth swelled in the heat of noon
As in a mother's womb—as when the seven-lipped
Nile shrinks to its source, so sun's heat wakens

The moss-green river side, and there the peasant
As he turns the soil finds under it a world
Of things that live, half-live, or creep or run
As though one body of earth were alive,
Half dead, so in all things
And in a single body, half motionless,
Inert, yet half alive. As heat and water
Become one body, so life begins; though fire
And water are at war, life's origins
Awake discordant harmonies that move
The entire world. Therefore when fires
Of newly wakened sun turned toward the earth
Where waters still receded from her sides,
All living things in multitudes of being
Became her progeny once more. Some were
Of ancient lineage and colors
And others were mysterious and new.

.   .   .

From mud and mire the green frog makes his way
Legless at first, but soon has legs to swim,
The rear long-legged leap from here to there.
Even the cub that the she-bruin carries
Is not a bear but something rolled together
Until its mother's tongue strokes it alive
To make it seem a creature like herself.
Look at the hatch of honeybees in cells
Formless until they stir with legs and wings,
Or Juno's peacock with its star-eyed tail,
Jove's eagle carrying thunderbolts and arrows,
Or Cytherea's doves in golden air—
Who'd think that their beginnings were concealed
Within the featureless white wall of egg?
Some say that when man's backbone rots away
In sleep within the tomb, the spine grows wary
And is a snake that crawls through open doors.

Ovid, *Transformations* 1.416-37,
15.375-90 (Horace Gregory)

207

III

THUNDER

First, then, the reason why the blue expanses of heaven are shaken by *thunder* is the clashing of clouds soaring high in the ether, when conflicting winds cause them to collide. A thunderclap does not issue from a clear stretch of sky: the normal source of that terrific crash and roll is the point where the advancing columns of cloud are most densely serried. Clouds cannot be composed of such dense bodies as make up stones or logs, nor of such flimsy ones as mist and drifting smoke. In the one case, they would be forced to fall like stones by the drag of their dead weight; in the other, they would be no better able than smoke to cohere or to contain icy snow and showers of hail. The noise they make above the levels of the outspread world is comparable to the intermittent clap of the awning stretched over a large theatre, when it flaps between poles and cross-beams; or to the loud crackling, reminiscent of rending paper, that it makes when riotous winds have ripped it. You can pick out the former sound in thunder, and you hear it again when hanging clothes or flying scraps of paper are whipped and whirled by the wind and swished through the air. At other times it happens that the clouds cannot so much collide head-on as pass side by side on different courses, scraping their bodies together protractedly. That is when our ears are rubbed by that dry crackling sound, long drawn out, until the clouds have drifted out of close quarters.

Lucretius, *On Reality* 6.96-120 (R. E. Latham)

IV

FERTILITY

Nor can the vain decrees of pow'rs above
Deny production to the act of love—
Or hinder fathers of that happy name,
Or with a barren womb the matron shame
(As many think, who stain with victims' blood
The mournful altars, and with incense load,
To bless the showery seed with future life,
And to impregnate the well-labor'd wife).
In vain they weary heav'n with prayer, or fly
To oracles, or magic numbers try;

For barrenness of sexes will proceed
Either from too condens'd, or wat'ry, seed.
The wat'ry juice too soon dissolves away,
And in the parts, projected, will not stay;
The too condens'd, unsoul'd unwieldy mass,
Drops short, nor carries to the destin'd place—
Nor pierces to the parts, nor, tho' injected home,
Will mingle with the kindly moisture of the womb.
For nuptials are unlike in their success;
Some men with fruitful seed some women bless,
And from some men some women fruitful are,
Just as their constitutions join or jar:
And many seeming barren wives have been,
Who after, match'd with more prolific men,
Have fill'd a family with prattling boys;
And many, not supplied at home with joys,
Have found a friend abroad to ease their smart,
And to perform the sapless husband's part.
So much it does import that seed with seed
Should of the kindly mixture make the breed;
And thick with thin, and thin with thick should join,
So to produce and propagate the line.
Of such concernment too is drink and food,
T' incrassate, or attenuate, the blood.
Of like importance is the posture too,
In which the genial feat of love we do;
For, as the females of the four-foot kind
Receive the leapings of their males behind,
So the good wives, with loins uplifted high,
And leaning on their hands, the fruitful stroke may try;
For in that posture will they best conceive,
Not when, supinely laid, they frisk and heave;
For active motions only break the blow,
And more of strumpets than of wives they show
When, answering stroke with stroke, the mingled liquors flow.
Endearments eager, and too brisk a bound,
Throws off the ploughshare from the furrow'd ground.
But common harlots in conjunction heave
Because 't is less their business to conceive

Than to delight, and to provoke the deed;
A trick which honest wives but little need.

Lucretius, *On Reality* 4.1233-77 (John Dryden)

V

HEREDITY

And when the woman's more prevailing juice
Sucks in the man's, the mixture will produce
The mother's likeness; when the man prevails,
His own resemblance in the seed he seals.
But when we see the new-begotten race
Reflect the features of each parent's face,
Then of the father's and the mother's blood
The justly temper'd seed is understood;
When both conspire, with equal ardor bent,
From every limb the due proportion sent,
When neither party foils, when neither foil'd,
This gives the blended features of the child.
    Sometimes the boy the grandsire's image bears;
Sometimes the more remote progenitor he shares;
Because the genial atoms of the seed
Lie long conceal'd ere they exert the breed;
And, after sundry ages past, produce
The tardy likeness of the latent juice.
Hence families such different figures take,
And represent the ancestors in face, and hair, and make,
Because of the same *seed* the voice, and hair,
And shape, and face, and other members are,
And the same antique mold the likeness does prepare.
Thus oft the father's likeness does prevail
In females, and the mother's in the male;
For, since the seed is of a double kind,
From that where we the most resemblance find
We may conclude the strongest tincture sent,
And that was in conception prevalent.

Lucretius, *On Reality* 4.1208-32
(John Dryden)

VI

DETACHMENT

What can life give of sweeter than to dwell
Serenely in the strongholds of the wise
High-towering, impregnable, and thence
Look out to far horizons and the tide
That hither-thither bears the sons of men
Jostling and struggling, birth with talents match'd
In strife to seize the prizes of the world?
O mortal hearts, so busy and yet so blind!
Life's a frail bark that sails on perilous seas,
Or a dim taper ring'd about with dark:
O foolish hearts, let be; nature but craves
Limbs without ache or ail, and minds unvext.

Lucretius, *On Reality* 2.7-19
(V.S. Vernon-Jones)

GREEK ART

When Minos landed on the coast of Crete,
He bled a hundred bulls to mighty Jove,
And decked his palace with the spoils of war.
And yet strange gossip tainted all his honours:
Proof that his wife was mounted by a bull
Was clear enough to all who saw her son,
Half-beast, half-man, a sulky, heavy creature.
To hide this symbol of his wife's mismating
He planned to house the creature in a maze,
An arbour with blind walls beyond the palace;
He turned to Daedalus, an architect,
Who was well known for artful craft and wit,
To make a labyrinth that tricked the eye.
Quite as Meander flows through Phrygian pastures,
Twisting its streams to sea or fountainhead,
The dubious waters turning left or right,
So Daedalus designed his winding maze;
And as one entered it, only a wary mind

23. The Emperor Caracalla. Naples, Museo Nazionale.

. . . sensual vibrancy easily jangled . . .

Could find an exit to the world again—
Such was the cleverness of that strange arbour.

　　　．　　　　　．　　　　　．

　Weary of exile, hating Crete, his prison,
Old Daedalus grew homesick for his country
Far out of sight beyond his walls—the sea.
"Though Minos owns this island, rules the waves,
The skies are open: my direction's clear.
Though he commands all else on earth below
His tyranny does not control the air."
So Daedalus turned his mind to subtle craft,
An unknown art that seemed to outwit nature:
He placed a row of feathers in neat order,
Each longer than the one that came before it
Until the feathers traced an inclined plane
That cast a shadow like the ancient pipes
That shepherds played, each reed another step
Unequal to the next. With cord and wax
He fixed them smartly at one end and middle,
Then curved them till they looked like eagles' wings.
And as he worked, boy Icarus stood near him,
His brilliant face lit up by his father's skill.
He played at snatching feathers from the air
And sealing them with wax (nor did he know
How close to danger came his lightest touch);
And as the artist made his miracles
The artless boy was often in his way.
At last the wings were done and Daedalus
Slipped them across his shoulders for a test
And flapped them cautiously to keep his balance,
And for a moment glided into air.

Ovid, *Transformations* 8.152-68,
183-202 (Horace Gregory)

WHERE GREEKS EXCEL . . .

Greece had a genius, Greece had eloquence,
For her ambition and her end was fame.
Our Roman youth is diligently taught
The deep mysterious art of growing rich,
And the first words that children learn to speak
Are of the value of the names of coin:
Can a penurious wretch, that with his milk
Hath suck'd the basest dregs of usury,
Pretend to generous and heroic thoughts?
And can rust and avarice write lasting lines?

Horace, *Dramatic Technique* 323-32
(Earl of Roscommon)

ATELIER TALK

Should painter attach to a fair human head
The thick, turgid neck of a stallion,
Or depict a spruce lass with the tail of a bass,
I am sure you would guy the rapscallion.

Believe me, dear Pisos, that just such a freak
Is the crude and preposterous poem
Which merely abounds in a torrent of sounds,
With no depth of reason below 'em.

'Tis all very well to give license to art—
The wisdom of license defend I;
But the line should be drawn at the fripperish spawn
Of a mere *cacoethes scribendi.*

It is too much the fashion to strain at effects—
Yes, that's what's the matter with Hannah!
Our popular taste, by the tyros debased,
Paints each barnyard a grove of Diana!

Should a patron require you to paint a marine,
Would you work in some trees with their barks on?
When his strict orders are for a Japanese jar,

Would you give him a pitcher like Clarkson?

Now, this is my moral: Compose what you may,
And fame will be ever far distant
Unless you combine with a simple design
A treatment in toto consistent.

Horace, *Dramatic Technique* 1-23 (Eugene Field)

METRICAL HOLIDAY

But yesterday, Licinius, we,
gamesters of metre, diced away
in poems a whole holiday.
We sat and scribbled cheerfully;
in turns we wrote each ribald line,
mixing our jokes with cups of wine.
Dear laughter! when we had to quit,
I left so burning with your wit
no food could drive pain's gap away,
no sleep could lid my eyes with peace,
my thoughts were wild and would not cease.
I tossed awake the whole night through.
I longed for dawn, I longed for you,
and wearied half to death I lay
in dazed impatience till the day.

Catullus, *Songs* 50.1-15 (Jack Lindsay)

DEDICATION

To whom
  send my book off
  all poised, pretty,
by heavy effort light
  and witty?

To you, Cornelius, I think
  who took for jewels my shined-up stones

though you were busying your ink
   on Everything in three thick tomes.

My little something
be received by her
(and you)
with whom beMused I wrote
words for an aeon
(or two).

Catullus, Songs 1 (G. W.)

AT THE SALON

Sempronia was a woman who had committed many crimes that showed her to have the reckless daring of a man. Fortune had favoured her abundantly, not only with birth and beauty, but with a good husband and children. Well educated in Greek and Latin literature, she had greater skill in lyre-playing and dancing than there is any need for a respectable woman to acquire, besides many other accomplishments such as minister to dissipation. There was nothing that she set a smaller value on than seemliness and chastity, and she was as careless of her reputation as she was of her money. Her passions were so ardent that she more often made advances to men than they did to her. Many times already she had broken a solemn promise, repudiated a debt by perjury, and been an accessary to murder. At once self-indulgent and impecunious, she had gone headlong from bad to worse. Yet her abilities were not to be despised. She could write poetry, crack a joke, and converse at will with decorum, tender feeling, or wantonness; she was in fact a woman of ready wit and considerable charm.

Sallust, The Conspiracy of Catiline 25
(S. A. Handford)

ON CICERO'S POETRY

"Fortune foretun'd the dying notes of Rome:
Till I, thy consul sole, consol'd thy doom."

His fate had crept below the lifted swords,
Had all his malice been to murther words.

Juvenal, *Satires* 10.122-24 (John Dryden)

THE WOULD-BE POET

Dickie-boy Trill
climbed helicon hill
to fetch a pail a poesy
the muses saw
and (being quick on the draw)
they knocked him arsover noesy

Catullus, *Songs* 105 (Frank O. Copley)

CAUTION

Why don't I send my book to you
Although you often urge me to?
The reason's good, for if I did
You'd send me yours—which God forbid!

Martial, *Epigrams* 7.77 (J. A. Pott)

THE WISE AUTHOR

Arthur, they say, has wit; for what?
For writing? No, for writing not.

Martial, *Epigrams* 8.20 (Jonathan Swift)

THE PLAGIARIST

I wrote that book you read us,
    as can readily be shown.
You read it, though, so vilely
    it begins to be your own.

Martial, *Epigrams* 1.38 (Paul Nixon)

217

TOUGH CHOICE

Gods love me, I can't rightly tell which hole
    I'd smell in Emil, mouth or ass.
It's hard to say, but I would judge the ass
    wins out for cleanliness and class:
it has no teeth. The mouth has half a yard
    of gums that grate like wagon crates;
it widens as, in summer, split in two,
    the cunt of a pissing mule will do.
He screws the girls and preens himself with charm—
    and isn't on a donkey farm?
The girl who touches him would kiss the stink
    of some sick hangman's ass, I think.

                Catullus, *Songs* 97 (Roy A. Swanson)

EVIDENCE

Am I a man, my boys? I'll ram
indisputable evidence
up, Aurelius, Furius, and down
the appropriate orifices—
you the receiver, and you the dispenser
of such goods, who thought
my pretty (pretty dirty) lines
a pansy poet's work.

Say—no one will argue—the poet's life
is to be pure; but why his poems?
Why give ten commandments to a text?
For poetry must be salted with wit,
with all that intrigues or tickles a bit
(not—superfluous labor—
to make youth effervesce;
my salt is meant for scouring
hairy rust off old limbs).

If, then, my lines have one or two
thousands of kisses, you think

only a fairy could cast such a spell?
Take warning!—indisputable, up and down
proof for you up- and down- men!

Catullus, *Songs* 16 (G. W.)

FACED DOWN

Vainly your fingers
coax men's tools.
Hand "makes a motion"
face overrules.

Martial, *Epigrams* 6.23 (G. W.)

INVOLUNTARY CONFESSION

Seven husbands' tombs
Chloe chiseled thus:
CHLOE SET THIS UP.
(What's more obvious?)

Martial, *Epigrams* 9.15 (Richard E. Braun)

"MARRIED" LIFE

No coupling, Lupus, with Charisi-anus.
You ask him why this long frustration?
"My period," he'll say; for diarrhea
Is homosexuals' menstruation.

Martial, *Epigrams* 11.88 (G. W.)

TO A BLUESTOCKING

From scenturies of rot you'll heave and ask
What pulls my power's nerves from out of my?
When dingy what you have of teeth; cross-hatched,

24. Satyr. Baltimore, Walters Art Gallery.

The drunken sire pursues, the dames retire;
Sometimes the drunken dames pursue the drunken sire.

And of your face digs wrinkles, age. And in
Between dry crags your anus yawns and dangles
Tidbits of filth, like a dyspeptic cow's.
Your chest down me knocks screwloose, whose flat knobs
Are flimsy as she-horses' teats; your slop-
py gut, thighs meagre, sprouting out into
Tremendous calves—Be gay, can't you, while your
Wax forbears lead your graveyard-bound parade?
And may no mamma toddle after you
Tricked in rotunder pearls. And what about
Those stoic tracts cuddling in silken pillows?
Does the illiterate stand with any less
Of fiber, spare the rod more quickly? If
You want this fascination from slack switch,
I fear, my dear, you'll have to play the licktor.

Horace, *Intermittent Metres* 8 (Nicholas Kilmer)

CONGRATULATIONS ON THE
SIMPLE LIFE

Furius, you own no slave, no bank,
no spider, bug, or fire, but own
a dad and second mother, two
whose teeth could grind up even stone.
And life with your old man is good,
and with his wife (a block of wood).
No wonder: you're all healthy, your
digestion's good, you have no fear
of fires, heavy losses, or
of crimes, or snares of poison, or
of other chance calamity.
But sun- and cold- and famine-worn,
you've bodies drier than a horn
or what has more aridity.
Why shouldn't you be benign and fit?
You're free from sweat and free from spit;
your nose is free from snot and slime.
To this fit state add fitter fact,

you're cleaner where your back is cracked
than salt bowls, and it's very clear
you hardly drop ten turds a year,
each hard as pebbles or a bean:
your hands can rub them and stay clean.
Count your blessings, Furius, you
shan't spurn or think them all too few—
and stop your prayers for sesterces;
you're blest enough with all of these.

Catullus, *Songs* 23 (Roy A. Swanson)

TO CAESAR: NO

Join your party?
I might,
mighty czar—

could I remember,
quite,
who you are.

Catullus, *Songs* 93 (G. W.)

SOCIETY ABORTIONS

You seldom hear of the rich mantle, spread
For the babe, born in the great lady's bed.
Such is the pow'r of herbs; such arts they use
To make them barren, or their fruit to lose.
But thou, whatever slops she will have brought,
Be thankful, and supply the deadly draught;
Help her to make manslaughter; let her bleed,
And never want for savin at her need.
For, if she holds till her nine months be run,
Thou mayst be father to an Ethiop's son.

Juvenal, *Satires* 6.594-600
(John Dryden)

MATRON

Cold Bassa leans and coos
at baby's little shoes.
Shows warmth of heart?
No. Masks a fart.

Martial, *Epigrams* 4.87 (G. W.)

SELF-DENIAL

Indeed, so well I've learned to fast
   That, sooth my love, I know not whether
I might not bring myself at last
   To—do without you altogether.

Martial, *Epigrams* 3.53 (Thomas Moore)

DRESSING THE PART

I

Cinna seems poor in show
   And he is so.

Martial, *Epigrams* 8.19
(Richard Lovelace)

II

Thy beard and head are of a different dye;
Short of one foot, distorted in an eye;
With all these tokens of a knave complete,
Should'st thou be honest, thou'rt a dev'lish cheat.

Martial, *Epigrams* 12.54
(Joseph Addison)

PUZZLEMENT

I

You're a pimp, you deal in slander,
you're an informer, forger, pander,
and gladiator-trainer. Funny
Vacerra, that you have no money.

Martial, *Epigrams* 11.66 (Jack Lindsay)

II

Sabby, old sock, you pain me
And why, I wonder, should this be?
    I cannot say: a mystery!
    You inexplicably pain me.

Martial, *Epigrams* 1.32 (G. W.)

ANCESTRY

Then please thy pride, and search the herald's roll,
Where thou shalt find thy famous pedigree
Drawn from the root of some old Tuscan tree—
And thou, a thousand off, a fool of long degree.

Persius, *Satires* 3.27-28 (John Dryden)

NO MYSTERY

I

That no fair woman will, wonder not why,
Clap (Rufus) under thine her tender thigh;
Not a silk gown shall once melt one of them,
Nor the delights of a transparent gemme.

A scurvy story kills thee, which doth tell
That in thine armpits a fierce goat doth dwell.
Him they all fear full of an ugly stench,
Nor's 't fit he should lie with a handsome wench;
Wherefore this Noses's cursed plague first crush,
Or cease to wonder why they fly you thus.

Catullus, *Songs* 69 (Richard Lovelace)

II

Naso, you are many men's man; and yet
 beside you no man's willing to be seen.
Naso, you are many men's man: "To let—
        you Queen!"

Catullus, *Songs* 112 (Jack Lindsay)

POETS IN THE UNDERWORLD

Whoever was the first to plant you, tree,
Did it on a black day; those impious hands
Trained you to massacre posterity
And bring disgrace upon our local lands.

I can imagine him—a homicide
Who'd strangled his own father, stabbed a guest
At night and smeared the hearth with blood, applied
The Colchic poisons, in a word professed

Every abomination that one could
Conceive of. Last, he placed you on my farm
To topple, miserable lump of wood,
Onto a master who deserves no harm.

No man is hourly armed against surprise.
The Carthaginian pilot who takes care
Passing the Bosphorus, forgets what lies
Beyond, and runs on hidden dooms elsewhere.

When Parthians flee, the legions are afraid
Of arrows; Parthians fear the captor's chain,

225

The strength of Rome; but death's an ambuscade
That has destroyed the world and shall again.

How close the realm of dusky Proserpine
Yawned at that instant! I half glimpsed the dire
Judge of the dead, the blest in their divine
Seclusion, Sappho on the Aeolian lyre

Mourning the cold girls of her native isle,
And you, Alcaeus, more full-throatedly
Singing with your gold quill of ships, exile
And war, hardship on land, hardship at sea.

The admiring shades accord the reverent hush
Due to them both; but when the theme is war
And tyrants banished, then the elbowing crush
Thickens, the ghostly hearers thirst for more.

No wonder, when such music can disarm
The hundred-headed hell-dog till he droops
His dark ears in bewilderment, can charm
The snakes that braid the Furies' hair in loops,

Yes, even beguile Prometheus and the sire
Of Pelops of their torments, while Orion,
Leaving the chase to listen to the lyre,
Forgets the shy lynx or the shadowy lion.

Horace, *Songs* 2.13 (James Michie)

THE LATIN LYRE

Back, lyre, to our labors!
If you ever lightened
an empty place and hour
with song under a tree, sing now
some Roman words to resonate forever.

Shape Latin as Alcaeus wrought
the Lesbian tongue—that man
who intermitted stormy war with song,
turned his imperiled bark in

to the glittering harbor
with melody to Bacchus, Muses, Venus and
her petulant-attentive radiant boy
(to the other boy as well, with dark locks—
Lycus—and dark liquid eyes).

Lyre, emblem of Apollo,
demanded at the table of the gods,
laboring to ease man's labors,
I sing this hymn to you
to make you sing.

Horace, *Songs* 1.32 (G. W.)

THE POET'S WEALTH

What boon, Apollo, what does the poet as
He pours the new wine out of the bowl at your
   New shrine request? Not bumper harvests
     (Prayer of Sardinian millionaires), nor

Huge herds of fine cows grazed in Calabria's
Heat, nor the Far East's goldware and ivory,
   Nor land that Liris, silent river,
     Nibbles away with its sleepy water.

To each his life-work. Let the Calenian
Prune back his vines. Let merchants with moneybags
   Swill out of pure gold cups the wines they
     Buy on the profits from Tyre and Sidon—

God's own elect: how else can they weather the
Atlantic three times yearly and come to port
   Unscathed? For me, though, olives, endives,
     Mallows—the last for a smooth digestion.

Here's what I crave most, son of Latona, then:
Good health, a sound mind, relish of life, and an
   Old age that still maintains a stylish
     Grip on itself, with the lyre beside me.

Horace, *Songs* 1.31 (James Michie)

THE ARTIST'S INTEGRITY

Persius to Self   "Maenas" and "Attis" in the mouth were bred,
  And never hatch'd within the lab'ring head.
  No blood from bitten nails those poems drew;
  But churn'd, like spittle, from the lips they flew.

Self   'Tis fustian all; 'tis execrably bad;
  But if they will be fools, must you be mad?
  Your satires, let me tell you, are too fierce;
  The great will never bear so blunt a verse.
  Their doors are barr'd against a bitter flout.
  Snarl, if you please, but you shall snarl without.
  Expect such pay as railing rhymes deserve,
  Y' are in a very hopeful way to starve.

.   .   .

Persius to Self   Yet old Lucilius never fear'd the times,
  But lash'd the city, and dissected crimes.
  Mutius and Lupus both by name he brought;
  He mouth'd 'em, and betwixt his grinders caught.
  Unlike in method, with conceal'd design,
  Did crafty Horace his low numbers join;
  And, with a sly insinuating grace,
  Laugh'd at his friend, and look'd him in the face;
  Would raise a blush where secret vice he found,
  And tickel, while he gently prob'd, the wound.
  With seeming innocence the crowd beguil'd,
  But made the desperate passes when he smil'd.
    Could he do this, and is my Muse controll'd
  By servile awe? Born free, and not be bold?
  At least I'll dig a hole within the ground,
  And to the trusty earth commit the sound:
  The reeds shall tell you what the poet fears
  ("King Midas has a snout, and ass's ears").
  This mean conceit, this darling mystery,
  Which thou think'st nothing, friend, thou shalt not buy;

228

Nor will I change for all the flashy wit
That flatt'ring Labeo in his "Iliads" writ.
     Thou, if there be a thou in this base town,
Who dares with angry Eupolis to frown
(He who, with bold Cratinus, is inspir'd
With zeal, and equal indignation fir'd),
Who at enormous villainy turns pale,
And steers against it with a full-blown sail,
Like Aristophanes—let him but smile
On this my honest work, though writ in homely style;
And if two lines or three in all the vein
Appear less drossy, read those lines again.
May they perform their author's just intent,
Glow in thy ears, and in thy breast ferment.

> Persius, *Satires* 1.104-10, 114-26
> (John Dryden)

THE POET'S FAME

This monument will outlast metal and I made it
More durable than the king's seat, higher than pyramids.
Gnaw of the wind and rain?
     Impotent
The flow of the years to break it, however many.

Bits of me, many bits, will dodge all funeral,
O Libitina-Persephone and, after that,
Sprout new praise. As long as
Pontifex and the quiet girl pace the Capitol
I shall be spoken where the wild flood Aufidus
Lashes, and Daunus ruled the parched farmland:

Power from lowliness: "First brought Aeolic song to Italian
    fashion"—
Wear pride, work's gain! O Muse Melpomene,
By your will bind the laurel.
     My hair, Delphic laurel.

> Horace, *Songs* 3.30 (Ezra Pound)

THE USES OF LITERATURE

(Cicero validates the Roman citizenship of a Greek poet, Aulus Licinius Archias):

If, my lords, I have any capacity (which I own to be but slender), if I have any merit as a speaker (which I do not deny to be indifferent), but—indifferent as it is—if from my early youth it was improved by a regular application to the study of the arts (which even at those years I found delightful), the defendant Aulus Licinius has a right to claim the fruit of all my qualifications, of all my abilities. For, as far as I can retrace the scenes of life, or revive the ideas of the age immediately succeeding childhood, he it was who, in the course of all my studies, prompted my application and directed my progress. If therefore my tongue (filed by his art and tutored by his precepts) ever relieved the oppressed, my duty and my gratitude direct me to defend the man who formed it to defend others.

And here lest some should be surprised at what I advance (as the turn of his genius, his eloquence, and his studies are different from mine), give me leave to say that, though I never wholly applied myself to poetry, yet in all the liberal professions there is an intellectual relation, a secret charm that, connecting the one to the other, combines them all.

Again, lest I am blamed for introducing—in a regular proceeding, in a public pleading, before a praetor the best of men and of magistrates, before impartial judges, in so full, so frequent an assembly—a style unknown to the forms of a trial and inconsistent with the practice of the bar, I beg to be indulged in what I hope you will conceive to be a decent liberty of speech by suiting it to the circumstances of my client. In pleading for an excellent poet and a man of letters, surrounded as I am by a crowd of learned Romans, encouraged by your patronage of arts and sciences and protected by such a judge, give me leave to enlarge upon the love of learning and the Muse, and to use an unprecedented language in supporting the character of a man whose lettered indolence has ever been averse to the bustle of public life. Indulge me, I say, in this; and I will prove, my lords, that as Archias *is* a citizen, he ought not to be disfranchised;—nay, though he had the misfortune of being an alien, you yourselves shall own that he is worthy the privileges of a Roman.

For as soon as Archias ceased to be a boy, and had bid adieu to the studies that tutor the youthful mind into the love of arts, his genius led him to poetry. His capacity soon distinguished him at Antioch, the place of his birth (which was noble) and a city once eminent and wealthy but still fertile in men of great learning and true taste. Afterwards, in his progress through the other parts of Asia and all over Greece, so much was he admired that, though they expected more than what they had heard, yet did they not expect so much as they saw and experienced of his genius.

Italy was then full of the professors of the fine arts and sciences, which were more assiduously then cultivated in the *country* of Italy than they now are in her *cities,* and the public tranquillity afforded them some shelter even here in Rome. Therefore the inhabitants of Tarentum, Rhegium, and Naples presented him with the privileges of their respective cities and with other marks of their regard, and every man who had the smallest discernment or taste was proud of his acquaintance and friendship. His fame thus spreading to places where his person was unknown, he came to Rome under the consulate of Marius and Catulus. To these he endeared himself: the actions of Marius afforded the noblest subject for poetic genius; and the other not only deserved to be the theme, but actually was the judge and friend, of the Muse. Afterwards the Luculli, while Archias was but seventeen years of age, invited him to their house. But, my lords, it was the virtues of the heart and humanity of his nature, not the charms of his Muse or the brightness of his genius, that recommended him to a family where he spent his youth and grew grey in the practice of every social virtue.

He was in these days favored by Marcus Metellus Numidicus and his son Pius, admired by Marcus Aemilius, familiar with the elder and the younger Catulus, courted by Lucius Crassus, and so endearingly intimate was he with the Luculli, Drusus, the Octavii, Cato, and all the Hortensian family that they thought no expression of their regard for him too great. Thus an acquaintance with Archias grew in some sense to be a fashion, courted not only by men of taste and discernment but by those who were blind to all his beauties and sought reputation by *pretending* a regard for his profession.

Having lived long in this manner, he went to Sicily with Lucius Lucullus and, having left that province in the same company, he came to Heraclea, which the strictest faith of nations and the sanctity of laws have joined with Rome. He expressed his desire of being enfranchised in that city, which was granted as well on account of his personal merit as at the recommendation of Lucullus. The terms on which, by the Plautian Law, any alien might be admitted a citizen of Rome, were as follows: provided they were enrolled by free cities, provided they had a dwelling in Italy at

231

the time of the law's passage, and provided they declared their enrollment before the praetor within sixty days. Archias for many years had resided in Italy, and he had declared before the praetor Quintus Marcellus, who was his intimate friend.

If the enfranchisement and the law is all I have to prove, here will I rest my defence, the trial is over. For what can you, his adversary, object to this fact? Lucullus, a man of the strictest honor, truth, and integrity, is here in court ready to affirm it—not as a matter agreeable to his opinion, but consistent with his knowledge; not as a thing he heard, but saw; not as an affair in which he had some concern, but what he actually transacted. Commissioners from Heraclea (all of them men of quality) are present, ready to produce the public mandates and declaration of their constituents that prove him an Heraclean by enrollment. But here you demand that the public archives of Heraclea should be produced, though we all know that they, and the office which contained them, were consumed by fire in the Italian war. How ridiculous therefore is it, not to plead to the evidence which we are ready to produce, and to insist upon our producing evidence which it is impossible we can command; to refuse what is recent in the minds of men, and to appeal to the authority of registers; to reject what is affirmed on the honor of an illustrious Roman and the unquestionable, the uncorruptible faith and oath of a free city, and to demand the evidence of registers which, at the same breath, you own may be and often are vitiated!

But he did not reside at Rome?—he who, for so many years before he obtained his enfranchisement, had made Rome the bank of all he was worth in the world! But he did not declare?—I affirm he did; nay, entered his declaration into those registers which, by their being in custody of the college of praetors, alone have a title to the authority of public archives. For, as the registers of Appius are said to have been very negligently kept, the corruption of his colleague before he was accused and his fate after he was condemned in a manner canceled the authority due to public records; yet such was the indefatigable application of Metellus, the most modest, most virtuous man alive, that he went before Lucius Lentulus the praetor and the other judges, and complained of the erasure of one name—therefore the name of Licinius is still to be read there.

If this is a fact, why should you doubt of his enfranchisement, especially as he was enrolled in another free city? If in Greece men of no consideration and possessing either no art at all (or a very mean one) were gratuitously enfranchised in their cities, is it possible that the Rhegians, the

Locrians, the Neapolitans, and the Tarentines would deny to a man who had the merit of superior genius to recommend him a compliment which they never scrupled to bestow on vulgar mechanics? How—when others, not only after their enfranchisement but even after the Papian Law, found means to creep into the registers of the municipal cities—shall he, who never claimed his privilege by virtue of his being enrolled in other cities (because he wished still to pass for an Heraclean), be rejected?

You demand to see the enrollment of our estate—as if it were doubtful that at the time of the last censors my client was in the army under that brave general Lucius Lucullus; in the time of their immediate predecessors he was in Asia, where the same general was quaestor; and under Julius and Crassus the people underwent no census. But as an enrollment in the census books does not constitute an enfranchisement, but only proves that a man thus enrolled assumed the character of a citizen, know that at the time in which you pretend that (even by his own confession) he had no right to the freedom of Rome, by our law he then made a will, he had access to the privileges of a Roman, and was recommended to the treasury by Lucius Lucullus, then consul and praetor. Find out therefore some other arguments, for neither by his own nor his friends' conduct can he ever be convicted.

You demand, Gratius, of me, Why I am bewitched by this man? I answer: because he supplies me with an agreeable relaxation for my spirits when fatigued with this battle of the Forum, and charms my ears when stunned with its noise. Do you imagine I could possibly furnish matter for my daily pleading on such a variety of heads, were not my understanding cultivated with learning; or that my mind could be equal to such a load of altercations, were it not sometimes unbent by my learned amusements? I own myself to be enchanted with these studies. Let those be ashamed who so bury themselves in learned dust as that their qualifications can neither be of use to society nor give credit nor reputation to themselves. But what have I to be ashamed of—I, my lords, who never have been detained by interest or indolence, distracted by pleasure or diverted by sleep, for so many years, from the offices of humanity? Then who can justly blame, who can censure me if, while others are pursuing the views of interest, gazing at festal shows and solemnities, exploring new pleasures, reposing the body or unbending the mind, while they are deep in the midnight revel, in dice or diversion, I spend the recollective hour in the pleasing review of these studies?

Farther I can urge in my own excuse—(to them it is owing that I thus speak, that I thus reason)—that no acquirements did I ever possess which have not been employed to relieve my friends. These may indeed be slender, but virtue is of a more exalted nature, that I feel; and from what source I derive it this breast informs me. For had not my youthful mind, from many precepts, from many writings drunk in *this* truth—that glory and virtue ought to be the darling, nay the only, wish in life; that to attain these the torments of the flesh, with the perils of death and exile, are to be despised—never for your deliverance had I exposed my person in so many encounters and to these daily conflicts with the worst of men. But on this head books are full, the voice of the wise is full, the example of antiquity is full. And all these the night of barbarism had still enveloped had it not been enlightened by the sun of science. How many pictures of the bravest men, not to be gazed at but to be imitated, have the Greek and Latin authors left us! It was by the lovely ideas which I drew from their excellence that I regulated my conduct as a magistrate, and simultaneously improved my head and my heart.

"How?" it may be said. "Were all those great men whose virtues are recorded skilled in the learning that you have so lavishly praised?" It is hard to say that they were, but I affirm one thing as certain: I own that I have known many who, without letters, by the almost divine intelligence of their own nature, have enjoyed every good quality, every amiable virtue; and of themselves have acquired the love and veneration of mankind. Nay, I will add that nature without learning is of more efficacy towards forming such a character than learning is without nature. But at the same time I do insist that, when intelligent improvable nature is assisted by polished education and regular study, then something inexpressibly beautiful, something inimitably excellent, is ever the consequence. Such was the divine Africanus, known to past ages; such the amiable Laelius and the temperate Furius; and such, known to this age, was Marcus Cato, that brave Roman and learned old man. All these had never applied to learning but from a consciousness that their innate virtue was improved and enlightened by study.

But were pleasure *without* utility to be the sole end of learning, yet must you own it to be the most generous, the most humane exercise of the rational faculties. Other exercises depend on the circumstances of time, age, and place; but these studies give nurture in youth and amusement in old age, in prosperity they grace and embellish, in adversity they shelter and support, delightful at home and easy abroad, they soften slumber, they shorten fatigue and enliven retirement. Though I myself never had

234

felt their efficacy nor could taste their excellence, yet must they be the object of my adoration when I see them beam from others.

Where amongst us is the mind so barbarous, where the breast so flinty, as of late to be unaffected with the death of Roscius the actor? He died indeed an old man, but a man whose art and elegance seemed to challenge immortality. Was he so universally esteemed and loved for the inimitable management of his limbs, and are we to overlook the divine enthusiasm of genius and the glowing energy of the soul? How often, my lords, have I seen this Archias—(for I presume upon your goodness as I am encouraged by your attention to this unusual method of pleading); how often, I say, have I seen him when, without the assistance of a pen, he poured forth a number of excellent lines on subjects that were transacting while he composed them! How often has he clothed the same subject in a different turn of words and expression! While whatever was the cool, the digested result of his study, reduced to writing, has in my hearing met with an approbation nothing short of what is due to the merit of antiquity itself! Has not this man then a right to my love, to my admiration, to all the means which I can employ in his defence? For we are instructed by all the greatest and most learned of mankind that education, precepts, and practice can in every *other* branch of learning produce excellence, but a poet is formed by the finger of nature, he is aroused by the mental vigor, and inspired by what we may call the spirit, of divinity itself. Therefore our Ennius has a right to give to poets the epithet of holy, because they are as it were lent to mankind by the indulgent bounty of the gods.

May you therefore, my lords, as you are men impassioned with the love of learning, suffer the name of Poet, which no barbarism ever profaned, with you to be sacred. Rocks and deserts are respondent to the voice; music has charms to soothe and tame the horrid savage—and shall we, with all the advantages of excellent education, be deaf to the voice of the bard? The Colophonians claim Homer for their countryman, the Chians assert him to be theirs, the Salaminians affirm him to be a Salaminian, but the Smyrnians prove him to be of Smyrna (therefore they have dedicated a temple to him in their city), and many other people draw their swords on one another upon the same account. Do they therefore claim a stranger, because a Poet, for their countryman (even though dead), and shall we reject this living poet as ours, who has a Roman heart and Roman laws to recommend him; especially as Archias employed the utmost efforts of his art and genius to make Rome immortal by his Muse?

For, when a youth, he sung the Cimbrian War, and touched with pleasure even the stubborn, the untractable soul of Marius. (Nor is there a breast so unsusceptible of poetry who is not pleased that the Muse should be the eternal herald of his praise. It is said that Themistocles, the greatest man of Athens, when asked what melody or whose voice he heard with the greatest pleasure, answered "That of the man who can best rehearse my virtues." Thus the same Marius had the highest esteem for Lucius Plotius, whose genius he thought was fit to celebrate his actions). The Mithradatic War, a war of such importance, such variety, of such action both by sea and land, is all painted by Archias in verses that not only do honor to Lucullus, the best of men and the greatest of Romans, but reflect lustre upon the dignity of Rome herself; for the Romans under Lucullus penetrated into Pontus, till then impregnable by means of its frontier, guarded by a monarch's arms and a situation almost inaccessible by nature; under him the Roman arms with an inconsiderable force routed the innumerable troops of the Armenians; to his conduct it was owing that the Romans had the glory of snatching and securing Cyzicus, the city of our dearest allies, from the fury of a monarch and out of the destructive jaws of a whole impending war; to our praise shall it ever be recorded and related that under Lucullus we sunk the enemy's ships, we slew their generals, and performed miracles in the sea fight of Tenedos; ours are the trophies, ours the glory, and ours the triumphs.

Therefore the genius that records the actions of our heroes, at the same time celebrates the glory of our country. Our Ennius was dear to the elder Africanus, and it is thought his statue was erected in marble amidst the monuments of that family. Not only the immediate subject of a poem, but even the glory of the Roman people derives a lustre from the art of the poet. Cato, the ancestor of the judge who sits here, is ranked among the gods—and so the highest honor is reflected on the conduct of the Romans. In short, all the Maximi, the Marcelli, and the Fulvii, whose virtues the Muse records, communicate a portion of their own glory to every man in Rome.

Did our ancestors then admit to the privileges of a Roman a native of Rudiae, and shall we eject out of Rome an Heraclean whom many cities have courted but whom the laws of Rome ascertain to be hers? Ridiculous is the mistake in imagining that the merit of a Greek poet is inferior to that of a Latin. Greek verses are read almost universally, the Latin are confined to the narrow bounds of Latium. Therefore, if the operations of the Roman arms are limited only by the limits of the earth, we ought to pant that our glory and fame should reach at least as far as our power is felt. These, as they are strong motives to the people in general whose actions are celebrated, so to the particular heroes who expose their lives in the field of honor they have still been found the principal incentives to danger and to toil.

What an army of writers is the great Alexander said to have carried along with him; yet when he stood by the tomb of Achilles at Sigeum, "Happy youth," he cried, "who found a Homer to celebrate your courage!" Irrefragably true!—for had it not been for the *Iliad,* the fame and the ashes of Achilles had been buried in the same grave. And did not Pompey the Great (whose virtues are equal to his fortune) in a military assembly enfranchise Theophanes of Mitylene, the poet of his praise?— and these brave fellows, rough and unpolished as they were, felt yet the emotions of glory and sent up an approving shout as sharing in the fame of the leader. Are we then to suppose that, if Archias had not by our laws been a citizen of Rome, he could not have obtained his enfranchisement from some general?

Would Sulla, when he admitted Gauls and Spaniards, have refused the suit of Archias?—Sulla, I say, who we once saw in an assembly, when a very obscure poet presented him a petition upon the merit of a hobbling epigram to his praise, ordered him instantly to be rewarded out of a personal estate which was then selling, on condition that he should scribble no more; would the man who thought that the labors even of a wretched poet deserved some reward have been ungrateful to the wit, the genius, and the excellency of Archias? Could neither he nor the Luculli have had interest enough with Metellus Pius, his intimate friend who was lavish of his enfranchisements, to obtain that boon—especially as that great man had such a passion for having his actions recorded in verse that he heard, with some degree of pleasure, the harsh uncouth things called verses of poets born at Cordoba?

Nor must we dissemble a truth which can never be darkened, and must be ever in our eye: the love of praise biases all mankind, and the greatest minds are most susceptible to a passion for glory. Those very philosophers who most preach up a contempt of glory prefix their names to their works, and the very performances in which thy run down ostentation and distinction are eminent proofs of their vanity and weakness. Decimus Brutus, that great man and excellent general, adorned the entrance of the temples and the monuments of his own family with the verses of Accius his intimate friend. The great Fulvius, who in his war with the Aetolians was attended by Ennius, made no scruple to consecrate the spoils of Mars to the Muses. In this city, therefore, if generals in their armor have dignified the name and worshipped at the shrine of the Muses, you, my lords, in your robes ought to assert their honor and protect their poets.

My lords, to encourage you to this, I will unbosom myself and confess my perhaps too keen (but virtuous) passion for glory. For all that, in conjunction with you, I effected during my consulate for the safety of this city and empire, for the lives of Romans and the liberties of my country, is the subject of a poem which Archias has begun on that subject. So much as I heard of it, which at once gave me surprise and pleasure, induced me to exhort him to complete it; for virtue requires no other reward for all her toils and dangers but this of praise and glory. Take this away, my lords, and what can remain—in this narrow, this scanty career of life—that has charms to prompt us to toils and dangers?

Surely if the mind could not launch into the prospect of futurity, were the operations of the soul to be limited to the space that bounds those of the body, she would not weaken herself by constant fatigues nor vex herself with continued watchings and anxieties, nor would she think even life itself worthy of a struggle. But a certain principle lives in the breast of every good man, whose unceasing hints prompt and inspirit him to the pursuit of a fame which is not commensurate to our moral existence but extending to the latest posterity.

Can we, who have undergone dangers for our country, think so narrowly as to imagine that, though from our entering to our leaving the world we have never breathed without anxiety and trouble, yet that all consciousness shall be buried in the grave with ourselves? If the greatest men have been careful to leave their busts and statues, these pictures not of their minds but of their bodies, ought we not to wish rather to transmit to posterity the resemblance of our wisdom and virtues, designed and finished by the most accomplished artists? For my part, while I acted as I did, even then I imagined that I disseminated and transmitted my actions to the remotest corners and the latest ages of the world. Whether therefore my consciousness of this shall cease in the grave or, as some learned men have thought, it shall survive as a property of the soul, yet still at this instant I feel from the reflection a flattering hope and a delightful sensation.

Therefore, my lords, retain the man whom the affections of his friends, his own virtues, and his own genius recommend (and how great his accomplishments are you may learn from the greatest men in Rome, who court him for their friend); and his plea is of such a nature as to be proved by the construction of the law, by the faith of municipal cities, the evidence of Lucullus, and the registers of Metellus. As the case thus stands, we are emboldened, my lords, if the intercession not only of men but of gods can have any weight, to hope that the man who has ever added lustre to you, your generals, and your country, who has undertaken to transmit to posterity an eternal memorial of your praise while your and my domestic dangers are yet recent, and whose character has ever been esteemed and pronounced sacred, shall be sheltered under your protection, that he may seem to be rather relieved by your humanity than oppressed by your rigor.

The matters of fact, my lords, which I have with my accustomed brevity and simplicity related, require I hope no farther proof. The manner in which, contrary to the usage of the Forum and the bar, I have enlarged upon the genius of my client and the general merits of his profession, will (I hope) by you be taken in good part, as I am sure they will by him who presides on your bench.

Cicero, Defence of Archias (W. Guthrie)

PART V

Duty, Empire, Reward

He was dispos'd to mirth, but on the sudden
A Roman thought hath struck him.

Antony and Cleopatra 1.2 (86-87)

Had Tawney directed his attentions to Rome, he might have discovered an anima naturaliter calvinistica. *The Romans certainly had a "puritan ethic" of work and service. Even Shakespeare's "noblest Roman of them all" obliges Tawney by taking usurious rates of interest. But we touch something older than Calvin, as old as man, in the Roman instinct that life exacts performance; that manhood is given only to be earned; that man's great distinction from the other animals lies in his ability to place conscious demands upon himself; that the supreme praise at the end is "Well done." Call it puritanism, if you will; without it, we shall earn even harsher names.*

The stern ideal of service is rhapsodically hymned in Cicero's "Dream of Scipio," in which the cosmic Emperor rewards the good soldier and citizen. The stars lead up to a Stoic "city of God"—a city later glimpsed in Vergil's underworld and in St. Augustine's major work. Even the earlier Confessions *of St. Augustine opens with a recitation of his heavenly Monarch's many titles; it resembles the address to the emperor at the beginning of epics by Statius and Lucan. Civic duty, citizenship, the demands of the state do not end, for the Roman, even in heaven.*

242

ROME

I

First of cities, and the home
of every god, the golden Rome.

Ausonius, *Hierarchy of Cities* 1 (G. W.)

I I

There is a place men call Earth's evening land
where Latin people first inhabited.

This thing, Rome, is simply men
who know what their past means.

Luck is a thing
brave men command.

Roman courage
is an endless sky.

Happier the people than their king,
for they can cry. His tears
are interdicted.

Ennius, *Fragments* (G. W.)

I I I

It was at Rome, and—but, Meliboeus, how say "Rome"
unless one sees it? I was a silly hick
who thought the city is our village magnified.
I guessed at large from small, as one supposes
shape of dog from that of pup, of goat from kid.
But I found a striding city of some higher air,
higher over other towns than cypresses drawn up
from tangled brush.

Vergil, *Eclogues* 1.19-25 (G. W.)

IV

Rome alone first vanquishes, then fondles,
and gave to our one race of men one name—
mother, not empress, of men,
ruling over citizens, not slaves,
knitting distant lands in one allegiance.
Sheltered by her living peace
we walk the world, tread far-off Thule,
and where we are is home,
even in the darkest corners of the globe.
We can quench our thirst with Rhone or with Orontes;
be, as we were meant to be, one fellowship.
And Rome's authority will have no end.

Claudian, *On Stilicho's Consulship,*
150-60 (G. W.)

THE ROMAN TONGUE

I

Were lady deities allowed to weep
for men, the Latin Muses would
for Naevius. For Orcus has him
and, that large speech lost,
all men are Latinless.

Naevius, *Epitaph for Himself* (G. W.)

II

No tears for me, no pomp of funeral hearse
escort my spirit to eternal night;
for every lip that flutters out my verse
breathes what was me alive again, in flight.

Ennius, *Epitaph for Himself* (G. W.)

III

Tragedy takes Plautus
and comedy is crying.
No play today.
Festival, fun, laughter,
the untuned tunefulness of verse,
inordinately all together weep.

Plautus, *Epitaph for Himself* (G. W.)

FATHER OF ROME

I

A PROPHECY TO AENEAS

So long as you are here and walk the earth
Even Troy itself shall not be total ruin;
For you shall still advance through flame and steel,
So you shall carry her, however far,
Until you find a strange yet greener country
More friendly to your will than thoughts of home.
Even as I speak I see our destiny,
The city of our sons and sons of sons,
Greater than any city we have known,
Or has been known or shall be known to men.

Ovid, *Transformations* 15.440-45
(Horace Gregory)

II

AENEAS' PRAYER

Thus far, by Fate's decrees and thy commands,
Through ambient seas and through devouring sands
Our exiled crew has sought the Ausonian ground;
And now, at length, the flying coast is found.
Thus far the fate of Troy, from place to place,

245

With fury has pursued her wandering race.
Here cease, ye powers, and let your vengeance end,
Troy is no more, and can no more offend.
And thou, O sacred maid, inspired to see
The event of things in dark futurity,
Give me what heaven has promised to my fate
To conquer and command the Latian state;
To fix my wandering gods, and find a place
For the long exiles of the Trojan race.

Vergil, *The Song of Aeneas*
6.58-68 (John Dryden)

III

THE PRICE OF ROME

Aeneas, escaping conquered Troy, is summoned by gods to Italy. On his way, a shipwreck casts him and his men helpless on the coast of Carthage, where the Queen befriends him —more than he knows:

Poor Dido burns, and stung with restless love
Runs raving to and fro through every street;
Runs like a hind which, in some covert grove
Where she securely graz'd in fruitful Crete,
A woodman shooting at far distance hit.
Drunk in her veins, the feather'd iron lies,
Nor he who made the wound doth know of it.
She through Dictaean woods and pastures hies
(But carries in her side the arrow which she flies).

She takes Aeneas with her up and down
And shows him the vast wealth she brought from Tyre,
The goodly streets and bulwarks of her town;
No less, a thousand times, did she desire
To show unto him too her amorous fire,
And oft began—but shame repress'd her tongue.
At night unto their banquets they retire,
And Troy's sad fall again she must have sung,
And at his charming lips again she fondly hung.

When everyone was parted to his rest,
And the dim moon trod on the heels of day
And setting stars show'd it high time to rest,
She in the empty house languish'd away
And on the couch, which he had presséd, lay:
Absent she sees him whom her thoughts admire,
Him absent hears, or on her lap doth stay
Ascanius, the true picture of his sire,
As if she so could cheat her impotent desire.

All works are at a stand. The youth for war
Provide no forts nor training exercise.
Huge beams and arches which half-finish'd are
Hang doubtful, in the air, to fall or rise,
And towers do threat at once both earth and skies.
Her whenas Jove's dear wife perceiv'd so drown'd
In witchcrafts (and that fame with loudest cries
Could not awake her from the pleasing swound),
She thus accosted Venus, and her mind did sound:

Juno's
speech
"Great glory sure, and goodly spoils ye gain,
You and your boy! A doughty enterprise
Ye have achiev'd, and worthy to remain
In lasting marble, if two deities
By subtlety one woman do surprise!
Nor am I ignorant that, to defend
Your race from fear of future enemies,
Y' are jealous of my walls. But to what end
Should so near friends as we eternally contend?

Nay rather let us knit eternal love,
And bind the peace more strong with Hymen's cord.
Ye have the thing for which so much ye strove—
My Dido with love's fiery shaft is gor'd;
Then rule we this joint town with one accord,
And who shall aid it most be now our strife.
Now let our Queen obey a Trojan lord,
And Tyrians (to preserve a lover's life)
Call *thee* their patroness as dowry of his wife."

Venus—who saw her drift was to translate

247

The
response
of Venus
To Carthaginians those imperial dues
Which were reserv'd for Italy by fate—
Made this reply: "Who madly would refuse
So advantageous match, and rather choose
To war with you?—if but the fair event
According to your wise forecast ensues.
But fates (I fear me) nor Jove will consent
That Tyrians and Trojans in one town be pent;

And yet perchance *you*, lying in his breast,
With a wife's rhetoric may his counsels sway:—
Then break the ice; I'll second the request."
Juno
con-
cludes
"Leave that to me," said she, "and for a way
T' effect our wishes, mark my plot I pray:
Tomorrow, when the sun shall be descried
To guild the mountains with his earliest ray,
Aeneas and the love-sick Queen provide
To have a solemn hunting in the forest wide.

Now I—when here they beat the coppice, there
The horsemen flutter—on their heads will pour
A pitchy cloud, and heav'n with thunder tear.
Their followers, for shelter from the shower,
By several paths along the plain shall scour.
Mask'd in dark night, unto one cave they two
Shall come. There I will be; and add your power,
Tie such a knot as only fates undo!
I'LL SEAL HER HIS. (Good Hymen shall be present too)."

The
hunt
Venus seems, nodding, to consent (and smiles
To see Dame Juno's craft). Meanwhile the morn
Arose; and the choice youth, with subtle toils,
Sharp hunting spears, fleet steeds in Barbary born,
And sure-nos'd hounds tun'd to the bugle-horn,
Are gone before. The lords at door expect
Whilst the Queen stays within, herself t'adorn.
Her palfrey stands with gold and scarlet deck'd
And champs the foaming bit, as scorning to be check'd.

Dido
appears,
At length she comes with a huge troop, her gown
Of Tyrian dye border'd with flowers of gold.

248

A quiver by her comely side hung down,
Gold ribboning her brighter hair enroll'd,
Gold buttons did her purple vesture hold.

and Ascanius, and Aeneas The Trojans too, and blithe Iulus went
(Above the rest far goodliest to behold).
Aeneas' self his gladding presence lent
And with his darken'd train did Dido's train augment.

As when Apollo leaves his winter seats
Of Lycia and Zanthus' floods to see
His country Delos, and his feast repeats—
(About his altars hum confusedly
Cretes, Dryopés, and ruddy nymphs, but he
Mount Cynthus strides and, plaiting, doth enlace
His flowing hair with gold and his lov'd tree;
His shafts jog at his side)—with no less grace
Aeneas march'd, such rays display'd his lovely face.

When in the mountains now engag'd they were
And pathless woods, lo! goats, from summits cast,
Run tumbling through the bushes; herds of deer
Another way come hurrying down as fast
And raise a cloud as through the dust they haste.
Hot-spurr'd Iulus, on his mettl'd horse
Outcracking all, now these now those men pass'd;
And wish'd, 'mongst those—(faint beasts and without
    force)—
Some lion or tusk'd boar would cross him in his course.

The storm Meanwhile loud thunder heav'n's pavilion tears,
Making a passage for the th'ensuing rain.
The Trojan youth and Tyrian followers
And Venus' Dardan grandchild through the plain
Seek several shelters. Rivers like a main
Rush from the mountains round. One cave that lord
Of Troy, and she who did in Carthage reign,
Lighted upon. Earth gives the signal word,
And Juno queen of marriage doth their hands accord.

The guilty heav'ns, as blushing to have been
An instrument this meeting to fulfill,

249

With flashing lightning shone; the nymphs were seen
To weep with all their streams, and from each hill
Were heard to murmur the presagéd ill.
That day did usher death and Dido's shame;
For now she's arm'd—"Let men say what they will!"—
Nor seeks as erst to hide her amorous flame:
She calls it wedlock, gives her fault an honest name.

*Aeneas remains with Dido, helping her raise the walls of her
new city, forgetful of his mission until Jove tells Mercury to
remind him of it:*

Jove to
Mercury
 "Go, son, as swift as winds; in Carthage light!
 Tell Venus' son—whom loit'ring there thou'lt see
 Unworthy of that fate which he doth slight—
 That his fair mother painted him to me
 Another man (and therefore twice did free
 From Grecian swords): one who with steady rein
 Should manage proud and warlike Italy
 And prove himself of Teucer's haughty strain,
And the triumph'd-o'er world under his laws maintain.

 If not at all this him with glory fires,
 Nor care of his own greatness he doth show,
 Why should he grudge his son the Roman spires?
 What makes he here? What seeks he from a foe?
 Latium, and them who there expect to grow
 From him, let him regard. Let him away.
 This is th'effect, from me this let him know."
 At once Jove ended and the son of May
His greater sire's commands prepar'd himself t'obey.

 First, golden wings unto his feet he binds
 Which over lands and over seas that swell
 Bear him aloft as speedy as the winds;
 Then takes his rod (with this he calls from hell
 Pale ghosts, sends others in sad shades to dwell,
 Gives sleep and takes it from the drowsy brain,
Mer-
cury's
flight
 And seals up eyes with death); he doth repel,
 By pow'r of this, the heav'ns which part in twain,
And through the watery clouds he sails as through the main.

250

He, soaring, the lank sides and crown disclos'd
Of craggy Atlas whose neck props the sky,
Atlas whose piney head, to storms expos'd,
Is bound about with clouds continually;
Thick on his agéd back the snow doth lie,
And down his dabell'd chin pour plenteous springs;
His beard in icicles grows horridly.
Here lights the god, pois'd on his hov'ring wings;
Towards the sea, from hence, his body headlong flings.

Like to a bird which round the shores doth glide
(And fishy rocks), skimming along the bay,
So flies 'tween earth and heav'n—and doth divide
The windy and sandy coast of Lybia
Leaving his mother's sire—the son of May;
Who, landing where the sheepcots lately were,
Sees how Aeneas doth the works survey,
Here building towers, and altering turrets there;
He by his side a sword all starr'd with gems did wear.

Upon his shoulder, to the air display'd,
A robe of Tyrian purple seem'd to flame,
Which Dido with her own fair hands had made,
And edged the seams with gold. "Here you do frame,"
Said Hermes, "(hind'ring your own crown and fame)
High towers of Carthage, and uxorious raise
Fair walls whereof another bears the name!
Mark now what Jove himself, whom heav'n obeys
And earth, by his wing'd messenger unto you says:

Mercury to Ae-neas

What make you here, loit'ring in Lybia?
If glory of great actions fire not you,
Nor your own interést nor fame you weigh,
Seek your heir's good! Iulus' hopes pursue,
To whom the Latian crown and Rome is due!"
This having said, Cyllenius vanish'd quite
From mortal eyes, and back to heaven flew.
Aeneas at the vision shakes with fright,
His tongue cleaves to his jaws, his hair stands bolt-upright.

He is on fire to go, and fly that land

Of sweet enchantments, being scared away
By no less warning than the god's command.
But ah! what shall he do? How dare t'essay
With words the amorous Queen? What should he say
For introduction? His swift-beating thought
In doubtful balance thousand things did lay,
And this way cast them, and then that way wrought:
At last this seem'd the best, when all ways he had sought—

Aeneas to his men He call'd Sergestus, Mnesteus, and the stout
Colanthus, bids them fit immediately
The fleet, and draw their companies about
The port, their arms prepar'd, not telling why;
Meanwhile himself, when no least jealousy
To the good Queen should thought of breach betray
In so great love, an entrance would espy—
The season of soft speech, and dext'rous way.
With readiness and joy they do him all obey.

But Dido found their plot—what's hid from lovers?
Herself, who doubts ev'n safe things, first doth see't
(And also tattling Fame to her discovers)
That Trojans are departing with their fleet.
She's mad, stark mad, and runs through ev'ry street—
Like Bacchus' she-priests when the god is in
And they to do him furious homage meet,
(Cithaeron yowling with their midnight din).
Then thus to Aeneas speaks, nor stays till he begin:

Dido to Aeneas "Did'st thou hope, too, by stealth to leave my land,
And that such treason could be unbetray'd?
Nor should my love—nor thy late plighted hand,
Nor Dido who would die—thy flight have stay'd?
Must, too, this voyage be in winter made
Through storms? O cruel to thyself and me!
Did'st thou not hunt *strange* lands, and sceptres sway'd
By others,—if old Troy reviv'd should be,—
Should Troy itself be sought through a tempestuous sea?

Me flyest thou? By these tears and thy right hand
(Since this is all's now left to wretched me),

252

By marriage's new joys and sacred band,
If aught I did could meritorious be,
If ever aught of mine were sweet to thee,
Pity our house—which must with my decay
Give early period to its sovereignty,
And put (I do beseech thee) far away
This cruel mind, if cruel minds hear them that pray.

For thee the Lybian nations me defy,
The kings of Scythia hate me, and my Tyre;
For thee I lost my shame, and (that whereby
Alone I might unto the stars aspire)
The chaster fame which I did once acquire.
To whom, my guest (for 'husband' is out of date),
Dost thou commit me ready to expire?
Why stay I?—till Pygmalion waste my state,
Or on Iarbas' wheel a captive Queen to wait?

Yet if before thou fled'st out of this place
Some child at least I unto thee had borne,
If in my court, resembling but thy face,
Some young Aeneas play'd, I should not mourn
As one so quite deluded or forlorn."
Here ceased she; but he, whom Jove had tied
With strict commands, his eyes did no way turn
But stoutly did his grief suppress and hide
Under his secret heart. Then thus in short replied:

Aeneas answers "For me, O Queen, I never will deny
But that I owe you more than you can say;
Nor shall I stick to bear in memory
Sweet Dido's name whilst memory doth stay
In this frail seat, whilst breath these limbs doth sway—
But to the point: I never did intend
(Pray charge me not with that) to steal away.
And much less did I wedlock bands pretend,
Neither to such a treaty ever condescend.

Would fates permit me mine own way to take
And please myself in choosing of a land,
Ilium out of her ashes I would rake
And glean my earth's sweet relics; Troy should stand,

The vanquish'd troops replanted by my hand,
And Priam's towers again to heav'n aspire;
But now have I the oracle's command
To seek great Italy. The same require
The destinies. My country's this, this my desire.

If you of Tyre with Carthage-towers are took,
Why should our seeking Latian fields offend?
May not the Trojans to new mansions look?
As oft as Night moist shadows doth extend
Over the earth, and golden stars ascend,
My father's chiding ghost affrights my sleep
('My son, on whom that realm is to descend . . .')
And those dear eyes do freshly seem to weep,
Complaining that from him his destin'd crown I keep.

And now Jove's son (by both their heads I swear)
Was sent to me; myself the god did see
In open day and with these ears did hear.
Then vex not with complaints yourself and me—
I GO AGAINST MY WILL TO ITALY."
Whilst thus he spake, she look'd at him askew,
Rolling her lightening eyes continually,
And him from head to foot did silent view
When, being thr'oughly hot, these thundering words ensue:

Dido's
curse
"Nor goddess was thy mother, nor the source
Of thy high blood renownéd Dardanus;
But some Hyrcanian tigress was thy nurse—
Out of the stony loins of Caucasus
Descended, cruel and perfidious.
For with what hopes should I thy faults yet cover?—
Did my tears make thee sigh; or bend, but thus,
Thine eyes; or sadness for my grief discover;
Or (if thou could'st not love) to pity yet a lover?

Whom first accuse I since these loves began?—
Jove is unjust, Juno her charge gives o'er;
Whom may a woman trust? I took this man
Homeless, a desp'rate wreck upon my shore,
And fondly gave him half the crown I wore;

His ships rebuilt; to his men new lives I lent.
And now the fates, the oracles—(what more?
It makes me mad)—Jove's son, on purpose sent,
Brings him, forsooth, a menace through the firmament,

As if the gods their blissful rest did break
With thinking on thy voyages! But I
Nor stop you nor confute the words you speak:
Go, chase, on rolling billows, realms that fly;
With fickle winds, uncertain Italy.
Some courteous rock (if heav'n just curses hear)
Will be revenger of my injury:
When thou, perceiving the sad fate draw near,
Shalt 'Dido, Dido!' call—who surely will be there.

For when cold death shall part (with dreary swoon)
My soul and flesh, my ghost, where'er thou be,
Shall hunt thee with dim torch, and light thee down
To thy dark conscience: I'LL BE HELL TO THEE,
And this glad news will make hell heav'n to me . . ."

Vergil, *The Song of Aeneas* 4
(Sir Richard Fanshawe)

IV

AENEAS ENTERS HEAVEN

The man resolved and steady to his trust,
Inflexible to ill, and obstinately just,
May the rude rabble's insolence despise,
Their senseless clamours and tumultuous cries;
    The tyrant's fierceness he beguiles,
And the stern brow, and the harsh voice defies,
    And with superior greatness smiles.
Not the rough whirlwind, that deforms
Adria's black gulf, and vexes it with storms,
    The stubborn virtue of his soul can move;
    Nor the red arm of angry Jove,
    That flings the thunder from the sky,
And gives it rage to roar, and strength to fly.
Should the whole frame of nature round him break,

25. Male portrait. Munich, Glyptothek.

. . . the expression of Donatello's St. George—frightened heroes, facing the dragon and their own fear . . .

In ruin and confusion hurl'd,
He, unconcern'd, would hear the mighty crack,
    And stand secure amid a falling world.
Such were the godlike arts, that led
    Bright Pollux to the bless'd abodes;
Such did for great Alcides plead,
    And gain'd a place among the gods;
Where now Augustus, mix'd with heroes, lies,
And to his lips the nectar bowl applies:
His ruddy lips the purple tincture show,
And with immortal stains divinely glow.
By arts like these did young Lyaeus rise:
His tigers drew him to the skies;
    Wild from the desert, and unbroke,
In vain they foam'd, in vain they stared,
In vain their eyes with fury glared;
He tamed them to the lash, and bent them to the yoke.

Such were the paths that Rome's great founder trod,
When in a whirlwind snatch'd on high,
He shook off dull mortality,
    And lost the monarch in the god.
Bright Juno then her awful silence broke,
And thus th' assembled deities bespoke:
"Troy," says the goddess, "perjured Troy has felt
The dire effects of her proud tyrant's guilt;
The towering pile, and soft abodes,
Wall'd by the hand of servile gods,
Now spreads its ruins all around,
And lies inglorious on the ground.
An umpire partial and unjust,
And a lewd woman's impious lust
Lay heavy on her head, and sink her to the dust.
Since false Laomedon's tyrannic sway
That durst defraud th' immortals of their pay,
Her guardian gods renounced their patronage,
    Nor would the fierce invading foe repel;
To my resentment, and Minerva's rage,
    The guilty king and the whole people fell.

257

And now the long protracted wars are o'er,
The soft adulterer shines no more;
No more does Hector's force the Trojans shield,
That drove whole armies back, and singly clear'd
     the field.
My vengeance sated, I at length resign
To Mars his offspring of the Trojan line:
Advanced to godhead, let him rise,
And take his station in the skies:
There entertain his ravish'd sight
With scenes of glory, fields of light:
Quaff with the gods immortal wine,
And see adoring nations crowd his shrine.
    The thin remains of Troy's afflicted host
In distant realms may seats unenvied find,
    And flourish on a foreign coast;
But far be Rome from Troy disjoin'd,
Removed by seas from the disastrous shore,
May endless billows rise between, and storms
       unnumber'd roar.
Still let the cursed, detested place
Where Priam lies, and Priam's faithless race,
Be cover'd o'er with weeds, and hid in grass.
There let the wanton flocks unguarded stray;
    Or, while the lonely shepherd sings,
Amid the mighty ruins play,
    And frisk upon the tombs of kings.
May tigers there, and all the savage kind
Sad solitary haunts and deserts find;
In gloomy vaults and nooks of palaces,
May th' unmolested lioness
Her brinded whelps securely lay,
Or, couch'd, in dreadful slumbers waste the day.
While Troy in heaps of ruins lies,
Rome and the Roman capitol shall rise;
Th' illustrious exiles unconfined
Shall triumph far and near, and rule mankind.
In vain the sea's intruding tide
Europe from Afric shall divide,
And part the sever'd world in two:

258

Through Afric's sands their triumphs they shall spread,
And the long train of victories pursue
　　To Nile's yet undiscover'd head.
Riches the hardy soldiers shall despise,
And look on gold with undesiring eyes,
Nor the disbowell'd earth explore
In search of the forbidden ore;
Those glittering ills, conceal'd within the mine
Shall lie untouch'd, and innocently shine.
To the last bounds that nature sets
The piercing colds and sultry heats,
The godlike race shall spread their arms,
Now fill the polar circle with alarms,
Till storms and tempests their pursuits confine;
Now sweat for conquest underneath the line.
This only law the victor shall restrain;
On these conditions shall he reign:
If none his guilty hand employ
To build again a second Troy,
If none the rash design pursue,
Nor tempt the vengeance of the gods anew.
A curse there cleaves to the devoted place,
That shall the new foundations rase;
Greece shall in mutual leagues conspire
To storm the rising town with fire,
And at their armies' head myself will show
What Juno, urged to all her rage, can do.
Thrice should Apollo's self the city raise,
And line it round with walls of brass;
Thrice should my favourite Greeks his works confound,
And hew the shining fabric to the ground:
Thrice should her captive dames to Greece return
And their dead sons and slaughter'd husbands mourn."
But hold, my muse, forbear thy towering flight,
Nor bring the secrets of the gods to light:
In vain would thy presumptuous verse
Th' immortal rhetoric rehearse;
The mighty strains, in lyric numbers bound,
Forget their majesty, and lose the sound.

Horace, *Songs* 3.3 (Joseph Addison)

259

REGULUS

In Africa, while Marcus Atilius Regulus was consul for the second time, the enemy captured him by a trick; the Carthaginian commander was Xanthippus the Spartan, serving under Hannibal's father Hamilcar. The enemy authorities then dispatched Regulus to Rome. His instructions were to meet the Senate, and request the return of certain aristocratic Carthaginian prisoners. In case, however, he should fail in his mission, he placed himself under oath to return to Carthage.

When Regulus arrived in Rome, the superficially advantageous course was obvious enough to him. But he rejected the advantage as unreal: as subsequent developments were to show. His interests *seemed* to require him to stay in his own country, at home with his wife and children —retaining his high position as consul, and treating the defeat he had suffered as a misfortune which anyone might experience in time of war. And what do you think refuted the supposition that these were advantages? I will tell you: his heroism and his fortitude. And no more impressive authorities could be imagined. For the whole point of these virtues is that they reject fear, rise above all the hazards of this life, and regard nothing that can happen to a human being as unendurable.

So what did Regulus do? He entered the Senate, and reported his instructions. But at first he refused to express his own opinion in the matter, because, as long as he was still bound by an oath sworn to the enemy, he refused to consider himself a member of the Senate. What happened next will cause him to be criticized for foolishness in acting against his own advantage. For he then proceeded to advise the Senate that the Carthaginian prisoners should not be sent back, since they were young men and capable officers whereas he himself was old and worn out. His advice prevailed, and the prisoners were not released.

So Regulus returned to Carthage. Even his love for his own homeland and his dear ones was not strong enough to hold him back. Yet he knew full well the refinements of torture which a ruthless foe had in store for him. Nevertheless he believed that he had to obey his oath. When he rejoined his captors, they gave him no sleep until death came to him. But even so he was better off than if he had stayed at home— an aged ex-consul who had fallen into the enemy's hands and then perjured himself.

Cicero, *On Duties* 3.26-27
(Michael Grant)

AUGUSTUS, HEIR OF REGULUS

If God's call is in the thunder clap,
then thunderous victories (out in the North,
off in the East) will teach
Britons and Persians who is god
on earth.

Have the men that Crassus died for
held barbarian girls in bed—
(O Rome of the Senate!
O ridiculed ancient ways!)—
made a family of our foes?

Can a Marsian be a Mede, Apulia's men
forget Rome's shrines,
the town that is a title,
the toga and the Virgins' Fire,
while god is god and Rome is Rome?

Regulus, prophetic in his warning,
treated all "terms" as precedents,
his own life as a pattern,
lest cowardice call back
to weak traditions,

he let young captives die,
   said: "I have seen our flags upon their towers!
   Swords unadorned with blood
   adorning Punic shrines!

I saw the ruling hands of citizens in chains,
and—through doors freely opening (not beat down)—
the enemy gone out to sow in peace
where our wars plowed.

'The bought-back soldier can fight best'?
But who will buy back honor;
can wool, its whiteness dyed,
be counterdyed to white?

Courage is true mint of men,
cannot be bought with any lesser coin.

Does a doe, delivered from the snare,
grow braver for its netted moments?

Shall men negotiate and slaughter
by turns? Can hands that wore the chain,
that bargained with bad merchants
for bad lives, grind Carthage down?

'Live on any terms' our terms?
A war negotiated like a bargain?
Then rise forever, Carthage! Great Rome is down,
it cannot humble you."

As one condemned he took the kisses
of his wife and weeping children;
with bent head steadied himself
to strengthen them

in passing what no other man
had moved in his own case—
that they send him, from the midst
of friends, to exile and to glory.

He knew what Carthaginians
could do to captured Romans,
yet he put off his dear ones,
easily brushed them all aside

as if he had (for friends) adjudicated, and,
his city legal-work all done,
were turning to congenial fields he farmed
where Spartans once had dwelt in Italy.

Horace, *Songs* 3.5 (G. W.)

A ROMAN OF THE OLD WAYS

He called his friend, with whom he loved at ease
to share his board, his talk, and his affairs,
companionably, when tired with lengthy hours
he left the imperious councils of the state

in holy senate or broad market-place.
Boldly, small things and great, or little jokes,
he told; his bitterness, his noble hopes,
he showed without reserve, at whim, in trust.
They often laughed, alone or with the world.
No thought could sway his mind to evil ends,
malice or guile; for he was cultured, staunch,
gentle, contented, fortunate, speaking well
and seldom: rich with buried treasure dug
from ancient years, the lore of past and present,
manifold ways of time, of gods and men:
which taught him wisdom in his speech and silence.

Ennius, *Annals* 234-50 (Jack Lindsay)

THE NOBLEST ROMAN

The passers-by whom Cato met when drunk, blushed when they discovered who it was, and (says Caesar) "You would have thought they had been found out by Cato, not Cato by them." What better tribute to Cato's prestige than to show him still awe-inspiring when drunk. . . .

Pliny (the Younger), *Letters* 3.12 (Betty Radice)

WAR

The trumpet stuttered its intimidating TA-ti-ti-ti-TA.

In a sluice of lances he is drenched,
his shield rained through,
its metal center pinging,
his helmet ringing like a bell.
But no one, in the press
of everyone on him,
can shred that man with iron.
The spears that fill the air he shivers
or shrugs off. He is all sweat
and no breath. With their worrying flight
of lances the Histrians

263

keep at him.

In the wrenched head gasping for a body
in the eyes
some half-light glitters still
toward the light.

Ennius, *Fragments* (G. W.)

SOLDIERS' SONG

A thousand, a thousand, a thousand,
A thousand, a thousand, a thousand,
We, with one warrior, have slain!
A thousand, a thousand, a thousand, a thousand,
Sing a thousand, over again!
  Soho!—let us sing
  Long life to our king
Who knocked over a thousand so fine.
  Soho!—let us roar,
  He has given us more
  Red gallons of gore
Than all Syria can furnish of wine!

Recorded in Flavius Vopiscus,
Life of Aurelian (Edgar Allan Poe)

CHILDE ROLAND

Thus strove the chief, on ev'ry side distress'd,
Thus still his courage, with his toils, increas'd:
With his broad shield oppos'd, he forc'd his way
Thro' thickest woods, and rous'd the beasts of prey.
Till he beheld, where, from Larissa's height,
The shelving walls reflect a glancing light . . .

Statius, *The Song of Thebes* 1.376-82
(Alexander Pope)

YOUTH TRAINED TO WAR

Let the boy, timber-tough from vigorous soldiering,
learn to endure lack amicably,
and let him, horseman feared for his javelin,
plague the ferocious men of Parthos;

let him live his life lower than heaven
in the midst of restless things. Seeing him
from enemy ramparts, may the warring tyrant's wife
and the young ripe woman breathe, "Ah,

let not our kingly lover, clumsy
in the swirl of combat, stroke the lion
rough-to-the-touch, whom fury for blood
thrusts through the thick of the slaughter!"

Sweet it is, and seemly, to die for country.
Death overtakes the runaway as well,
and does not spare the coward backs
and knees of youths who are not warlike.

Manliness, not knowing the taint of defeat,
flashes forth with unsullied glory,
neither lifts nor lowers the axes
at a whisper from the scatterbrained mob.

Manliness, that throws open heaven to those
undeserving of death, plots its course
by a route denied to most, and on pinion
soaring scorns the common crowd, the damp earth.

There is, for faithful silence, too,
sure reward. I will forbid the man who spreads abroad
occult Ceres' sacred rites
to exist beneath a roof or to unmoor a frail craft

with me. Often slighted Jupiter
involves the unpolluted with the impure;
rarely does Poena not catch the wicked man,
though he has the head start, and her step is hesitant.

Horace, Songs 3.2 (John Updike)

SCHOLAR VERSUS SOLDIER

Will any man alive make a doubt that military accomplishments give much more dignity to a candidate for the consulate than any excellence in the civil law? You get up long before daylight to give counsel to your clients; he, that he may arrive in good time with his army to the end of his march. You are awaked by the crowing of a cock, he by the sounding of trumpets. You draw up a process, he marshals an army. You make out securities for clients, he for towns and camps. He knows how to guard against the attacks of an enemy, you against the inconvenience of a drain or a water spout. He is employed in enlarging territory, you in regulating it. And if I may speak my sentiments, it is but just that military glory should have the preference of any other. To this the renown of the Roman people and the eternal glory of the city is owing; it was this that forced the world to submit to our empire; it is military glory that guards, protects, and covers all these our domestic transactions, all these noble studies of ours, and all this pre-eminence and application in the Forum —for no sooner does the least whisper of any public disorder arise than all those arts of ours are silenced.

Cicero, *Defense of Murena* 22 (W. Guthrie)

MILITARY DISCIPLINE

On his arrival in Africa, he took over from Spurius Albinus, now acting consul, an indolent and unwarlike army, in no fit state to face danger or toil, readier to brag than to fight, and so undisciplined and ill behaved that it plundered its allies and allowed itself to be plundered by the enemy. Its demoralized condition caused its new commander so much anxiety that he could entertain little hope of being helped much by its numerical strength. Although the time available for the summer campaign had been shortened by the postponement of the elections and he had no doubt that his fellow citizens were awaiting its result with eager impatience, he decided not to take the field until he had inured the men to hard labour by putting them through a course of old-fashioned training. For Albinus had been so dismayed by the disaster which had befallen his brother Aulus and his army that he had determined not to move out of the Province; and for most of that part of the campaigning season during which he was in command he had kept the soldiers in permanent camps, moving them only when the bad smell or lack of fodder compelled him. The camps were not fortified, nor were watches posted in accordance with military routine; and men absented themselves from duty whenever they pleased. Camp-followers and soldiers roamed about together at all hours of day and night, plundering the fields, taking forcible possession of farmhouses, and trying which of them could carry off most cattle and slaves to barter with traders for imported wine and other commodities. They even sold their corn rations and bought what bread they needed each day. In short, every imaginable vice that one would expect to find among a set of dissipated idlers was to be found in that army—and some new ones as well.

In handling this difficult situation Metellus seems to have shown his greatness and prudence no less than in the actual conduct of the war, steering a judicious course between popularity-seeking and undue severity. He started, it is said, by putting a stop to practices which encouraged idleness. No one, he decreed, was to sell bread or any other cooked food in camp; the camp-followers were sent about their business; both ordinary privates and front-line troops were forbidden to keep servants or beasts of burden either in camp or on the march; and other irregular practices were strictly controlled. Furthermore, he moved camp daily, making a series of cross-country marches, and each new camp was fortified with a rampart and trench, as though the enemy were close at hand. At night he placed sentry-posts at short intervals and went the rounds himself, accompanied by his officers. On the march, too, he moved to and fro between the head and the tail of the column, often keeping for some time in the middle, to see that no one left the ranks, that the men kept close together round their standards, and that each soldier carried his food and arms. By these methods he was able to prevent breaches of discipline, and without having to inflict many punishments he soon restored the army's morale.

Sallust, *The War with Jugurtha* 44-45 (S. A. Handford)

VETERANS' REUNION

Pompeius, chief of all my friends, with whom
I often ventured to the edge of doom
    When Brutus led our line,
    With whom, aided by wine

And garlands and Arabian spikenard,
I killed those afternoons that died so hard—
  Who has new-made you, then,
  A Roman citizen

And given you back your native gods and weather?
We two once beat a swift retreat together
  Upon Philippi's field,
  When I dumped my poor shield,

And courage cracked, and the strong men who frowned
Fiercest were felled, chins to the miry ground.
  But I, half-dead with fear,
  Was wafted, airborne, clear

Of the enemy lines, wrapped in a misty blur
By Mercury, not sucked back, as you were,
  From safety and the shore
  By the wild tide of war.

Pay Jove his feast, then. In my laurel's shade
Stretch out the bones that long campaigns have made
  Weary. Your wine's been waiting
  For years: no hesitating!

Fill up the polished goblets to the top
With memory-drowning Massic! Slave, unstop
  The deep-mouthed shells that store
  Sweet-smelling oil and pour!

Who'll run to fit us out with wreaths and find
Myrtle and parsley, damp and easily twined?
  Who'll win the right to be
  Lord of the revelry

By dicing highest? I propose to go
As mad as a Thracian. It's a joy to throw
  Sanity overboard
  When a dear friend's restored.

Horace, *Songs* 2.7
(James Michie)

CIVIL WAR

I
CAUSES

The causes first I purpose to unfold
Of these garboils, whence springs a long discourse;
And what made madding people shake off peace.
The Fates are envious, high seats quickly perish,
Under great burdens falls are ever grievous;
Rome was so great it could not bear itself.
So when this world's compounded union breaks,
Time ends, and to old Chaos all things turn,
Confused stars shall meet, celestial fire
Fleet on the floods, the earth shoulder the sea,
Affording it no shore, and Phoebe's wain
Chase Phoebus, and enrag'd affect his place,
And strive to shine by day and full of strife
Dissolve the engines of the broken world.
All great things crush themselves; such end the gods
Allot the height of honour; men so strong
By land and sea, no foreign force could ruin.
O Rome, thyself art cause of all these evils,
Thyself thus shiver'd out to three men's shares!
Dire league of partners in a kingdom last not.
O faintly-join'd friends, with ambition blind,
Why join you force to share the world betwixt you?
While th' earth the sea, and air the earth sustains,
While Titan strives against the world's swift course,
Or Cynthia, night's queen, waits upon the day,
Shall never faith be found in fellow kings:
Dominion cannot suffer partnership.
This needs no foreign proof nor farfetch'd story:
Rome's infant walls were steep'd in brother's blood;
Nor then was land or sea, to breed such hate;
A town with one poor church set them at odds.

Caesar's and Pompey's jarring love soon ended,

'Twas peace against their wills; betwixt them both
Stepp'd Crassus in. Even as the slender isthmos,
Betwixt the Aegean, and the Ionian sea,
Keeps each from other, but being worn away,
They both burst out, and each encounter other;
So whenas Crassus' wretched death, who stay'd them,
Had fill'd Assyrian Carra's walls with blood,
His loss made way for Roman outrages.
Parthians, y'afflict us more than ye suppose;
Being conquer'd, we are plagu'd with civil war.
Swords share our empire: Fortune, that made Rome
Govern the earth, the sea, the world itself,
Would not admit two lords; for Julia,
Snatch'd hence by cruel Fates, with ominous howls
Bare down to hell her son, the pledge of peace,
And all bands of that death-presaging alliànce.
Julia, had heaven given thee longer life,
Thou hadst restrain'd thy headstrong husband's rage,
Yea, and thy father too, and, swords thrown down,
Made all shake hands, as once the Sabines did:
Thy death broke amity, and train'd to war
These captains emulous of each other's glory.
Thou fear'd'st, great Pompey, that late deeds would dim
Old triumphs, and that Caesar's conquering France
Would dash the wreath thou wor'st for pirates' wreck:
Thee war's use stirr'd, and thoughts that always scorn'd
A second place. Pompey could bide no equal,
Nor Caesar no superior: which of both
Had justest cause, unlawful 'tis to judge:
Each side had great partakers; Caesar's cause
The gods abetted, Cato lik'd the other.
Both differ'd much. Pompey was struck in years,
And by long rest forgot to manage arms,
And, being popular, sought by liberal gifts
To gain the light unstable commons' love,
And joy'd to hear his theatre's applause:
He lived secure, boasting his former deeds,
And thought his name sufficient to uphold him:
Like to a tall oak in a fruitful field,

Bearing old spoils and conquerors' monuments,
Who, though his root be weak, and his own weight
Keep him within the ground, his arms all bare,
His body, not his boughs, send forth a shade;
Though every blast it nod, and seem to fall,
When all the woods about stand bolt upright,
Yet he alone is held in reverence.
Caesar's renown for war was loss; he restless,
Shaming to strive but where he did subdue;
When ire or hope provok'd, heady and bold;
At all times charging home, and making havoc;
Urging his fortune, trusting in the gods,
Destroying what withstood his proud desires,
And glad when blood and ruin made him way:
So thunder, which the wind tears from the clouds,
With crack of riven air and hideous sound
Filling the world, leaps out and throws forth fire,
Affrights poor fearful men, and blasts their eyes
With overthwarting flames, and raging shoots
Alongst the air, and, not resisting it,
Falls, and returns, and shivers where it lights.

II
CROSSING RUBICON

Now Caesar overpass'd the snowy Alps;
His mind was troubled, and he aim'd at war:
And coming to the ford of Rubicon,
At night in dreadful vision fearful Rome
Mourning appear'd, whose hoary hairs were torn,
And on her turret-bearing head dispers'd,
And arms all naked; who, with broken sighs,
And staring, thus bespoke: "What mean'st thou, Caesar?
Whither goes my standard? Romans if ye be,
And bear true hearts, stay here!" This spectacle
Struck Caesar's heart with fear; his hair stood up,
And faintness numb'd his steps there on the brink.
He thus cried out: "Thou thunderer that guard'st
Rome's mighty walls, built on Tarpeian rock!
Ye gods of Phrygia and Iülus' line,

Quirinus' rites, and Latian Jove advanc'd
On Alba hill! O vestal flames! O Rome,
My thought's sole goddess, aid mine enterprise!
I hate thee not, to thee my conquests stoop:
Caesar is thine, so please it thee, thy soldier.
He, he afflicts Rome that made me Rome's foe."
This said, he, laying aside all lets of war,
Approach'd the swelling stream with drum and ensign:
Like to a lion of scorch'd desert Afric,
Who, seeing hunters, pauseth till fell wrath
And kingly rage increase, then, having whisk'd
His tail athwart his back, and crest heav'd up,
With jaws wide-open ghastly roaring out,
Albeit the Moor's light javelin or his spear
Sticks in his side, yet runs upon the hunter.
    In summer-time the purple Rubicon,
Which issues from a small spring, is but shallow,
And creeps along the vales, dividing just
The bounds of Italy from Cisalpine France.
But now the winter's wrath, and watery moon
Being three days old, enforc'd the flood to swell,
And frozen Alps thaw'd with resolving winds.
The thunder-hoof'd horse, in a crookèd line,
To scape the violence of the stream, first waded;
Which being broke, the foot had easy passage.
As soon as Caesar got unto the bank
And bounds of Italy, "Here, here," saith he,
"An end of peace; here end polluted laws!
Hence leagues and covenants! Fortune, thee I follow!
War and the Destinies shall try my cause."
This said, the restless general through the dark,
Swifter than bullets thrown from Spanish slings,
Or darts which Parthians backward shoot, march'd on;
And then, when Lucifer did shine alone,
And some dim stars, he Ariminum enter'd.
Day rose, and view'd these tumults of the war:
Whether the gods or blustering south were cause
I know not, but the cloudy air did frown.
The soldiers having won the market-place,

272

There spread the colours with confusèd noise
Of trumpets' clang, shrill cornets, whistling fifes.
The people started; young men left their beds,
And snatch'd arms near their household-gods hung up,
Such as peace yields; worm-eaten leathern targets,
Through which the wood peer'd, headless darts, old swords
With ugly teeth of black rust foully scarr'd.
But seeing white eagles, and Rome's flags well known,
And lofty Caesar in the thickest throng,
They shook for fear, and cold benumb'd their limbs,
And muttering much, thus to themselves complain'd:
"O walls unfortunate, too near to France!
Predestinate to ruin! all lands else
Have stable peace: here war's rage first begins;
We bide the first brunt. Safer might we dwell
Under the frosty bear, or parching east,
Waggons or tents, than in this frontier town.
We first sustain'd the uproars of the Gauls
And furious Cimbrians, and of Carthage Moors:
Where men are ready lingering ever hurts.
In ten years wonn'st thou France: Rome may be won
With far less toil, and yet the honour's more;
Few battles fought with prosperous success
May bring her down, and with her all the world.
Nor shalt thou triumph when thou com'st to Rome,
Nor Capitol be adorn'd with sacred bays;
Envy denies all; with thy blood must thou
Aby thy conquest past: the son decrees
To expel the father: share the world thou canst not;
Enjoy it all thou mayst." Thus Curio spake;
And therewith Caesar, prone enough to war,
Was so incens'd as are Elean steeds—
With clamours who, though lock'd and chain'd in stalls,
Souse down the walls, and make a passage forth.
Straight summon'd he his several companies
Unto the standard: his grave look appeas'd
The wrestling tumult, and right hand made silence;
And thus he spake: "You that with me have borne
A thousand brunts, and tried me full ten years,

273

See how they quit our bloodshed in the north,
Our friends' death, and our wounds, our wintering
Under the Alps! Rome rageth now in arms
As if the Carthage Hannibal were near;
Cornets of horse are muster'd for the field;
Woods turn'd to ships; both land and sea against us.
Had foreign wars ill-thriv'd, or wrathful France
Pursu'd us hither, how were we bested,
When, coming conqueror, Rome afflicts me thus?
Let come their leader whom long peace hath quail'd,
Raw soldiers lately press'd, and troops of gowns,
Babbling Marcellus, Cato whom fools reverence!
Must Pompey's followers, with strangers' aid
(Whom from his youth he brib'd) needs make him king?
And shall he triumph long before his time,
And, having once got head, still shall he reign?
What should I talk of men's corn reap'd by force,
And by him kept of purpose for a dearth?
Who sees not war sit by the quivering judge,
And sentence given in rings of naked swords,
And laws assail'd, and arm'd men in the senate?
'Twas his troop hemm'd in Milo being accus'd;
And now, lest age might wane his state, he casts
For civil war, wherein through use he's known
To exceed his master, that arch-traitor Sulla.
As brood of barbarous tigers, having lapp'd
The blood of many a herd, whilst with their dams
They kennell'd in Hyrcania, evermore
Will rage and prey; so, Pompey, thou, having lick'd
Warm gore from Sulla's sword, art yet athirst:
Jaws fleshed with blood continue murderous.
Speak, when shall this thy long-usurped power end?
What end of mischief? Sulla teaching thee,
At last learn, wretch, to leave thy monarchy!
What, now Sicilian pirates are suppress'd,
And jaded king of Pontus poison'd slain,
Must Pompey as his last foe plume on me,
Because at his command I wound not up
My conquering eagles? say I merit naught,

274

Yet, for long service done, reward these men,
And so they triumph, be't with whom ye will.
Whither now shall these old bloodless souls repair?
What seats for their deserts? what store of ground
For servitors to till? what colonies
To rest their bones? say, Pompey, are these worse
Than pirates of Sicilia? they had houses.
Spread, spread these flags that ten years' space have conquer'd!
Let's use our tried force: they that now thwart right,
In wars will yield to wrong: the gods are with us;
Neither spoil nor kingdom seek we by these arms,
But Rome, at thraldom's feet, to rid from tyrants."
This spoke, none answer'd, but a murmuring buzz
Th' unstable people made: their household-gods
And love to Rome (though slaughter steel'd their hearts,
And minds were prone) restrain'd them; but war's love
And Caesar's awe dash'd all. Then Laelius,
The chief centurion, crown'd with oaken leaves
For saving of a Roman citizen,
Stepp'd forth, and cried: "Chief leader of Rome's force,
So be I may be bold to speak a truth,
We grieve at this thy patience and delay.
What, doubt'st thou us? even now when youthful blood
Pricks forth our lively bodies, and strong arms
Can mainly throw the dart, wilt thou endure
These purple grooms, that senate's tyranny?
Is conquest got by civil war so heinous?
Well, lead us, then, to Syrtes' desert shore,
Or Scythia, or hot Libya's thirsty sands.
This band, that all behind us might be quail'd,
Hath with thee pass'd the swelling ocean,
And swept the foaming breast of Arctic Rhine.
Love over-rules my will; I must obey thee,
Caesar: he whom I hear thy trumpets charge,
I hold no Roman; by these ten blest ensigns
And all thy several triumphs, shouldst thou bid me
Entomb my sword within my brother's bowels,
Or father's throat, or women's groaning womb,
This hand, albeit unwilling, should perform it;

Or rob the gods, or sacred temples fire,
These troops should soon pull down the church of Jove;
If to encamp on Tuscan Tiber's streams,
I'll boldly quarter out the fields of Rome;
What walls thou wilt be levell'd with the ground,
These hands shall thrust the ram, and make them fly,
Albeit the city thou wouldst have so raz'd
Be Rome itself." Here every band applauded,
And, with their hands held up, all jointly cried
They'll follow where he please. The shouts rent heaven,
As when against pine-bearing Ossa's rocks
Beats Thracian Boreas, or when trees bow down
And rustling swing up as the winds fetch breath.
When Caesar saw his army prone to war,
And Fates so bent, lest sloth and long delay
Might cross him, he withdrew his troops from France,
And in all quarters musters men for Rome.

III
CAESAR TURNS THE WORLD ON ROME

They by Lemannus' nook forsook their tents;
They whom the Lingones foil'd with painted spears,
Under the rocks by crookèd Vogesus;
And many came from shallow Isara,
Who, running long, falls in a greater flood,
And, ere he sees the sea, loseth his name;
The yellow Ruthens left their garrisons;
Mild Atax, glad it bears not Roman boats,
And frontier Varus that the camp is far,
Sent aid; so did Alcides' port, whose seas
Eat hollow rocks, and where the north-west wind
Nor zephyr rules not, but the north alone
Turmoils the coast, and enterance forbids;
And others came from that uncertain shore
Which is nor sea nor land, but ofttimes both,
And changeth as the ocean ebbs and flows—
Whether the sea roll'd always from that point
Whence the wind blows, still forcèd to and fro,

276

Or that the wandering main follow the moon,
Or flaming Titan, feeding on the deep,
Pulls them aloft, and makes the surge kiss heaven,
Philosophers, look you; for unto me,
Thou cause, whate'er thou be, whom God assigns
This great effect, art hid. They came that dwell
By Nemes' fields and banks of Satirus,
Where Tarbell's winding shores embrace the sea;
The Santons that rejoice in Caesar's love;
Those of Bituriges, and light Axon pikes;
And they of Rhine and Leuca, cunning darters,
And Sequana that well could manage steeds;
The Belgians apt to govern British cars;
Th' Arverni, too, which boldly feign themselves
The Roman's brethren, sprung of Ilian race;
The stubborn Nervians stain'd with Cotta's blood;
And Vangions who, like those of Sarmata,
Wear open slops; and fierce Batavians,
Whom trumpet's clang incites; and those that dwell
By Cinga's stream, and where swift Rhodanus
Drives Araris to sea; they near the hills,
Under whose hoary rocks Gebenna hangs;
And, Trevier, thou being glad that wars are past thee;
And you, late-shorn Ligurians, who were wont
In large-spread hair to exceed the rest of France;
And where to Hesus and fell Mercury
They offer human flesh, and where Jove seems
Bloody like Dian, whom the Scythians serve.
And you, French Bardi, whose immortal pens
Renown the valiant souls slain in your wars,
Sit safe at home and chant sweet poesy.
And, Druides, you now in peace renew
Your barbarous customs and sinister rites:
In unfell'd woods and sacred groves you dwell;
And only gods and heavenly powers you know,
Or only know you nothing; for you hold
That souls pass not to silent Erebus
Or Pluto's bloodless kingdom, but elsewhere
Resume a body; so (if truth you sing)

Death brings long life. Doubtless these northern men,
Whom death, the greatest of all fears, affright not,
Are blest by such sweet error; this makes them
Run on the sword's point, and desire to die,
And shame to spare life which being lost is won.
You likewise that repuls'd the Caÿc foe,
March towards Rome; and you, fierce men of Rhine,
Leaving your country open to the spoil.

IV
FEAR IN ROME

Vain fame increased true fear, and did invade
The people's minds, and laid before their eyes
Slaughter to come, and, swiftly bringing news
Of present war, made many lies and tales:
One swears his troops of daring horsemen fought
Upon Mevania's plain, where bulls are graz'd;
Other that Caesar's barbarous bands were spread
Along Nar flood that into Tiber falls,
And that his own ten ensigns and the rest
March'd not entirely, and yet hide the ground;
And that he's much chang'd, looking wild and big,
And far more barbarous than the French, his vassals;
And that he lags behind with them, of purpose,
Borne 'twixt the Alps and Rhine, which he hath brought
From out their northern parts, and that Rome,
He looking on, by these men should be sack'd.
Thus in his fright did each man strengthen fame,
And, without ground, fear'd what themselves had feign'd.
Nor were the commons only struck to heart
With this vain terror; but the court, the senate,
The fathers' selves leap'd from their seats, and, flying,
Left hateful war decreed to both the consuls.
Then, with their fear and danger all-distract,
Their sway of flight carries the heady rout,
That in chain'd troops break forth at every port:
You would have thought their houses had been fir'd,
Or, dropping-ripe, ready to fall with rain.

278

So rush'd the inconsiderate multitude
Thorough the city, hurriedly headlong on,
As if the only hope that did remain
To their afflictions were t' abandon Rome.
Look how, when stormy Auster from the breach
Of Libyan Syrtes rolls a monstrous wave,
Which makes the main-sail fall with hideous sound,
The pilot from the helm leaps in the sea,
And mariners, albeit the keel be sound,
Shipwreck themselves; even so, the city left,
All rise in arms; nor could the bed-rid parents
Keep back their sons, or women's tears their husbands:
They stayed not either to pray or sacrifice;
Their household-gods restrain them not; none lingered,
As loath to leave Rome whom they held so dear:
Th' irrevocable people fly in troops.
O gods, that easy grant men great estates,
But hardly grace to keep them! Rome, that flows
With citizens and captives, and would hold
The world, were it together, is by cowards
Left as a prey, now Caesar doth approach.
When Romans are besieged by foreign foes,
With slender trench they escape night-stratagems,
And sudden rampire rais'd of turf snatched up,
Would make them sleep securely in their tents.
Thou, Rome, at name of war runn'st from thyself,
And wilt not trust thy city-walls one night:
Well might these fear, when Pompey feared and fled.

V

PORTENTS

Now evermore, lest some one hope might ease
The commons' jangling minds, apparent signs arose,
Strange sights appeared; the angry threatening gods
Filled both the earth and seas with prodigies.
Great store of strange and unknown stars were seen
Wandering about the north, and rings of fire
Fly in the air, and dreadful bearded stars,

And comets that presage the fall of kingdoms;
The flattering sky glittered in often flames,
And sundry fiery meteors blazed in heaven,
Now spear-like long, now like a spreading torch;
Lightning in silence stole forth without clouds,
And, from the northern climate snatching fire,
Blasted the Capitol; the lesser stars,
Which wont to run their course through empty night,
At noon-day mustered; Phoebe, having filled
Her meeting horns to match her brother's light,
Struck with th' earth's sudden shadow, waxèd pale;
Titan himself, throned in the midst of heaven,
His burning chariot plunged in sable clouds,
And whelmed the world in darkness, making men
Despair of day; as did Thyestes' town,
Mycenae, Phoebus flying through the east.
Fierce Mulciber unbarrèd Aetna's gate,
Which flamèd not on high, but headlong pitched
Her burning head on bending Hespery.
Coal-black Charybdis whirled a sea of blood.
Fierce mastives howled. The vestal fires went out;
The flame in Alba, consecrate to Jove,
Parted in twain, and with a double point
Rose, like the Theban brothers' funeral fire.
The earth went off her hinges; and the Alps
Shook the old snow from off their trembling laps.
The ocean swelled as high as Spanish Calpe
Or Atlas' head. Their saints and household-gods
Sweat tears, to show the travails of their city:
Crowns fell from holy statues. Ominous birds
Defiled the day; and wild beasts were seen,
Leaving the woods, lodge in the streets of Rome.
Cattle were seen that muttered human speech;
Prodigious births with more and ugly joints
Than nature gives, whose sight appals the mother;
And dismal prophecies were spread abroad:
And they, whom fierce Bellona's fury moves
To wound their arms, sing vengeance; Cybel's priests,
Curling their bloody locks, howl dreadful things.
Souls quiet and appeas'd sighed from their graves;

Clashing of arms was heard; in untrod woods
Shrill voices schright; and ghosts encounter men.
Those that inhabited the suburb-fields
Fled: foul Erinnys stalked about the walls,
Shaking her snaky hair and crookèd pine
With flaming top; much like that hellish fiend
Which made the stern Lycurgus wound his thigh,
Or fierce Agave mad; or like Megaera
That scar'd Alcides, when by Juno's task
He had before look'd Pluto in the face.
Trumpets were heard to sound; and with what noise
An armèd battle joins, such and more strange
Black night brought forth in secret.

Lucan, *The Song of Pharsalus* 1
(Christopher Marlowe)

CONSTITUTIONAL REFORM

In Rome there was something like panic; with one party as much alarmed by the situation as the other, everything came to a standstill. The commons, abandoned as they were by their friends in the army, feared violence at the hands of the senatorial party, who, in their turn, were afraid of the commons still left in the city, and could hardly make up their minds if they would rather see them stay or go. Moreover, how long would the deserters be content to remain inactive? What would happen if, in the present situation, there were a threat of foreign invasion? Clearly the only hope lay in finding a solution for the conflicting interests of the two classes in the state: by fair means or foul the country must recover its internal harmony. The senatorial party accordingly decided to employ Menenius Agrippa as their spokesman to the commons on the Sacred Mount—he was a good speaker, and the commons liked him as he was one of themselves. Admitted to the deserters' camp, he is said to have told them, in the rugged style of those far-off days, the following story. "Long ago, when the members of the human body did not, as now they do, agree together, but had each its own thoughts and the words to express them in, the other parts resented the fact that they should have the worry and trouble of providing everything for the belly, which remained idle, surrounded by its ministers, with nothing to do

26. Augustus. Rome, Museo Vaticano.

. . . political choreography . . .

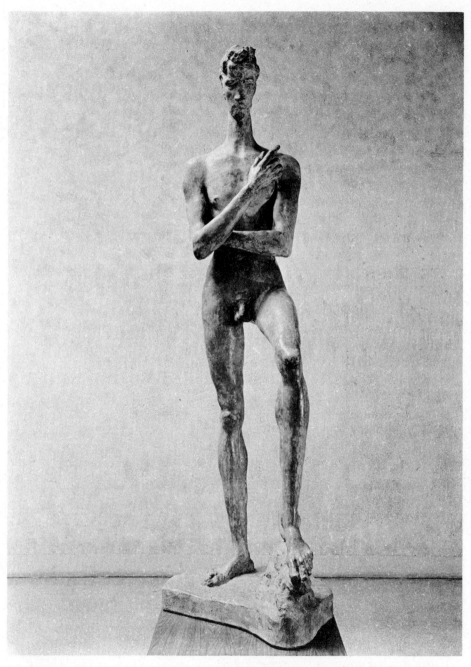

27. William Lehmbruck, *Standing Youth*. New York, The Museum of Modern Art.

. . . as the lonely head on a work of Lehmbruck looks,
from far off, down its own elongated limbs . . .

but enjoy the pleasant things they gave it. So the discontented members plotted together that the hand should carry no food to the mouth, that the mouth should take nothing that was offered it, and that the teeth should accept nothing to chew. But alas! while they sought in their resentment to subdue the belly by starvation, they themselves and the whole body wasted away to nothing. By this it was apparent that the belly, too, has no mean service to perform: it receives food, indeed; but it also nourishes in its turn the other members, giving back to all parts of the body, through all its veins, the blood it has made by the process of digestion; and upon this blood our life and our health depend."

This fable of the revolt of the body's members Menenius applied to the political situation, pointing out its resemblance to the anger of the populace against the governing class; and so successful was his story that their resentment was mollified. Negotiations began and an agreement was reached on the condition that special magistrates should be appointed to represent the commons; these officers—"tribunes of the people"— should be above the law, and their function should be to protect the commons. . . .

Livy, *Rome from Its Foundation*
2.32-33 (Aubrey de Sélincourt)

SOCIAL CONTRACT

As time went by, men began to build huts and to use skins and fire. Male and female learnt to live together in a stable union and to watch over their joint progeny. Then it was that humanity first began to mellow. Thanks to fire, their chilly bodies could no longer so easily endure the cold under the canopy of heaven. Venus subdued brute strength. Children by their wheedling easily broke down their parents' stubborn temper. Then neighbours began to form *mutual alliances,* wishing neither to do nor to suffer violence among themselves. They appealed on behalf of their children and womenfolk, pointing out with gestures and inarticulate cries that it is right for everyone to pity the weak. It was not possible to achieve perfect unity of purpose. Yet a substantial majority kept faith honestly. Otherwise the entire human race would have been wiped out there and then instead of being propagated, generation after generation, down to the present day.

Lucretius, *On Reality* 5.1011-27 (R. E. Latham)

THE NATURAL LAW

And so, the experts think that law is practical wisdom, whose function it is to order right action and forbid transgression, and they think it derives its Greek name (*nomos*) from a word (*nemein*) implying giving each one his own, while I think our word (*lex*) is derived from the verb "to choose" (*legere*). For they emphasize equal distribution when they talk about law, and we emphasize choice, but actually both ideas belong in the definition. If this definition is correct, as I at least always think of it as being, it is right that we should derive the origin of justice from law, for law is a natural force, it is the thinking mind of the man of practical wisdom, it is the standard of judgment for justice and injustice. But since our whole discussion is concerned with the people's thinking on the subject, we shall have to use ordinary speech from time to time and say that law is what the mob calls it, that which decrees its meaning in writing either by commanding or by forbidding. But let *us* derive the beginning of established justice from that highest law which was born centuries before any law was written down or any state founded.

.   .   .

I won't be too long about it. This is where it leads. That provident, sagacious, complex, sharp-witted animal, with so long a memory, so full of reason and judgment, which we call man, has been brought to birth by God the all-highest in very exalted circumstances. For he is the only one of all the numerous natural types of living creatures who shares in the power of reason and thought, which the others are entirely without. Moreover, what is more divine than reason, not merely in man, but in all heaven and earth? And when reason has reached the finish of maturity, it is properly called wisdom. Therefore, since nothing is better than reason, and since it exists both in man and in God, the prime link between man and God is the bond of reason. Moreover, those who share reason, share right reason also. And since law is right reason, we ought to think that law also links man with the gods. Furthermore, those who share law, share justice also. Moreover, those who share law and justice ought to be considered to belong to the same state, all the more so if they obey the commands of the same authorities. Moreover, they obey this heavenly hierarchy, this divine mind, this omnipotent God, so that this whole universe ought to be considered a single state shared by gods

285

and men. And as in states, by a system which I will discuss in its proper place, one's status is determined by one's family relationships, so in nature, but much more magnificently and pre-eminently, men are bound together by their family relationship to the gods.

.　　.　　.

But among the peoples of the world much legislation is passed which is pernicious and unhealthy. What are we to say about that? Do these deserve to be called laws any more than if a set of brigands had held a meeting and passed them? For doctors' prescriptions cannot be said to be sound if ignorant, unskilled practitioners prescribe poisons instead of proper medicines; similarly in a nation, any chance piece of legislation cannot be called a law, even though the populace has accepted it, ruinous as it is. Law then is the distinction between what is just and what is unjust, expressed in accordance with Nature, the oldest and chiefest of all things. And in accordance with Nature human laws are set up, punishing the wicked, preserving and protecting the good.

Cicero, *The Laws* 1.19, 22-23; 2.13
(Paul MacKendrick)

BROTHERHOOD OF MAN

I

The fact that no one wants to live in complete solitude, not even if pleasures are his in infinite abundance, makes it easy for us to understand that we have been born for close human association, a sort of natural community. Moreover we have a natural impulse to be as useful as possible to the maximum number of people, especially in the teaching of philosophy and in handing on to posterity the precepts of practical wisdom. And so our propensity for teaching as well as learning is so strong that it is hard to find any one who does not pass on to others what he knows himself. And just as Nature has given bulls the instinct to fight for their calves with all their might and main against lions, even so those who have the resources and the ability (like Hercules and

Bacchus) are naturally spurred on to the preservation of the human race. And even when we give Jupiter the title of Best and Greatest, or when we worship him as Savior, as God of Hospitality, as Supporter of Armies, what we mean is that the security of mankind is in his keeping. It would be terribly inappropriate to demand that the immortal gods cherish us and care for us while we ourselves are negligent and mean in our treatment of one another. Therefore just as we use our limbs [by instinct] before we learn why we have them, so we are linked by a natural instinct in the bonds of a civil community; if it were not so, there would be no room for justice or benevolence. But though the Stoics believe that bonds of justice exist between man and man, they do not think that there is any such link between man and the beasts. So Chrysippus well says that all other animals are born for the use of men and gods, but that men exist to live together in society, so that men may without injustice use beasts to their own advantage. And since man's nature is such that a sort of universal law of common citizenship links him to the human race, the man who abides by this law will be just, the man who departs from it unjust. But just as, though the theatre is public property, each spectator may be said to have a right to the seat he occupies, even so in our one world there is no objection to the law which grants to each man the ownership of private property.

·   ·   ·

In every moral act . . . the most illustrious thing, and the one that has the widest range, is the tie that binds man to man, a sort of alliance for the distribution of advantages. This natural human affection has its origin at our very birth, because our parents love us, and our whole family is linked by marriage and blood relationship. Gradually it creeps beyond the walls of the individual house, first to blood relations, then to relations by marriage, then to friends, neighbors, fellow citizens, and allied states, and finally to the whole compass of the human race. This affection of the soul, which gives to each his own and handsomely and equitably protects this close-linked alliance of man with man that I have been talking about, is called justice, and linked to it are piety, benevolence, liberality, kindness, courtesy, and the like.

Cicero, *Supreme Good and Evil*
3.65-67, 5.65 (Paul MacKendrick)

287

II

"Have you time to grieve
for others' pain
as thine?"

"I am a man,
what's any man's
is mine."

Terence, *The Masochist* 75-77 (G. W.)

POLICY AT WAR WITH PRINCIPLE

THE POLITICIAN'S DILEMMA

I am just as devoted to Cato as you are, but with the best intentions and from the highest principles he sometimes does the State harm. He talks as if he were living in Plato's Republic instead of on Romulus' dunghill. . . .

Cicero, *Letter to Atticus, June, 60 B.C.*

Cicero hovers between contending factions—the Senate and the triumvirate: I have not the heart to write any more about politics. I am not at all pleased with myself, and it hurts me a great deal to write. I keep my end up, not discreditably considering the general servility, but not courageously considering my distinguished past. . . .

Letter to Atticus, Summer, 59 B.C.

Cicero deserts the constitutional but ineffectual party of the Senate: But good-bye to good, honest, straightforward policy. It is incredible the disloyalty of those "leaders"—leaders as they want to be and would be if they had a spark of loyalty. I felt it, I knew it: had they not led me on, then ratted and thrown me over? Even so I resolved to collaborate with them in politics. But they have proved the same as ever, and at long last, under your guidance, I have come to my senses. You will say that you warned and advised me with a view to policy only, not writing. But the truth is, I wanted to commit myself bindingly to this new connection, and leave myself no loophole for slipping back to those people, who even now, when they ought to pity me, do not cease to envy. . . . Since those who have no power are unwilling to befriend me, I will endeavour to make friends with those who have power. You will say, "I wish you had long ago." I know you wanted it, and that I have been a perfect ass. But now the time has come for me to befriend myself, since there is no prospect of friendship from them on any terms. . . .

Letter to Atticus, May, 56 B.C.

I write somewhat briefly on this topic, because the state of affairs is not to my liking. But I do write nevertheless, to impress upon you a lesson which, with all my life-long devotion to literature, I have discovered from experience rather than from books: learn before you come to grief that one should not contemplate safety without honour, nor yet honour without safety. . . .

Letter to Lentulus Spinther, August, 56 B.C.

Calm reigns in the Forum, but it is the calm of a decrepit rather than a contented state. As for my speeches in the Senate, they are such that others agree with them more than I do myself. . . .

Letter to Quintus, his brother, June 3, 54 B.C.

After his hard decision to support the triumvirate, Cicero finds he must choose, now, between the great rivals within that faction—Pompey or Caesar: My idea was that by attaching myself to Pompey I should never be forced to do anything unconstitutional, and by agreeing with Caesar I should avoid any clash with Pompey, they were so closely allied. But now, on your own showing, and in my view as well, they are on the brink of an open conflict. Each of them is counting on me:—Caesar may be only pretending; Pompey at least has no doubts, rightly supposing that his present political attitude has my warm approval. At any rate, each of them sent me a letter, which arrived with yours, from which it appeared that neither set more store by anyone than by me. But what am I to do? I don't mean in the long run: if it comes to open warfare, I see that it would be better to lose with Pompey than to win with Caesar. But what about the debate which will be in progress when I arrive? . . . Have I avoided this trap all through the past two years, when Caesar's province has been under debate, only to stumble now into the thick of the trouble? To ensure that someone else has to give his opinion first, I am very much inclined to begin taking steps about my Triumph, and so have a good excuse for remaining outside the capital. And yet they will do everything they can to elicit my opinion. . . .

Letter to Atticus, October 16, 50 B.C.

Meanwhile Caelius, Cicero's principal source of information in Rome, was giving very Caesarian advice: You will of course realise that, in a case of internal dissension, men should support the side that is in the right so long as it is a matter of politics and not fighting, but the stronger side when it comes to open warfare, considering then that might is right.

Letter from Caelius to Cicero, August, 50 B.C.

Nonetheless, Cicero joins what is clearly the losing side—Pompey's: We ought to have resisted Caesar while he was still weak—and it would have been easy; now he has eleven legions, all the cavalry he wants, the peoples north of the Po, the city mob, and all these Tribunes of the People and young men gone to the bad—himself a leader of supreme prestige and daring. Either we must fight him, or we must make his candidature legal. "Fight," you say, "rather than be slaves." What's the use? If you lose, you'll be outlawed; if you win, you'll still be slaves. "What will you do then?" Why, what livestock do: when scattered, make for your own sort. As the cow joins the cattle-herd, I shall join the patriots, or so-called patriots, even if they stampede to destruction.

Letter to Atticus, December 18, 50 B.C.

But how is one to oppose a Caesar? Can one justly destroy the state in order to "save" it from a tyrant? These are the questions Cicero asked himself two months after Caesar had brought a Roman army over the Rubicon against Rome: Should one remain in one's country even under a tyranny? Are all means justifiable to abolish a tyranny, even if there is danger of ruining the state? Should one take precautions to prevent the tyrannicide becoming tyrant himself? Should one, if one's country is under a tyranny, try to help it by words and biding one's time, or by war? Is one doing one's duty if one retires to some other place and remains there so long as one's country is under a tyranny, or should one brave any danger for the sake of liberation? Should one invade one's

290

country, or blockade it, if it is under a tyranny? Should one enroll one-self in the ranks of the loyalists, even if one does not oneself approve of war as a means of abolishing tyranny? Should one in public matters share the dangers of one's benefactors and friends, even if one believes their fundamental policy to be mistaken?

Letter to Atticus, March 12, 49 B.C.

A confrontation with Caesar: I followed your advice on both points: I spoke in such a way as to earn Caesar's respect rather than his grati-tude, and I persisted in my resolve—no going to Rome. Where I was wrong was in thinking he would be amenable: I never saw anyone less so. My decision, he said, amounted to condemning him, and if I did not come, others would be more reluctant. I said their position was different. After much argument he said, "Then come there and discuss peace." "On my terms?" I asked. "Who am I," he answered, "to dictate to you?" "Then," said I, "I shall take the line that the Senate objects to your going to Spain or transferring forces to Greece; and I shall express deep sympathy for Pompey." He interposed, "I cannot have such things said." "So I imagined," I replied, "but I don't want to be there precisely be-cause I must either say such things and many others which I would not leave unsaid if I were present, or not go at all." The upshot was that, by way of ending the interview, he asked me to think it over. I could hardly refuse, and so we parted. The result is that I don't think he's very pleased with me. But I was very pleased with myself, a feeling which I had long got out of the way of having.

Letter to Atticus, March 29, 49 B.C.

More Caesarian advice from Caelius: It would be sheer idiocy now to go against the victor, whom you were careful not to injure when the issue was still in doubt, and to join, now that they are in flight, men whom you refused to join while they were putting up a stand. Beware of deciding too hastily which is the best cause through anxiety to be on the side of "the best people." But if I cannot altogether convince you, at least wait until the result of our Spanish operations is known: I may inform you that when Caesar arrives the whole peninsula will be in our hands. What hope the Pompeians have if they lose Spain, I do not know: and what your idea is in joining a lost cause, upon my word I fail to see. . . . Think it over again and again, Cicero, before you completely ruin yourself and those you love; don't fall open-eyed into a pit from which you can see there is no escape. But if you are influenced by what the nobles will say, or feel unable to bear the arrogance and swagger of certain persons, my advice is that you choose some town unaffected by the war, and live there until these issues are decided, as presently they will be. In that case I shall consider you have acted wisely, and at the same time you will avoid offending Caesar.

Letter from Caelius to Cicero, April 16, 49 B.C.
from Cicero, *Letters* (L. P. Wilkinson)

But Cicero continued on the losing side—and survived, this time. He was to make a similar choice against Antony, who was not so lenient toward his enemies as Caesar. That ended the debate between principle and policy.

"CONFLICT OF INTEREST" CODE

You want to know what I think about your continuing to practise in the law courts while you hold the office of tribune. It depends entirely on the view you take of the tribunate—an "empty form" and a "mere title," or an inviolable authority which should not be called in question by anyone, not even the holder. When I was tribune myself, I acted on the assumption (which may have been a wrong one) that my office really meant something. I therefore gave up all my court work, for I thought it unsuitable for a tribune to stand while others were seated, when it was really every man's duty to rise and give place to him; to be cut short by the water-clock though he had the power to command anyone's silence; and, although it was sacrilege to interrupt him, to be exposed to insults which he could not pass over without an appearance of weakness, nor counter without seeming to abuse his power. I had also to face the difficulty of how to react if my client or my opponent were to appeal to me as tribune, whether to lend my aid by interposing my veto, or to keep silent as if I had laid down my office and resumed my status of private citizen. For these reasons I chose to be tribune to all rather than give my professional services to a few; but your own decision, as I said before, can only depend on your idea of the tribunate and the part you intend to play: a wise man will choose one within his capacity to play to the end.

Pliny (the Younger), *Letters* 1.23 (Betty Radice)

LAW: LETTER AND SPIRIT

I understand from your letter that Sabina in making us her heirs left us no instructions that her slave Modestus was to be given his freedom, but even so left him a legacy in the words: "To Modestus whom I have ordered to be set free"; and you would like to hear my view. I have consulted the legal experts, and it was their unanimous opinion that Modestus should receive neither his freedom, as it was not expressly granted, nor his legacy, as it was bequeathed to him while his status was that of a slave. But it seems to me obvious that it was a mistake on Sabina's part, and I think we ought to act as if she had set out in writing what she believed she had written. I am sure you will agree with me, for you are always most scrupulous about carrying out the intention of the deceased. Once understood, it should be legally binding on an honest heir, as honour puts us under an obligation as binding as necessity is for other people. Let us then allow Modestus to have his liberty and enjoy his legacy as if Sabina had taken every proper precaution. She did in fact do so by her wise choice of heirs.

Pliny (the Younger), *Letters* 4.10 (Betty Radice)

RELAX INTO WISDOM

Descended of an ancient line,
    That long the Tuscan scepter sway'd,
Make haste to meet the generous wine,
    Whose piercing is for thee delay'd:
The rosy wreath is ready made;
    And artful hands prepare
The fragrant Syrian oil, that shall perfume thy hair.

When the wine sparkles from afar,
    And the well-natur'd friend cries, "Come away!"
Make haste, and leave thy business and thy care;
    No mortal int'rest can be worth thy stay.

Leave for a while thy costly country seat;
    And, to be great indeed, forget
The nauseous pleasures of the great:
    Make haste and come;

293

Come, and forsake thy cloying store;
   Thy turret that surveys, from high,
The smoke, and wealth, and noise of Rome;
   And all the busy pageantry
That wise men scorn, and fools adore:
Come, give thy soul a loose, and taste the pleasure of the poor.

Sometimes 't is grateful to the rich to try
A short vicissitude, and fit of poverty:
   A savory dish, a homely treat,
   Where all is plain, where all is neat,
   Without the stately spacious room
The Persian carpet, or the Tyrian loom,
Clear up the cloudy foreheads of the great.

   The sun is in the Lion mounted high;
     The Syrian star
     Barks from afar,
   And with his sultry breath infects the sky;
The ground below is parch'd, the heav'ns above us fry.
   The shepherd drives his fainting flock
   Beneath the covert of a rock,
   And seeks refreshing rivulets nigh:
   The sylvans to their shades retire,
Those very shades and streams new shades and streams re-
     quire,
And want a cooling breeze of wind to fan the raging fire.

   Thou, what befits the new Lord May'r,
   And what the city faction dare,
   And what the Gallic arms will do,
   And what the quiver-bearing foe,
   Art anxiously inquisitive to know;
   But God has, wisely, hid from human sight
     The dark decrees of future fate,
     And sown their seeds in depth of night:
He laughs at all the giddy turns of state,
   When mortals search too soon, and fear too late.

   Enjoy the present smiling hour,
   And put it out of Fortune's pow'r;
The tide of bus'ness, like the running stream,

294

Is sometimes high, and sometimes low,
A quiet ebb, or a tempestuous flow,
  And always in extreme.
  Now with a noiseless gentle course
  It keeps within the middle bed;
Anon it lifts aloft the head,
And bears down all before it with impetuous force;
    And trunks of trees come rolling down,
    Sheep and their folds together drown:
  Both house and homestead into seas are borne;
  And rocks are from their old foundations torn,
And woods, made thin with winds, their scatter'd honors
    mourn.

Happy the man, and happy he alone,
    He, who can call to-day his own;
    He who, secure within, can say:
  "To-morrow do thy worst, for I have liv'd to-day.
    Be fair, or foul, or rain, or shine,
    The joys I have possess'd, in spite of fate, are mine.
    Not Heav'n itself upon the past has pow'r;
But what has been, has been, and I have had my hour."

Fortune, that with malicious joy
    Does man her slave oppress,
Proud of her office to destroy,
    Is seldom pleas'd to bless:
Still various, and unconstant, still,
But with an inclination to be ill,
    Promotes, degrades, delights in strife,
    And makes a lottery of life.
    I can enjoy her while she's kind;
    But when she dances in the wind,
    And shakes her wings, and will not stay,
    I puff the prostitute away:
    The little or the much she gave is quietly resign'd;
      Content with poverty, my soul I arm;
      And virtue, tho' in rags, will keep me warm.

        What is 't to me,
    Who never sail in her unfaithful sea,

295

If storms arise, and clouds grow black;
If the mast split, and threaten wreck?
Then let the greedy merchant fear
For his ill-gotten gain;
And pray to gods that will not hear,
While the debating winds and billows bear
His wealth into the main.
For me, secure from Fortune's blows,
(Secure of what I cannot lose,)
In my small pinnace I can sail,
Contemning all the blust'ring roar;
And running with a merry gale,
With friendly stars my safety seek,
Within some little winding creek;
And see the storm ashore.

Horace, *Songs* 3.29 (John Dryden)

"HEART, WITH AN EASY HUMOUROUSNESS . . ."

Peace and calm seas the voyager begs the gods for
When storms blow up in mid-Aegean, and black clouds
Muffle the moon, and sailors miss the usual
  Stars in the sky;

And peace is what the battle-maddened Thracians
And the fierce Parthians with their painted quivers
Pray for—the peace no gold or gems or purple,
  Grosphus, can buy.

A pasha's bribes, a consul's rodded lictors
Can soon disperse a riot of the people,
But not the grey mob of the mind, the worries
  Circling the beams

Of fretted ceilings. He lives well on little
Whose family salt-dish glitters on a plain-laid
Table; no fears or ugly longings steal his
  Innocent dreams.

296

Why do we aim so high, when time must foil our
Brave archery? Why hanker after countries
Heated by foreign suns? What exile ever
    Fled his own mind?

Care, that contagion, clambers up the bronze-prowed
Galley, keeps level with the galloping squadron,
Outruns the stag and leaves the cloud-compelling
    East wind behind.

Happy with here and now, scorning hereafter,
Heart, with an easy humourousness attemper
The bitterness of things. Nothing is perfect
    Seen from all sides.

Death snatched away Achilles in his glory,
Long-drawn-out age wasted Tithonus inchmeal,
And any day may keep from you some blessing
    Which it provides

Me with. Sicilian cattle moo, a hundred
Herds, in your meadow, mares trained for the race-track
Neigh in your stalls, you dress in Tyrian purple,
    Double-dyed woof;

But I am rich too: Fate, an honest patron,
Has given me a small farm, an ear fine-tuned to
The Grecian Muses, and a mind from vulgar
    Envy aloof.

            Horace, *Songs* 2.16 (James Michie)

TRUE ROYALTY

Not riches makes a king, or high renown;
Not garnished weed, with purple Tyrian dye;
Not lofty looks, or head enclos'd with crown;
Not glitt'ring beams with gold, and turrets high.

A king is he that fear hath laid aside,
And all the affects that in the breast are bred;
Whom impotent ambition doth not guide,

Nor fickle favor hath of people led;
Nor all that West in metals' mines hath found,
Or channel clear of golden Tagus shows,
Nor all the grain that threshed is on ground
That with the heat of Libyac harvest glows;
Nor whom the flash of lightning flame shall beat,
Nor Eastern wind that smites upon the seas,
Nor swelling surge with rage of wind replete,
Or greedy gulph of Adria displease;
Whom not the prick of soldier's sharpest spear
Or pointed pike in hand hath made to rue,
Nor whom the glimpse of sword might cause to fear,
Or bright drawn blade of glitt'ring steel subdue;
Who in the seat of safety sets his feet,
Beholds all haps how under him they lie,
And gladly runs his fatal day to meet,
Nor aught complains or grudgeth for to die.

Though present were the princes everyone
The scatter'd Dakes to chase that wonted be,
That shining seas beset with precious stone
And Red Sea coasts do hold, like blood to see;
Or they which else the Caspian mountains high
From Sarmats strong with all their power withheld;
Or he that on the flood of Danubie
In frost afoot to travel dare be bold;
Or Seres in whatever place they lie,
Renowned with fleece that there of silk doth spring,
They never might the truth hereof denie:
It is the mind that only makes a king.

There is no need of sturdy steeds in war,
No need with arms, or arrows else to fight
That Parthus wonts with bow to fling from far,
While from the field he falsely feigneth flight;
Nor yet to siege no need it is to bring
Great guns in carts to overthrow the wall,
That from far off their batt'ring pellets fling.
A king is he that feareth naught at all.
Each man himself this kingdom gives at hand.

298

Let whoso list with mighty mace to reign
In tickle top of court delight to stand.
Let me the sweet and quiet rest obtaine;
So, set in place obscure and low degree,
Of pleasant rest I shall the sweetness know.
My life, unknown to them that noble be,
Shall in the step of secret silence go.
Thus, when my days at length are overpast,
And time without all troublous tumult spent,
An aged man, I shall depart at last
In mean estate, to die full well content.
But grievous is to him the death that, when
So far abroad the bruit of him is blown
That known he is too much to other men,
Departeth yet unto himself unknown.

Seneca, *Thyestes* 344-403 (Jasper Heywood)

THE MIDDLE WAY

The things of middle sort, and of a mean degree,
Endure above the rest and longest days do see,
The man of mean estate most happy is of all,
Who, pleaséd with the lot that doth to him befall,
Doth sail on silent shore, with calm and quiet tide,
And dreads with bruiséd barge on swelling seas to ride—
Not launching to the deep (where bottom none is found),
May with his rudder search, and reach, the *shallow* ground.

Seneca, *Agamemnon* 102-7 (John Studley)

HEAVEN'S EMPEROR

I

And now th' Almighty Father of the Gods
Convenes a council in the blest abodes.
Far in the bright recesses of the skies,

299

High o'er the rolling heav'ns, a mansion lies
Whence, far below the gods at once survey
The realms of rising and declining day
And all th' extended space of earth and air and sea.
Full in the midst, and on a starry throne,
The Majesty of Heav'n superior shone;
Serene he look'd, and gave an awful nod,
And all the trembling spheres confess'd the god.

At Jove's assent, the deities around
In solemn state the consistory crown'd.
Next a long order of inferior pow'rs
Ascend from hills and plains and shady bow'rs,
Those from whose urns the rolling rivers flow,
And those that give the wand'ring winds to blow.
Here all their rage, and ev'n their murmurs cease,
And sacred silence reigns, and universal peace.
A shining synod of majestic gods
Gilds with new lustre the divine abodes;
Heav'n seems improv'd with a superior ray,
And the bright arch reflects a double day.

The monarch then his solemn silence broke,
The still creation listen'd while he spoke,
Each sacred accent bears eternal weight,
And each irrevocable word is fate.

Statius, *The Song of Thebes* 1.197-213
(Alexander Pope)

I I

O thou whose pow'r o'er moving worlds presides,
Whose voice created, and whose wisdom guides,
On darkling man in pure effulgence shine,
And cheer the clouded mind with light divine.
'Tis thine alone to calm the pious breast
With silent confidence and holy rest:
From thee, great God, we spring, to thee we tend,
Path, motive, guide, original, and end.

Boethius, *The Comfort Philosophy Gives*
3.9 (Samuel Johnson)

III

Great are you, Lord, and greatly to be praised; great your strength, and of your wisdom who can take the measure? Yet *man* would praise you, man but a part of the whole of things you made, man who bears his own death cased around him, the blazon of his sin, visible proof that you beat back the proud. Yet he would praise you, man, this part of your whole creation. You stir him to it, to taste the joy of praising you, since you made us for you, and we are troubled at heart until our hearts are quieted in you.

Give me, Lord, to find and understand what is first—to call you to me or to praise you? to know you or call you to me? How call, without knowing you are there to hear the call?—to call in ignorance is to call for one thing and be answered by another. Are you called near in order to be known? Yet "how shall they call on one they do not believe in?" And "how could they know unless one tells them?"

"Those men shall praise God who seek him." In the seeking they find, and in the finding they shall praise. So I shall seek you, Lord, by calling to you; and call you to me by believing in you. For I *had* a preacher to tell me of you: that faith cries to you which you first gave me, the faith you breathed into me by the mediation of your son's humanity, itself mediated to me by the words of your preacher.

Still, how shall I call out to my God, the God who is my lord, since I call him into me when I cry out for him; and what space is there in me which he can enter into, he my God? How can that God enter me who made the sky and the earth? Is there, then, my God and Lord, that in me which could hold you? Indeed, do the sky and earth you made, and made me only in them, hold you? Or, since nothing that is could continue to be without you, do all things that exist hold you? And since I am, how shall I cry for you to come to me, I who would not be here to cry, unless you were already here? For I am not as low as hell, and even there you are present: "Should I go down to the abyss, you are there." I could not be, my God, could not begin to be but by you in me. Or rather is my being a being *in* you, out of whom and through and in whom everything comes to be and is? So it is, Lord, it must be so; and so to what new place am I calling you, I who exist in you? Or *from* where? Whither should I retreat, away from sky and earth, to call you to me, my God, who said, "I fill the sky and the earth"?

Do *they* hold you, the sky and the earth, since you fill them; or is something left over when you fill them, something they cannot hold?

And where would you spill over what is left of you when earth and sky are filled? Or do you need no vessel because you hold all things, and fill all your vessels by being *their* vessel? For the vessels filled with you do not support you; nor, when they break, are you spilled out. And when you are poured out over us, you are not drained down, but draw us up; you do not trickle away, but collect us in strength.

When you fill everything, do you fill it with all of you; or, if all things made cannot hold you, do they hold one part of you—all the same part, or each its own part; does the larger thing hold more of you, the smaller hold less; can you be parted into more or less? Rather, are you everywhere, all of you; while you are held, all of you, by nothing anywhere?

What then is my God? What to say but he is God, the Lord? "Who is lord but the Lord, or who can be god but our God?" High above all, and best; mighty above all, almighty; most hidden from us, yet closest to us; supreme in beauty and in strength; most fixed and most elusive; changeless, the author of change in everything; never old, never young, you give all things their youth, and surprise the proud with gradual age; ever in act, ever at rest; acquiring, yet not through want; carrying, filling, sheltering; creating, nourishing, giving final form; seeking though there is nothing for you to acquire; you are in love, without love's torment; jealous, from perfect security; your sorrow is not a suffering, your wrath not a disturbance; your actions alter, not your aims; you find what was never lost, and take it back; not poor, you delight in gifts; not greedy, demand payment; you let us overpay you, so you may owe *us* (yet who has anything not yours to give you?); you pay debts you do not owe, remit debts without loss . . .

What have I said, my God and life and sweet taste of holiness; or what can anyone say who tries to speak of you? Yet beware, you who speak not, where those who speak best are as the dumb.

St. Augustine, *Confessions* 1.1-4 (G. W.)

THE REWARD FOR ROMAN GREATNESS

Now, it is a familiar occurrence that constant thinking and speaking of an object beget in us during sleep something like what Ennius records as his personal experience regarding Homer, of whom, you know, he would continually think and speak during his waking hours. Well, that

28. Augustus. Baltimore, Walters Art Gallery.

. . . a busyness that eats at them . . .

night, in consequence no doubt of our conversation the evening before, Africanus appeared to me under a form with which I was familiar from his mask, rather than from his personal looks. A shiver ran through my frame as soon as I recognized him; but he reassured me, saying: "Courage, my dear Scipio; cast aside all fear and transmit to posterity what I will now impart to you."

"Do you descry yonder city which I forced under the yoke of Rome, but which now renews its old hostility and cannot be at rest?" And here he pointed to Carthage from a high starry place which was bathed in light. "'Little more than a common soldier," he continued, "you now come to lay siege to it; but before two years elapse you will be consul, and after that level the city with the ground. The surname to which you are now but heir will then be the reward of your personal merit. After the destruction of Carthage you will celebrate a triumph, then be censor, and go on an embassy to Egypt, Syria, Asia, and Greece. Finally, though absent from Rome, you will be re-elected consul and, by the destruction of Numantia, bring a gigantic war to its close. After your triumphal entry into the Capitol, however, you will find the State in a ferment as the result of the policy of my nephew. In that critical hour, dear Scipio, it will be your duty to display in the service of your country your fine gifts of mind and heart and your brilliant statesmanship.

"Nevertheless, fate, I see, has destined you for a perilous career in those days; when you reach the age of eight times seven solar years, and when in the course of nature these two numbers—both of which are perfect, though each for a different reason—accomplish the product so big with fate for you, then the entire commonwealth will turn to you and your name alone. The senate, all patriots, and the Latin allies will look to you; you will be the only man who can save the country. In a word, in the capacity of dictator, you will have to restore order in the State— if, indeed, you escape the murderous hands of your kinsmen."

(Here Laelius uttered a cry; the others broke out in sobs; Scipio alone smiled gently and said: "Please, be still; do not wake me from my trance, but have a little patience and hear me to the end.")

"However, to buoy you up in your endeavor to safeguard the constitution, mark well: all those who save, aid, or extend their country have a definite place set apart for them in Heaven where they may enjoy eternal life and happiness. No mere earthly institutions are viewed with greater favor by that supreme deity which rules the entire world than associations or communities of men, styled commonwealths, based on constitutional rights. Their rulers and saviors go forth hence and hither they return."

I was thoroughly frightened by this time, fearing not so much death as snares laid by my kin. Nevertheless, I inquired of Africanus whether he was still alive, and whether my father Paulus was, as well as others who, we thought, had ceased to be. "Of course they are," he replied. "In fact, they are truly alive who have taken their flight out of the captivity of the body as out of a prison house. Your so-called life on earth is in reality but death. Why, look at your father Paulus coming to meet you!"

At the sight of my dear father I cried like a child. But he pressed me to his bosom and kissed away my tears.

My grief was now assuaged and I found my voice again. Then I pleaded: "Please, good and sainted father, since here is life worthy of the name, as I have just heard Africanus say, why must I tarry on earth? Why may I not hasten to join you here?"

"Not so," he replied. "You cannot gain admission to this place, unless that deity, whose temple is all this realm as far as eye can reach, release you from the shackles of your body. It is the natural destiny of man to cultivate that globe, called Earth, which you descry in the centre of this vast space. He has been given a spirit—a spark from those eternal fires called stars and constellations, which are circular and globe-shaped and animated by divine intelligences, and which with wonderful velocity spin about in their established orbits. Like all god-fearing men, therefore, my dear Publius, you have to keep that spirit in the prison of your body and must not quit life on earth until you are summoned by him who gave you your spirit: otherwise you shirk a plain duty assigned by God to man.

"Like your grandsire here, my dear Scipio, and like myself, the author of your being, cultivate justice and a sense of duty. In the shape of filial affection and love of kin, dutifulness plays an important part in the world, but its rôle of patriotism is of vastly greater moment. Life spent in the service of one's country is a direct passport to Heaven, to this assembly, I mean, of all those whose earthly career is closed. Stripped of their mortality, they now inhabit the place you see yonder" (it was a belt of dazzling brightness blazing amidst the stars), "which by a term borrowed from the Greek you call the Milky Way."

Looking from this vantage ground, all else appeared to me to be of wondrous beauty. There were stars which we have never seen from the

305

earth, and the dimensions of all were such as we have never dreamt of. The smallest was that which, farthest from Heaven and nearest the earth, shone with a borrowed light. In size the celestial bodies far surpassed the earth. Indeed, the latter was so insignificant by comparison that I was disgusted with our empire, which is but a speck on the surface of the globe.

As I looked at the earth still more intently, Africanus interrupted me: "How long, I wonder, will your mind be fixed upon the earth? Do you not see what sort of region you have come to?

"Look, there is the universe, a system of nine circles, or rather spheres. One of these, the outermost, is Heaven, which contains within it all the rest, and is none other than the supreme deity, all-embracing, all-enclosing. In it are fixed the stars that roll in their eternal paths. Beneath it are seven spheres revolving the other way and in a direction opposite to that of Heaven. The star which on earth they call Saturn occupies one of them. Next comes the star called Jupiter, whose lustre means fortune and prosperity to the human race. Then there is one which you call Mars, of a reddish glow and a source of mischief to mankind. Again, farther down, the Sun lords it nearly midway between Heaven and Earth, the leader, prince, and ruler of all the other lights, the soul and principle of order in the world of such dimensions that his light illumes and fills the universe. Two orbs, Venus and Mercury, are his faithful satellites. Lastly, in the lowest course, revolves the Moon lit up by the rays of the Sun. Beneath her there is naught but what is frail and mortal, save souls—a gift of the gods to the human race. Above the Moon all things are eternal. The Earth, the ninth sphere and the hub of the universe, does not rotate at all, being at the lowest point of the whole system. To its centre all masses tend by reason of their gravity."

I was in an ecstasy of delight over this grand panorama. When I came to myself, I asked: "Tell me, what is this loud and sweet harmony that fills my ears?"

Whereupon he explained: "This music is produced by the friction and revolution of those very spheres. As the unequal intervals between them are arranged according to a fixed law of proportion, and as the high tones agreeably blend with the low, various sweet harmonies are bound to result therefrom. Such colossal revolutions cannot, of course, be swiftly executed in silence, and it is but natural that the extremes should elicit deep sounds at one end and high ones at the other. Accordingly, that highest starry orb of Heaven, whose revolution is comparatively swift, moves with a high and shrill sound, whereas this lowest lunar orb rotates with a deep sound. The Earth, of course, the ninth sphere, remains fixed and stationary, occupying as it does the centre of the universe. These eight orbs, two of which have the same musical value, produce seven different sounds—a number, by the way, which is the key of almost everything. Inspired bards reproduce this celestial strain on stringed instruments and thus pave the way for their own return to this place; so do other men of brilliant parts who spend their life on earth in the pursuit of things divine.

"Men's ears have been stunned by this music and, in consequence, are now deaf to it. Indeed, none of your senses is so blunt as hearing. In the vicinity of the so-called Catadupa Falls, for example, where the Nile comes rushing down from high mountains, the people that live near-by have lost their sense of hearing owing to the deafening noise. As for this music of the spheres, it is so overpowering, by reason of the amazing speed with which the cosmos spins round, that no human ear can endure it, any more than you can look straight into the sun, whose brightness would blunt the keenness of your sight."

Much as I marvelled at this explanation, I still kept turning my eyes in the direction of the earth. Then Africanus resumed:

"You are still lost, I see, in the contemplation of that comfortable home of man. If the earth appears to you small, as it really is, keep your gaze riveted upon this Heaven, and care not a straw for earthly things. How can you gain celebrity, how win a desirable kind of fame, merely from the approval of the world? You cannot help seeing that the earth is peopled but sparsely and in limited areas, and that vast stretches of wilderness intervene between the specks, I might almost call them, that are inhabited. Moreover, the inhabitants of the earth are scattered in such wise that among the different groups no report can travel from one place to another. Nay, some people live in a different zone from you, others live under different meridians, while still others are your antipodes. Surely, you cannot expect any glory from them.

"The earth, you will further notice, is girt round about with something like belts. Two of the zones, which are in entirely opposite parts of the earth and which at either end lie directly under the poles of the heavens, are buried, as you see, under ice and snow; while the middle zone, which is at once the largest, scorches under a tropical sun. There remain only two zones fit for habitation; of these the southern, whose inhabitants are your antipodes, is cut off from all communication with your race; of the other, situated in the North, which you inhabit—see what a slender strip forms your empire! In fact, the whole earth inhabited by you is but a small island that narrows towards the poles and widens at the sides, floating in that sea which on earth you call the Atlantic, the Great Sea, or the Ocean, but the small extent of which is in striking contrast with the pride of its name.

"Now, from these lands that are known and settled, has your name or that of any one of us been able to cross that Caucasus which you see, or be wafted across yonder Ganges? Will your name be heard in the other, remote countries of the East, or the West, or anywhere in the South or the North? Leave these out of account, and you certainly realize what a narrow theatre it is in which your glory is so eager to display itself. And then, those that actually speak of us—how long, I pray, will they keep it up?"

"Yes, even if all successive generations were willing to transmit to their descendants the fame of every one of us as they received it from their sires, still we can acquire no glory for any length of time, much less forever, on account of the flood and conflagration of the earth, which must recur at certain times.

"Besides, what does it really matter that you are going to reap golden opinions from generations yet unborn, when you have been unknown to fame in the past? And yet, the men of the past were not fewer in number and were certainly a superior race; a consideration that gains weight from the fact that at best no one can even for the space of 'one year' live in the memory of those very persons whom our name is able to reach.

"We, superficially enough, measure the length of a 'year' by the complete return of the sun, that is, of one star only. But when all the stars have returned to their starting-points and have restored, after long periods, the former configuration of the entire heavens, then that can be truly termed 'the current year.' I hardly venture to surmise how many generations of men may be contained within it. As in olden times the sun was seen to suffer a total eclipse when the spirit of Romulus penetrated this very realm, so, when the sun undergoes another eclipse in the same part of the heavens and on the same date, then you may consider 'one year' expired, because then all the stars and constellations will have returned to their original starting-points. Now, of that 'year,' mark you, not the twentieth part has as yet elapsed; and consequently, if you despair of your return to this place, which is the goal of great and eminent men, how hollow, I ask, must be your reputation on earth if it can barely extend over a small fraction of 'one year'? Be resolved, then, to aim high; keep a steady eye on this, your eternal home; lend not an ear to the foolish talk of the vulgar crowd nor stake the hope of your life on mere worldly recompense. No; Virtue, by her own native charms, should woo you on to true distinction. As for the world's judgment, wash your hands thereof. Of course the world will have its say; but all that sort of talk is limited to those narrow strips of land that you see; and besides, it has never outlived any individual forever, but dies away with man's dying breath and is lost in the silence of a forgetful posterity."

When he had finished speaking, I protested: "Aye, dear Africanus, from my boyhood up I have trodden in the footsteps of my father and in yours, and have never compromised your honor. Nevertheless, since a path to Heaven's gate is open to all zealous patriots, I am determined to redouble my energy and vigilance now that so splendid a reward is held out."

"Yes, use your best endeavors," he replied; "and mark well: it is not 'you' that is mortal, but this body of clay; nor are 'you' he whom that outward form of yours represents. Your spirit is your true Self, not that figure which can be pointed out with the finger. Believe me, then, you are a god—if indeed a god is the force that lives and feels in us, that remembers and foresees, that rules, governs, and moves the body over which it presides, even as the supreme deity yonder rules this world. And as nothing short of an eternal deity quickens the world which has an element of mortality in it, so an eternal spirit quickens your brittle frame.

"That which always moves is eternal. That, on the contrary, which imparts motion to something else, but is itself set in motion by an extraneous force, must cease to live as soon as its motion ceases. Consequently, that alone which moves by inherent power never ceases to move, for the reason that it never deserts itself. Nay, it is precisely the source and principle of movement for all other things that move. Now, a principle has no beginning; for all things spring from a principle, while itself cannot spring from another: that would not be a principle which owed its origin to something else. But, if it never comes into being, neither does it ever cease to be. For a principle once extinct will neither spring again from aught else (because it is from a principle that all things must spring) nor will it in turn bring anything into being. It follows, then, that the principle of all motion is in that being which moves by inherent power. But that can neither be born nor can it ever die: otherwise, you have to admit that the whole fabric of the heavens and all creation may some day come to a dead stop and never again find a force to give them a fresh start.

"Since it is evident, then, that that alone is eternal which has the source of its movement within itself, who will deny that the human soul is such a self-moving thing? For whatever is moved by an extraneous force is lifeless; whereas whatever has life moves by its own inherent power. Indeed, this power of self-movement is of the very essence of the soul. And therefore, if of all things the soul is the only one to move by inherent power, it has surely never had a beginning and is in consequence eternal.

"Pray exercise this immortal spirit in the noblest occupations. The noblest occupation, to be sure, is the service of your country. On the wings of such patriotic aspirations the spirit will fly the more swiftly to this, its true imperishable home. It will take wing the sooner if, while yet an inmate of the body, it will struggle forth and by the contemplation of the outer world deliver itself, as much as may be, from the bondage of the flesh. The souls of those slaves to sensual lust, those votaries of sin, who follow the lure of their passions into a life of pleasure and trample underfoot the rights of God and man—those souls, I repeat, after leaving the house of clay, still prowl about the earth and do not return to this place until after many a weary century of pain."

Here Africanus vanished, and my dream was ended.

Cicero, *The Dream of Scipio* (James A. Kleist, S.J.)

CENTERED

Blessed is he that has come to the heart of the world and is
    humble.
  He shall stand alone; and beneath
His feet are implacable fate, and panic at night, and the
    strumble
  Of the hungry river of death.

Vergil, *Georgics* 2.490-92 (Hilaire Belloc)

PART VI

The Dark Side

Idealism and cruelty are the lunar light and dark of the Roman mind. There is nothing so cruel as a disappointed idealist; and the Romans were masters of disappointment. They fed on it, and grew strong—and slightly twisted. They were harsh on themselves and on others: Roma ferox dare jura Medis. *Their ruling genius easily became a ruling mania. Their sensual vibrancy was easily jangled, tuned to weird music. Living with death took its toll on the men who had been sobered by it into a unique, dark greatness. The poetry turns us again toward the portrait busts—which are battered, now, by time. But they began battered.*

THE NOBILITY AND TORMENT
OF MAN

[It is man] for whose sake it should seem that Nature made and produced all other creatures besides: though this great favour of hers, so bountiful and beneficial in that respect, hath cost them full dear. Insomuch, as it is hard to judge, whether in so doing she hath done the part of a kind mother, or a hard and cruel stepdame. For first and foremost, of all other living creatures, man she hath brought forth all naked, and clothed him with the goods and riches of others. To all the rest, given she hath sufficient to clad them everyone according to their kind: as namely, shells, cods, hard hides, pricks, shag, bristles, hair, down feathers, quills, scales, and fleeces of wool. The very trunks and stems of trees and plants, she hath defended with bark and rind, yea and the same sometimes double, against the injuries both of heat and cold: man alone, poor wretch, she hath laid all naked upon the bare earth, even on his birthday, to cry and wraule presently from the very first hour that he is born into the world: in such sort, as among so many living creatures, there is none subject to shed tears and weep like him. And verily to no

29. Colosseum, Rome.

. . . like the Colosseum, Roman culture has a large external simplicity . . .

30. Internal passage-ways of the Colosseum.

. . . a labyrinthine internal life, and subterranean
passages prowled by animals . . .

babe or infant is it given once to laugh before he is forty days old, and that is counted very early and with the soonest. Moreover, so soon as he is entered in this manner to enjoy the light of the sun, see how he is immediately tied and bound fast, and hath no member at liberty, a thing that is not practised upon the young whelps of any beast among us, be he never so wild. The child of man thus untowardly born, and who another day is to rule and command all other, lo how he lyeth bound hand and foot, weeping and crying, and beginning his life with misery, as if he were to make amends and satisfaction by his punishment unto Nature, for this only fault and trespass, that he is born alive. O folly of all follies, ever to think (considering this simple beginning of ours) that we were sent into this world to live in pride and carry our head aloft. The first hope that we conceive of our strength, the first gift that time affordeth us, maketh us no better yet than four-footed beasts. How long is it ere we can go alone? how long before we can prattle and speak, feed ourselves, and shew our meat strongly? what a while continueth the mould and crown of our heads to beat and pant, before our brain is well settled; the undoubted mark and token that bewrayeth our exceeding great weakness above all other creatures? What should I say of the infirmities and sicknesses that soon seize upon our feeble bodies? what need I speak of so many medicines and remedies devised against these maladies: besides the new diseases that come every day, able to check and frustrate all our provision of physic whatsoever? As for all other living creatures, there is not one, but by a secret instinct of nature knoweth his own good, and whereto he is made able: some make use of their swift feet, others of their flight wings: some are strong of limb; others are apt to swim, and practise the same: man only knoweth nothing unless he is taught; he can neither speak, nor go, nor eat, otherwise than he is trained to it: and to be short, apt and good at nothing he is naturally, but to pule and cry. And hereupon it is, that some have been of this opinion, that better it had been, and simply best for a man, never to have been born, or else speedily to die. None but we do sorrow and wail, none but we are given to excess and superfluity infinitely in everything, and shew the same in every member that we have. Who but we again are ambitious and vainglorious? who but we are covetous and greedy of gathering good? We and none but we desire to live long and never to die, are superstitious, careful of our sepulture and burial, yea, and what shall betide us when we are gone. Man's life is most frail of all others, and in least security he liveth: no creature lusteth more after

315

everything than he: none feareth like unto him, and he is more troubled and amazed in his fright: and if he be set once upon anger, none more raging and wood than he. To conclude, all other living creatures live orderly and well, after their own kind: we see them flock and gather together, and ready to make head and stand against all others of a contrary kind: the lions as fell and savage as they be, fight not one with another: serpents sting not serpents, nor bite one another with their venomous teeth: nay the very monsters and huge fishes of the sea, war not amongst themselves in their own kind: but believe me, man at man's hand receiveth most harm and mischief.

Pliny (the Elder), *The Encyclopedia,*
Vol. 7 (Philemon Holland)

ONCE GONE

More life, Lesbia, and more love
(despite their envy).
Suns come and go and come again.
We come and go, and once
gone, we are forever
gone, so
KISS kiss kiss kiss kiss kiss kiss
keep them coming, the going things, the kisses
so none can curse us for them,
for none can count the
kisses kisses kisses kisses kisses.

Catullus, *Songs* 5 (G. W.)

IN DEATH'S SHADOW

No man more blest! O night, not dark for me,
beloved bed, scene of such dear delight!
To lie and talk there in the lamp's soft flickering,
and then to learn ourselves by touch, not sight—
to have her hold me with her breasts uncovered,
or, slipping on her tunic, balk my hand;

to have her kiss my eyes awake and murmur,
Why must you sleep? and make her sweet demand.
Shifting our arms, moving to new embraces,
we kissed a thousand kisses multiplied;
then, with the lamp rekindled, fed our senses
on new delights—the eye is love's best guide.
For Paris himself, they say, seeing Helen naked
on Menelaus' bed, loved at first sight;
Endymion, naked, roused the cold Diana,
naked to lie with her throughout the night.
Put on your tunic if you will, my Cynthia;
these furious hands will rip it into shreds.
You'll have bruised arms to show your mother, sweetheart;
when did frustration ever cool hot heads?
Youth's in those light ripe breasts, not yet gone flabby
as women's do when they have borne a child.
O let us love until we are each other—
we on whom Fate these few swift hours has smiled.
It will not be for long. A night will take us
which must refuse to brighten into dawn.
Strain closer to me, lock me in a nearness
that will not fail when time would have it gone.
Remember doves, how they are one in passion,
yoked, as we are, the male and female one?
Love is a frenzy, and it has no limit;
no love, if it is true, is ever done.
Let earth bear winter fruit and shock the farmer,
or let the sun god drive the steeds of night,
rivers run backward, or the seas be shrivelled,
fish dead in unaccustomed air and light—
these things will chance before I love another.
Living, I'll praise her; dead, dream of no other.

A single year of such nights, should she grant it—
for this I'd give up three-score-and-ten.
If there were many, I would be immortal;
if there were even one, a god again.
Ah, men are fools who do not pass their life so,
limbs languorous and heavy with much wine.
Did they, there'd be no need for swords and warships,

for sailors' bones to steep in Actium's brine;
no need for Rome to break her heart with Romans
die in the shambles of a civil war.
No god was ever outraged by our wine cups—
men can say this for us, if nothing more.
Do not renounce life while its light is in you.
Given all your kisses, still I'd have too few.
See how the withering wreath lets fall its petals
to float within the cup—O Cynthia, you
and I are lovers blest and hopeful, but
who knows what day may see that last door shut?

Propertius, *Elegies* 2.15 (Constance Carrier)

OURSELVES AND ALL THAT'S OURS

As woods whose change appears
Still in their leaves, throughout the sliding years,
The first-born dying, so the aged state
Of words decays, and phrases born but late,
Like tender buds shoot up, and freshly grow.
Ourselves, and all that's ours, to death we owe:
Whether the sea receiv'd into the shore,
That from the north the navy safe doth store,
A kingly work; or that long barren fen
Once rowable, but now doth nourish men
In neighbor towns, and feels the weighty plough;
Or the wild river, who hath changed now
His course, so hurtful both to grain and seeds,
Being taught a better way. All mortal deeds
Shall perish: so far off it is, the state,
Or grace of speech, should hope a lasting date.
Much phrase that now is dead, shall be reviv'd,
And much shall die, that now is nobly liv'd,
If Custom please; at whose disposing will
The power and rule of speaking resteth still.

Horace, *Dramatic Technique* 60-72
(Ben Jonson)

318

SPRING AND DEATH

The snows are fled away, leaves on the shaws
  And grasses in the mead renew their birth,
The river to the river-bed withdraws,
  And altered is the fashion of the earth.

The Nymphs and Graces three put off their fear
  And unapparelled in the woodland play.
The swift hour and the brief prime of the year
  Say to the soul, *Thou wast not born for aye*.

Thaw follows frost; hard on the heel of spring
  Treads summer sure to die, for hard on hers
Comes autumn with his apples scattering;
  Then back to wintertide, when nothing stirs.

But oh, whate'er the sky-led seasons mar,
  Moon upon moon rebuilds it with her beams;
Come *we* where Tullus and where Ancus are
  And good Aeneas, we are dust and dreams.

Torquatus, if the gods in heaven shall add
  The morrow to the day, what tongue has told?
Feast then thy heart, for what thy heart has had
  The fingers of no heir will ever hold.

When thou descendest once the shades among,
  The stern assize and equal judgment o'er,
Not thy long lineage nor thy golden tongue,
  No, nor thy righteousness, shall friend thee more.

Night holds Hippolytus the pure of stain,
  Diana steads him nothing, he must stay;
And Theseus leaves Pirithous in the chain
  The love of comrades cannot take away.

Horace, Songs 4.7 (A. E. Housman)

MUCH IN LITTLE

Dark thy clear glass with old Falernian wine,
  And heat with softest love thy softer bed.

He, that but living half his days, dies such,
Makes his life longer than 'twas given him, much.

Martial, *Epigrams* 8.77, lines 5-8 (Ben Jonson)

ALEXANDER THE GREAT

One world suffic'd not Alexander's mind:
Coop'd up, he seem'd in earth and seas confin'd;
And, struggling, stretch'd his restless limbs about
The narrow globe, to find a passage out.
Yet, enter'd in the brick-built town, he tried
The tomb, and found the strait dimensions wide.

Juvenal, *Satires* 10.168-72 (John Dryden)

YOUTH AND DEATH

Nisus, the guardian of the portal, stood,
Eager to gild his arms with hostile blood;
Well skill'd in fight the quivering lance to wield,
Or pour his arrows through th' embattled field:
From Ida torn, he left his sylvan cave,
And sought a foreign home, a distant grave.
To watch the movements of the Daunian host,
With him Euryalus sustains the post;
No lovelier mien adorn'd the ranks of Troy,
And beardless bloom yet graced the gallant boy;
Though few the seasons of his youthful life,
As yet a novice in the martial strife,
'T was his, with beauty, valour's gifts to share—
A soul heroic, as his form was fair:
These burn with one pure flame of generous love;
In peace, in war, united still they move;
Friendship and glory form their joint reward;
And now combined they hold their nightly guard.

"What god," exclaim'd the first, "instils this fire?
Or, in itself a god, what great desire?

My labouring soul, with anxious thought oppress'd,
Abhors this station of inglorious rest;
The love of fame with this can ill accord,
Be't mine to seek for glory with my sword.
Seest thou yon camp, with torches twinkling dim,
Where drunken slumbers wrap each lazy limb?
Where confidence and ease the watch disdain,
And drowsy Silence holds her sable reign?
Then hear my thought:—In deep and sullen grief
Our troops and leaders mourn their absent chief;
Now could the gifts and promised prize be thine
(The deed, the danger, and the fame be mine),
Were this decreed, beneath yon rising mound,
Methinks, an easy path perchance were found;
Which past, I speed my way to Pallas' walls,
And lead Aeneas from Evander's halls."

With equal ardour fired, and warlike joy,
His glowing friend address'd the Dardan boy:—
"These deeds, my Nisus, shalt thou dare alone?
Must all the fame, the peril, be thine own?
Am I by thee despised, and left afar,
As one unfit to share the toils of war?
Not thus his son the great Opheltes taught;
Not thus my sire in Argive combats fought;
Not thus, when Ilion fell by heavenly hate,
I track'd Aeneas through the walks of fate:
Thou know'st my deeds, my breast devoid of fear,
And hostile life-drops dim my gory spear.
Here is a soul with hope immortal burns,
And life, ignoble life, for *glory* spurns.
Fame, fame is cheaply earn'd by fleeting breath:
The price of honour is the sleep of death."

Then Nisus:—"Calm thy bosom's fond alarms:
Thy heart beats fiercely to the din of arms.
More dear thy worth and valour than my own,
I swear by him who fills Olympus' throne!
So may I triumph, as I speak the truth,
And clasp again the comrade of my youth!

But should I fall,—and he who dares advance
Through hostile legions must abide by chance,—
If some Rutulian arm, with adverse blow,
Should lay the friend who ever loved thee low,
Live thou, such beauties I would fain preserve.
Thy budding years a lengthen'd term deserve.
When humbled in the dust, let some one be,
Whose gentle eyes will shed one tear for me;
Whose manly arm may snatch me back by force,
Or wealth redeem from foes my captive corse;
Or, if my destiny these last deny,
If in the spoiler's power my ashes lie,
Thy pious care may raise a simple tomb,
To mark thy love, and signalize my doom.
Why should thy doting wretched mother weep
Her only boy, reclined in endless sleep?
Who, for thy sake, the tempest's fury dared,
Who, for thy sake, war's deadly peril shared;
Who braved what woman never braved before,
And left her native for the Latian shore."

"In vain you damp the ardour of my soul,"
Replied Euryalus; "it scorns control!
Hence, let us haste!"—their brother guards arose,
Roused by their call, nor court again repose;
The pair, buoy'd up on Hope's exulting wing,
Their stations leave, and speed to seek the king.

Now o'er the earth a solemn stillness ran,
And lull'd alike the cares of brute and man;
Save where the Dardan leaders nightly hold
Alternate converse, and their plans unfold.
On one great point the council are agreed,
An instant message to their prince decreed;
Each lean'd upon the lance he well could wield,
And poised with easy arm his ancient shield;
When Nisus and his friend their leave request
To offer something to their high behest.
With anxious tremors, yet unawed by fear,
The faithful pair before the throne appear:

Iulus greets them; at his kind command,
The elder first address'd the hoary band.

"With patience" (thus Hyrtacides began)
"Attend, nor judge from youth our humble plan.
Where yonder beacons half expiring beam,
Our slumbering foes of future conquest dream,
Nor heed that we a secret path have traced,
Between the ocean and the portal placed.
Beneath the covert of the blackening smoke,
Whose shade securely our design will cloak!
If you, ye chiefs, and fortune will allow,
We'll bend our course to yonder mountain's brow,
Where Pallas' walls at distance meet the sight,
Seen o'er the glade, when not obscured by night:
Then shall Aeneas in his pride return,
When hostile matrons raise their offspring's urn;
And Latian spoils and purpled heaps of dead
Shall mark the havoc of our hero's tread.
Such is our purpose, not unknown the way;
Where yonder torrent's devious waters stray,
Oft have we seen, when hunting by the stream,
The distant spires above the valleys gleam."

Mature in years, for sober wisdom famed,
Moved by the speech, Alethes here exclaim'd,—
"Ye parent gods! who rule the fate of Troy,
Still dwells the Dardan spirit in the boy;
When minds like these in striplings thus ye raise,
Yours is the godlike act, be yours the praise;
In gallant youth, my fainting hopes revive,
And Ilion's wonted glories still survive."
Then in his warm embrace the boys he press'd.
And, quivering, strain'd them to his aged breast;
With tears the burning cheek of each bedew'd,
And, sobbing, thus his first discourse renew'd:
"What gift my countrymen, what martial prize,
Can we bestow, which you may not despise?
Our deities the first best boon have given—
Internal virtues are the gift of Heaven.

What poor rewards can bless your deeds on earth,
Doubtless await such young, exalted worth.
Aeneas and Ascanius shall combine
To yield applause far, far surpassing mine."

Iulus then:—"By all the powers above!
By those Penates who my country love!
By hoary Vesta's sacred fane, I swear,
My hopes are all in you, ye generous pair!
Restore my father to my grateful sight,
And all my sorrows yield to one delight.
Nisus! two silver goblets are thine own,
Saved from Arisba's stately domes o'erthrown!
My sire secured them on that fatal day,
Nor left such bowls an Argive robber's prey:
Two massy tripods, also, shall be thine;
Two talents polish'd from the glittering mine;
An ancient cup, which Tyrian Dido gave,
While yet our vessels press'd the Punic wave:
But when the hostile chiefs at length bow down,
When great Aeneas wears Hesperia's crown,
The casque, the buckler, and the fiery steed
Which Turnus guides with more than mortal speed,
Are thine; no envious lot shall then be cast,
I pledge my word, irrevocably past:
Nay more, twelve slaves, and twice six captive dames,
To soothe thy softer hours with amorous flames,
And all the realms which now the Latins sway,
The labours of to-night shall well repay.
But thou, my generous youth, whose tender years
Are near my own, whose worth my heart reveres,
Henceforth affection, sweetly thus begun,
Shall join our bosoms and our souls in one;
Without thy aid, no glory shall be mine;
Without thy dear advice, no great design;
Alike through life esteem'd, thou godlike boy,
In war my bulwark, and in peace my joy."

To him Euryalus:—"No day shall shame
The rising glories which form this I claim.

324

Fortune may favour, or the skies may frown,
But valour, spite of fate, obtains renown.
Yet, ere from hence our eager steps depart,
One boon I beg, the nearest to my heart:
My mother, sprung from Priam's royal line,
Like thine ennobled, hardly less divine,
Nor Troy nor king Acestes' realms restrain
Her feeble age from dangers of the main:
Alone she came, all selfish fears above,
A bright example of maternal love.
Unknown the secret enterprise I brave,
Lest grief should bend my parent to the grave;
From this alone no fond adieus I seek,
No fainting mother's lips have press'd my cheek;
By gloomy night and thy right hand I vow
Her parting tears would shake my purpose now:
Do thou, my prince, her failing age sustain,
In thee her much-loved child may live again;
Her dying hours with pious conduct bless,
Assist her wants, relieve her fond distress:
So dear a hope must all my soul inflame,
To rise in glory, or to fall in fame."
Struck with a filial care so deeply felt,
In tears at once the Trojan warriors melt;
Faster than all, Iulus' eyes o'erflow!
Such love was his, and such had been his woe.
"All thou hast ask'd, receive," the prince replied;
"Nor this alone, but many a gift beside.
To cheer thy mother's years shall be my aim,
Creusa's style but wanting to the dame.
Fortune an adverse wayward course may run,
But bless'd thy mother in so dear a son.
Now, by my life!—my sire's most sacred oath—
To thee I pledge my full, my firmest troth,
All the rewards which once to thee were vow'd,
If thou shouldst fall, on her shall be bestow'd."
Thus spoke the weeping prince, then forth to view
A gleaming falchion from the sheath he drew;

Lycaon's utmost skill had graced the steel,
For friends to envy and for foes to feel:
A tawny hide, the Moorish lion's spoil,
Slain midst the forest, in the hunter's toil,
Mnestheus to guard the elder youth bestows,
And old Alethes' casque defends his brows.
Arm'd, thence they go, while all th' assembled train,
To aid their cause, implore the gods in vain.
More than a boy, in wisdom and in grace,
Iulus holds amidst the chiefs his place:
His prayer he sends; but what can prayers avail,
Lost in the murmurs of the sighing gale?

The trench is pass'd, and, favour'd by the night,
Through sleeping foes they wheel their wary flight.
When shall the sleep of many a foe be o'er?
Alas! some slumber who shall wake no more!
Chariots and bridles, mix'd with arms, are seen;
And flowing flasks, and scatter'd troops between:
Bacchus and Mars to rule the camp combine;
A mingled chaos this of war and wine.
"Now," cries the first, "for deeds of blood prepare,
With me the conquest and the labour share:
Here lies our path; lest any hand arise,
Watch thou, while many a dreaming chieftain dies:
I'll carve our passage through the heedless foe,
And clear thy road with many a deadly blow."
His whispering accents then the youth repress'd,
And pierced proud Rhamnes through his panting breast:
Stretch'd at his ease, th' incautious king reposed;
Debauch, and not fatigue, his eyes had closed:
To Turnus dear, a prophet and a prince,
His omens more than augur's skill evince;
But he, who thus foretold the fate of all,
Could not avert his own untimely fall.
Next Remus' armour-bearer, hapless, fell,
And three unhappy slaves the carnage swell;
The charioteer along his courser's sides
Expires, the steel his sever'd neck divides;
And, last, his lord is number'd with the dead:

Bounding convulsive, flies the gasping head;
From the swoll'n veins the blackening torrents pour;
Stain'd is the couch and earth with clotting gore.
Young Lamyrus and Lamus next expire,
And gay Serranus fill'd with youthful fire;
Half the long night in childish games was pass'd;
Lull'd by the potent grape, he slept at last:
Ah! happier far had he the morn survey'd,
And till Aurora's dawn his skill display'd.

In slaughter'd fold, the keepers lost in sleep,
His hungry fangs a lion thus may steep;
'Mid the sad flock, at dead of night he prowls,
With murder glutted, and in carnage rolls:
Insatiate still, through teeming herds he roams;
In seas of gore the lordly tyrant foams.

Nor less the other's deadly vengeance came,
But falls on feeble crowds without a name;
His wound unconscious Fadus scarce can feel,
Yet wakeful Rhaesus sees the threatening steel;
His coward breast behind a jar he hides,
And vainly in the weak defence confides;
Full in his heart, the falchion search'd his veins,
The reeking weapon bears alternate stains;
Through wine and blood, commingling as they flow,
One feeble spirit seeks the shades below.
Now where Messapus dwelt they bend their way,
Whose fires emit a faint and trembling ray;
There, unconfined, behold each grazing steed,
Unwatch'd, unheeded, on the herbage feed:
Brave Nisus here arrests his comrade's arm,
Too flush'd with carnage, and with conquest warm:
"Hence let us haste, the dangerous path is pass'd;
Full foes enough to-night have breathed their last:
Soon will the day those eastern clouds adorn;
Now let us speed, nor tempt the rising morn."

What silver arms, with various art emboss'd,
What bowls and mantles in confusion toss'd,
They leave regardless! yet one glittering prize

327

Attracts the younger hero's wandering eyes;
The gilded harness Rhamnes' coursers felt,
The gems which stud the monarch's golden belt:
This from the pallid corse was quickly torn,
Once by a line of former chieftains worn.
Th' exulting boy the studded girdle wears,
Messapus' helm his head in triumph bears;
Then from the tents their cautious steps they bend,
To seek the vale where safer paths extend.

Just at this hour, a band of Latian horse
To Turnus' camp pursue their destined course:
While the slow foot their tardy march delay,
The knights, impatient, spur along the way:
Three hundred mail-clad men, by Volscens led,
To Turnus with their master's promise sped:
Now they approach the trench, and view the walls,
When, on the left, a light reflection falls;
The plunder'd helmet, through the waning night,
Sheds forth a silver radiance, glancing bright.
Volscens with question loud the pair alarms:—
"Stand, stragglers! stand! why early thus in arms?
From whence? To whom?" —He meets with no reply;
Trusting the covert of the night, they fly:
The thicket's depth with hurried pace they tread,
While round the wood the hostile squadron spread.

With brakes entangled, scarce a path between,
Dreary and dark appears the sylvan scene:
Euryalus his heavy spoils impede,
The boughs and winding turns his steps mislead;
But Nisus scours along the forest's maze
To where Latinus' steeds in safety graze,
Then backward o'er the plain his eyes extend,
On every side they seek his absent friend.
"O God! my boy," he cries, "of me bereft,
In what impending perils art thou left!"
Listening he runs—above the waving trees,
Tumultuous voices swell the passing breeze;
The war-cry rises, thundering hoofs around

Wake the dark echoes of the trembling ground.
Again he turns, of footsteps hears the noise;
The sound elates, the sight his hope destroys:
The hapless boy a ruffian train surround,
While lengthening shades his weary way confound;
Him with loud shouts the furious knights pursue,
Struggling in vain, a captive to the crew.
What can his friend 'gainst thronging numbers dare?
Ah! must he rush his comrade's fate to share?
What force, what aid, what stratagem essay,
Back to redeem the Latian spoiler's prey?
His life a votive ransom nobly give,
Or die with him for whom he wish'd to live?
Poising with strength his lifted lance on high,
On Luna's orb he cast his frenzied eye:—
"Goddess serene, transcending every star!
Queen of the sky, whose beams are seen afar!
By night heaven owns thy sway, by day the grove,
When, as chaste Dian, here thou deign'st to rove;
If e'er myself, or sire, have sought to grace
Thine altars with the produce of the chase,
Speed, speed my dart to pierce yon vaunting crowd,
To free my friend, and scatter far the proud."
Thus having said, the hissing dart he flung;
Through parted shades the hurtling weapon sung;
The thirsty point in Sulmo's entrails lay,
Transfix'd his heart, and stretch'd him on the clay:
He sobs, he dies,—the troop in wild amaze,
Unconscious whence the death, with horror gaze.
While pale they stare, through Tagus' temples riven,
A second shaft with equal force is driven:
Fierce Volscens rolls around his lowering eyes;
Veil'd by the night, secure the Trojan lies.
Burning with wrath, he view'd his soldiers fall.
"Thou youth accurst, thy life shall pay for all!"
Quick from the sheath his flaming glaive he drew,
And raging, on the boy defenceless flew.
Nisus no more the blackening shade conceals,
Forth, forth he starts, and all his love reveals;

Aghast, confused, his fears to madness rise,
And pour these accents, shrieking as he flies:
"Me, me,—your vengeance hurl on me alone;
Here sheathe the steel, my blood is all your own.
Ye starry spheres! thou conscious Heaven! attest!
He could not—durst not—lo! the guile confest!
All, all was mine,—his early fate suspend;
He only loved too well his hapless friend:
Spare, spare, ye chiefs! from him your rage remove;
His fault was friendship, all his crime was love."
He pray'd in vain; the dark assassin's sword
Pierced the fair side, the snowy bosom gored;
Lowly to earth inclines his plume-clad crest,
And sanguine torrents mantle o'er his breast:
As some young rose, whose blossom scents the air,
Languid in death, expires beneath the share;
Or crimson poppy, sinking with the shower,
Declining gently, falls a fading flower;
Thus, sweetly drooping, bends his lovely head,
And lingering beauty hovers round the dead.

But fiery Nisus stems the battle's tide,
Revenge his leader, and despair his guide;
Volscens he seeks amidst the gathering host,
Volscens must soon appease his comrade's ghost;
Steel, flashing, pours on steel, foe crowds on foe;
Rage nerves his arm, fate gleams in every blow;
In vain beneath unnumber'd wounds he bleeds,
Nor wounds, nor death, distracted Nisus heeds;
In viewless circles wheel'd, his falchion flies,
Nor quits the hero's grasp till Volscens dies;
Deep in his throat its end the weapon found,
The tyrant's soul fled groaning through the wound.
Thus Nisus all his fond affection proved—
Dying, revenged the fate of him he loved;
Then on his bosom sought his wonted place,
And death was heavenly in his friend's embrace!

Celestial pair! if aught my verse can claim,
Wafted on Time's broad pinion, yours is fame!

Ages on ages shall your fate admire,
No future day shall see your names expire,
While stands the Capitol, immortal dome!
And vanquish'd millions hail their empress, Rome!

Vergil, *The Song of Aeneas*
9.176-449 (George Gordon Byron)

SLAIN INNOCENTS

To Stygian havens go, Ye-of-shade-and-night!
Go, hurtless souls, whom mischief hath oppress'd—
Ev'n in first porch of life-but-lately-had—
And father's fury. Go, unhappy kind!
O little children, by the way (full sad)
Of journey knowen
Go! See the angry kings!

Seneca, *Mad Hercules* 1131-37
(Jasper Heywood)

MOMENTARY

Not faster in the summer's ray
The spring's frail beauty fades away,
Than anguish and decay consume
The smiling virgin's rosy bloom.
Some beauty's snatch'd each day, each hour;
For beauty is a fleeting flower:
Then how can wisdom e'er confide
In beauty's momentary pride?

Seneca, *Hippolytus* 761-71 (Samuel Johnson)

BRIGHT DIMINUTION

All that parental nature labored forth,
however firm, gives way
brittled by time, used to uselessness

331

with each innumerable touch.

Old rivers eat new ways,
the linear insistent stream frays out
(earth raveling along its sides).

Rough cliffs are smoothed
with brushings of the waterfall.

The plough is slimmer
by each furrow curled.

The rich man's ring
is brilliantly rubbed
away.

Sulpicious Lupercus Servasius (G. W.)

ALL IS TO THEE INCLINED

This wand'ring heap in wide lands far away
Shall go to ghosts; and all shall give their sails
To slow Cocytus. All is to thee 'nclined,
Both what the fall and rise of sun doth see.
Spare us that come! To thee we, Death, are 'signed!
Though *thou* be slow, *ourselves* yet haste do we!

Seneca, *Mad Hercules* 868-73 (Jasper Heywood)

WHY BREAK THE HEART
WITH STARS?

Don't ask don't, Lucy, don't
Ask it isn't right to
Know the gods' good time.
Don't play Babylonian numbers.
Sit still for however snows many
    (This may be the last now that sponges
    Tyrrhenian sea rocks with . . .)
                     maybe
God gives you.

Think a minute
(Have another?)

Long wasting hopes
Short lives shorten.
White time falls as our lips speak.
Today : take it : hoping brings few tomorrows.

> Horace, *Songs* 1.11
> (Nicholas Kilmer)

TANTALUS

But then each branch his plenteous riches all
lets lower down; and apples from on high
with lither leaves they flatter like to fall,
and famine stir . . .

> Seneca, *Thyestes* 162-65
> (Jasper Heywood)

THE LAW OF MUTABILITY

This let me further add, that Nature knows
No steadfast station, but or ebbs or flows:
Ever in motion; she destroys her old,
And casts new figures in another mold.
Ev'n times are in perpetual flux, and run,
Like rivers from their fountain, rolling on;
For time, no more than streams, is at a stay:
The flying hour is ever on her way;
And, as the fountain still supplies her store,
(The wave behind impels the wave before,)
Thus in successive course the minutes run,
And urge their predecessor minutes on,
Still moving, ever new: for former things
Are set aside, like abdicated kings;
And every moment alters what is done,
And innovates some act till then unknown.

"Nor those, which elements we call, abide,
Nor to this figure, nor to that, are tied;
For this eternal world is said of old
But four prolific principles to hold,
Four different bodies; two to heaven ascend,
And other two down to the center tend.
Fire, first, with wings expanded mounts on high,
Pure, void of weight, and dwells in upper sky;
Then Air, because unclogg'd in empty space,
Flies after Fire, and claims the second place;
But weighty Water, as her nature guides,
Lies on the lap of Earth, and Mother Earth subsides.
　　"All things are mix'd of these, which all contain,
And into these are all resolv'd again:
Earth rarefies to Dew; expanded more,
The subtile Dew in Air begins to soar;
Spreads as she flies, and weary of her name
Extenuates still, and changes into Flame.
Thus having by degrees perfection won,
Restless they soon untwist the web they spun,
And Fire begins to lose her radiant hue,
Mix'd with gross Air, and Air descends to Dew;
And Dew, condensing, does her form forego,
And sinks, a heavy lump of Earth, below.
　　"Thus are their figures never at a stand,
But chang'd by Nature's innovating hand;
All things are alter'd, nothing is destroy'd,
The shifted scene for some new show employ'd."

Ovid, *Transformations* 15.177-85, 237-55
(John Dryden)

ONE MORE SPRING

Winter to Spring: the west wind melts the frozen rancour,
　The windlass drags to sea the thirsty hull;
Byre is no longer welcome to beast or fire to ploughman,
　The field removes the frost-cap from his skull.

Venus of Cythera leads the dances under the hanging
  Moon and the linked line of Nymphs and Graces
Beat the ground with measured feet while the busy Fire god
  Stokes his red-hot mills in volcanic places.

Now is the time to twine the spruce and shining head with
    myrtle,
  Now with flowers escaped the earthy fetter,
And sacrifice to the woodland god in shady copses
  A lamb or a kid, whichever he likes better.

Equally heavy is the heel of white-faced Death on the pauper's
  Shack and the towers of kings, and O my dear
The little sum of life forbids the ravelling of lengthy
  Hopes. Night and the fabled dead are near

And the narrow house of nothing past whose lintel
  You will meet no wine like this, no boy to admire
Like Lycidas who to-day makes all young men a furnace
  And whom tomorrow girls will find a fire.

                    Horace, *Songs* 1.4 (Louis MacNeice)

THE TORTURE OF LUST

Thus, therefore, he who feels the fiery dart
Of strong desire transfix his amorous heart,
(Whether some beauteous boy's alluring face—
Or lovelier maid, with unresisted grace,
From her each part—the winged arrow sends),
From whence he first was struck he thither tends;
Restless he roams, impatient to be freed,
And eager to inject the sprightly seed;
For fierce desire does all his mind employ,
And ardent love assures approaching joy.
Such is the nature of that pleasing smart,
Whose burning drops distil upon the heart
The fever of the soul shot from the fair,
And the cold ague of succeeding care.
If absent, her *idea* still appears,

335

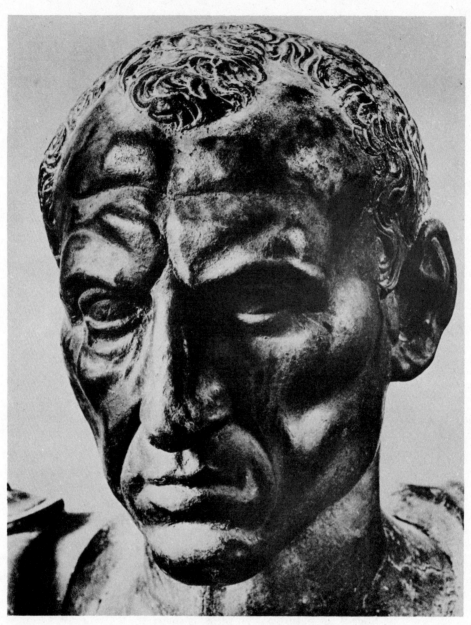

31. Bronze portrait. Rome, Museo Nazionale.

. . . idealism and cruelty the lunar light
and dark of the Roman mind . . .

And her sweet name is chiming in your ears.
But strive those pleasing phantoms to remove,
And shun th' aërial images of love
That feed the flame: when one molests thy mind,
Discharge thy loins on all the leaky kind;
For that's a wiser way than to restrain
Within thy swelling nerves that hoard of pain.
For every hour some deadlier symptom shows,
And by delay the gath'ring venom grows,
When kindly applications are not us'd:
The viper Love must *on* the wound be bruis'd.
On that one object 't is not safe to stay,
But force the tide of thought some other way;
The squander'd spirits prodigally throw,
And in the common glebe of nature sow.
Nor wants he all the bliss that lovers feign,
Who takes the pleasure and avoids the pain;
For purer joys in purer health abound,
And less affect the sickly than the sound.

When love its utmost vigor does employ,
Ev'n then 't is but a restless wand'ring joy;
Nor knows the lover in that wild excess,
With hands or eyes, what first he would possess,
But strains at all, and, fast'ning where he strains,
Too closely presses with his frantic pains.
With biting kisses hurts the twining fair,
Which shows his joys imperfect, unsincere;
For, stung with inward rage, he flings around,
And strives t' avenge the smart on that which gave the wound.
But love those eager bitings does restrain,
And mingling pleasure mollifies the pain.
For ardent hope still flatters anxious grief,
And sends him to his foe to seek relief:
Which yet the nature of the thing denies;
For love, and love alone of all our joys,
By full possession does but fan the fire,
The more we still enjoy, the more we still desire.
Nature for meat and drink provides a space,
And, when received, they fill their certain place;
Hence thirst and hunger may be satisfied.

But this repletion is to love denied:
Form, feature, color, whatsoe'er delight
Provokes the lover's endless appetite,
These fill no space, nor can we thence remove
With lips, or hands, or all our instruments of love;
In our deluded grasp we nothing find
But thin aërial shapes that fleet before the mind.
As he who, in a dream, with drought is curst
And finds no reàl drink to quench his thirst,
Runs to imagin'd lakes his heat to steep,
And vainly swills and labors in his sleep,
So love with phantoms cheats our longing eyes,
Which hourly seeing never satisfies:
Our hands pull nothing from the parts they strain,
But wander o'er the lovely limbs in vain.
Nor when the youthful pair more closely join,
When hands in hands they lock, and thighs in thighs they
        twine,
Just in the raging foam of full desire,
When both press on, both murmur, both expire,
They grip, they squeeze, their humid tongues they dart,
As each would force their way to th' others heart:
In vain; they only cruise about the coast;
For bodies cannot pierce, nor be in bodies lost
As, sure, they strive to be when both engage
In that tumultuous momentary rage;
So 'tangled in the nets of love they lie,
Till man dissolves in that excess of joy.
Then, when the gather'd bag has burst its way,
And ebbing tides the slacken'd nerves betray,
A pause ensues; and nature nods awhile,
Till with recruited rage new spirits boil;
And then the same vain violence returns,
With flames renew'd th' erected furnace burns;
Again they in each other would be lost,
But still by adamantine bars are cross'd.
All ways they try, successless all they prove,
To cure the secret sore of ling'ring love.

Lucretius, *On Reality* 4.1052-1120 (John Dryden)

338

ODI ET AMO

I

Of course I hate what I love, and can't explain,
for how is one to syllogize his pain?

Catullus, *Songs* 85 (G. W.)

I I

Now love and hate my light breast each way move,
But victory, I think, will hap to love.
I'll hate, if I can; if not, love 'gainst my will:
Bulls hate the yoke, yet what they hate have still.
I fly her lust, but follow beauty's creature;
I loathe her manners, love her body's feature.
Nor with thee, nor without thee, can I live,
And doubt to which desire the palm to give.
Or less fair, or less lewd, would thou might'st be!
Beauty with lewdness doth right ill agree.
Her deeds gain hate, her face entreateth love:
Ah, she doth more worth than her vices prove!
Spare me, oh by our fellow bed, by all
The gods who by thee to be perjur'd fall,
And by thy face, to me a power divine,
And by thine eyes whose radiance burns out mine!
Whate'er thou art, mine art thou: choose this course—
With me willing, or to love by force?
Rather I'll hoist up sail and use the wind,
That I may love yet, though against my mind.

Ovid, *Love Affairs* 3.11,
lines 33-52 (Christopher Marlowe)

NO ESCAPE

Escape! There is, O Idiot, no escape,
Flee if you like into Tanais,

339

desire will follow you thither,
Though you heave into the air upon the gilded Pegasean back,
Though you had the feathery sandals of Perseus
To lift you up through split air,
The high tracks of Hermes would not afford you shelter.

Amor stands upon you, Love drives upon lovers,
a heavy mass on free necks.

Propertius, *Elegies* 2.30, lines 1-8 (Ezra Pound)

THROUGH NIGHT'S STREETS

I

Last night I wandered drunk along the roadways,
and with no slave to catch me if I fell—
when small boys swarmed around me. I was frightened,
too frightened to count them—why, I cannot tell.
Some carried little torches, some had arrows,
and some had fetters ready for the limb,
and all were naked. One, more arrogant, shouted,
"Now seize him! We have all been warned of him—
he is the one that woman was denouncing"—
and then a rope circled this neck of mine
and my tormentors closed in, with one yelling,
"Death to the man who says we're not divine!
You don't deserve it, but she's waited for you,
while you, you fool, sought for another's door.
Her hair escapes the purple ribbon that binds it,
her eyes, sleep-heavy, search for you once more.
She lies in all the fragrance of Arabia,
or in the greater fragrance made by love.
Spare him, now, brothers! he has given his promise;
we'll take him to the house we're guardians of,
and give him over into her safekeeping.
Henceforth stay home when all sane folk are sleeping."

Propertius, *Elegies* 2.29 (Constance Carrier)

II

The day's noise was draining away in my mind
            and the light from behind my eyes
when savage Cypris grabbed a handful of my hair
        and yanked me up
        and gave me hell, so:
        "You, my creature, my cocksman, my gash-hound,
        you I catch sleeping alone?
                    Get on with it!"
So I leap up and barefoot, bathrobe flapping,
I rush down every alley in town
                and reach the end of none.
Like a man chasing a bus, running one minute,
        the next ashamed to run,
afraid to go home,
        terrified of looking silly
                standing here like this
                in the middle of an empty street
                hearing not one human voice
                not a sound but an occasional backfire
                    not so much as a dog.
Am I the only man in the city without a bed of my own?
Have I no option, hard goddess, but your imperium?

                    Petronius, *Songs* 99 (Tim Reynolds)

PRAYING FOR RELEASE

I

it's true isn't it
when people think back on the good things they've done
there's pleasure in it
            (you did what was right
            you kept your word
            you never took god's name in vain
            in order to cheat your fellow man)

341

then you've got lots to look forward to,
Catullus, in life's long years ahead
it was a love that knew no gratitude
but out of it great joy will come to you
for whatever, kindly, men to any man can say
or do, you said, you did
and all to a thankless heart entrusted died
why why then longer cut and lash yourself
in heart be hard, from where you are come back
the gods say no? well stop it anyway
its hard long suddenly love to lay aside
its hard but do it any way you will
this only health, this win, win on, win through
do this if this you can't, if this you can

> god if you know mercy
> if to any ever
> at the final door of death
> you've given the strength that saved
> me wretched look upon
> and if my life was good
> let this sickness pass
> this death let pass from me

down, under, down, the creeping numbness dulls
outdriven out of all my soul delight
I ask no longer that she love me too
or (anyway she can't) that she be pure
for my own health I hope and to lay down
the burden of this filthy foul disease

> god dear god grant me this
> for I was loyal ever

Catullus, *Songs* 76 (Frank O. Copley)

II

Miserable Catullus, stop being foolish
And admit it's over,
The sun shone on you those days
When your girl had you

When you gave it to her
        like nobody else ever will.
Everywhere together then, always at it
And you liked it and she can't say
        she didn't.
Yes, those days glowed.
Now she doesn't want it: why
        should you, washed out,
Want to? Don't trail her,
Don't eat yourself up alive,
Show some spunk, stand up
        and take it.
So long, girl. Catullus
        can take it.
He won't bother you, he won't
        he bothered:
But you'll be, nights.
What do you want to live for?
Whom will you see?
Who'll say you're pretty?
Who'll give it to you now?
Whose name will you have?
Kiss what guy? bite whose
    lips?
Come on, Catullus, you can
        take it.

Catullus, *Songs* 8 (Louis Zukofsky)

III

look down down
if you want to find my heart, Lesbia.
you brought it down
it killed itself trying to do
what hearts are supposed to do
now it couldn't love you
if you were virtue in person
nor cease to want you
if you did everything

Catullus, *Songs* 75 (Frank O. Copley)

JEALOUSY

My heart goes black and burning, Lydia Tom's
Pink neck and flexing arms praising. That
My mind and mood will not take sitting down.

Strange . . . there's a tear falling. The supple flames
Take me that way. No, you'll tear me open
There with your white bright drifting shoulders marked

With burly wine-pulled fingers, and your lips
Battered and scarred by your new gnashing boy.
Do you think—Child, listen to me—this bully

Will crush your sweet mouth forever? Happy
Three times and more whose bond unbroken holds nor parts
No quarrelled word until: love's last day breaks.

Horace, *Songs* 1.13 (Nicholas Kilmer)

LOST

Furius and Aurelius, Catullus's comrades,
Whether he penetrate the ultimate Indies,
Where the rolling surf on the shores of Morning
    Beats and again beats,
Or in the land of Bedouin, the soft Arabs,
Or Parthians, the ungentlemanly archers,
Or where the Nile with seven similar streamlets
    Colors the clear sea;
Or if he cross the loftier Alpine passes
And view the monuments of almighty Caesar—
The Rhine, and France, and even those remotest
    Shuddersome British—
Friends, prepared for all of these, whatever
Province the celestial ones may wish me,
Take a little bulletin to my girl friend,
    Brief but not dulcet:
Let her live and thrive with her fornicators,
Of whom she hugs three hundred in an evening,
With no true love for any, leaving them broken-

Winded the same way.
She need not look, as once she did, for my love.
By her own fault it died, like a tumbling flower
At the field's edge, after the passing harrow
Clipped it and left it.

Catullus, *Songs* 11 (Robert Fitzgerald)

MOTIVATION

Not that I trust you,
but I trusted you with her
(whom I had lost).

Not that we were friends,
not from respect for you,
but from the fact that she
I longed for
was no sister to you,
not your mother;
to take her were a sin
out of your class.
I forgot, your class
is omnivorous,
and I was *almost* a friend,
which was reason enough
for you.

Catullus, *Songs* 91 (G. W.)

DESPOTISM

At last [Sextus] was able to feel that he had the town, as it were, in his
pocket, and was ready for anything. Accordingly he sent a confidential
messenger to Rome, to ask his father what step he should next take, his
power in Gabii being, by God's grace, by this time absolute. Tarquin, I
suppose, was not sure of the messenger's good faith: in any case, he said
not a word in reply to his question, but with a thoughtful air went out
into the garden. The man followed him, and Tarquin, strolling up and

down in silence, began knocking off poppy-heads with his stick. The messenger at last wearied of putting his question and waiting for the reply, so he returned to Gabii supposing his mission to have failed. He told Sextus what he had said and what he had seen his father do: the king, he declared, whether from anger, or hatred, or natural arrogance, had not uttered a single word. Sextus realized that though his father had not spoken, he had, by his action, indirectly expressed his meaning clearly enough; so he proceeded at once to act upon his murderous instructions. All the influential men in Gabii were got rid of—some being brought to public trial, others executed for no better reason than that they were generally disliked. Many were openly put to death; some, against whom any charge would be inconvenient to attempt to prove, were secretly assassinated. A few were either allowed, or forced, to leave the country, and their property was confiscated as in the case of those who had been executed. The confiscations enriched the more fortunate —those, namely, to whom Sextus chose to be generous—with the result that in the sweetness of personal gain public calamity was forgotten, until at long last the whole community, such as it now remained, with none to advise or help it, passed without a struggle into Tarquin's hands.

Livy, *Rome from Its Foundation* 1.54 (Aubrey de Sélincourt)

THE ART OF SURVIVAL
UNDER TYRANTS

At this juncture, when everyone else was untruthfully disclaiming friendship with Sejanus, a gentleman outside the senate called Marcus Terentius bravely accepted the imputation. "In my position," he observed to the senate, "it might do me more good to deny the accusation than to admit it. And yet, whatever the results, I will confess that I was Sejanus' friend: I sought his friendship, and was glad to secure it. I had seen him as a joint-commander of the Guard with his father. Then I saw him conducting the civil as well as the military administration. His kinsmen, his relations by marriage, gained office. Sejanus' ill-will meant danger and pleas for mercy. I give no examples. At my own peril only, I speak for all who took no part in his final plans. For we honoured, not Sejanus of Vulsinii, but the member of the Claudian and

346

Julian houses into which his marriage alliances had admitted him—your son-in-law, Tiberius, your partner in the consulship, your representative in State affairs.

"It is not for us to comment on the man whom you elevate above others, and on your reasons. The gods have given you supreme control —to us is left the glory of obeying! Besides, we only see what is before our eyes: the man to whom you have given wealth, power, the greatest potentialities for good and evil—and nobody will deny that Sejanus had these. Research into the emperor's hidden thoughts and secret designs is forbidden, hazardous, and not necessarily informative. Think, senators, not of Sejanus' last day, but of the previous sixteen years. We revered even Satrius Secundus and Pomponius. We thought it grand even if Sejanus' ex-slaves and door-keepers knew us. You will ask if this defence is to be valid for all, without discrimination. Certainly not. But draw a fair dividing-line! Punish plots against the State and the emperor's life. But, as regards friendship and its obligations, if we sever them at the same time as you do, Tiberius, that should excuse us as it·excuses you." This courageous utterance, publicly reflecting everyone's private thoughts, proved so effective that it earned Terentius' accusers, with their criminal records, banishment and execution.

.　　. .　　.

The reputation of Caratacus had spread beyond the islands and through the neighbouring provinces to Italy itself. These people were curious to see the man who had defied our power for so many years. Even at Rome his name meant something. Besides, the emperor's attempts to glorify himself conferred additional glory on Caratacus in defeat. For the people were summoned as though for a fine spectacle, while the Guard stood in arms on the parade ground before their camp. Then there was a march past, with Caratacus' petty vassals, and the decorations and neck-chains and spoils of his foreign wars. Next were displayed his brothers, wife, and daughter. Last came the king himself. The others, frightened, degraded themselves by entreaties. But there were no downcast looks or appeals for mercy from Caratacus. On reaching the dais he spoke in these terms.

"Had my lineage and rank been accompanied by only moderate success, I should have come to this city as friend rather than prisoner, and you would not have disdained to ally yourself peacefully with one so

347

nobly born, the ruler of so many nations. As it is, humiliation is my lot, glory yours. I had horses, men, arms, wealth. Are you surprised I am sorry to lose them? If you want to rule the world, does it follow that everyone else welcomes enslavement? If I had surrendered without a blow before being brought before you, neither my downfall nor your triumph would have become famous. If you execute me, they will be forgotten. Spare me, and I shall be an everlasting token of your mercy!"

Claudius responded by pardoning him and his wife and brothers.

Tacitus, *Annals* 6.8-9, 12.36-37 (Michael Grant)

FEMALE AUDACITY

I

On Ceres' feast, restrain'd from their delight,
Few matrons, there, but curse the tedious night;
Few whom their fathers dare salute, such lust
Their kisses have, and come with such a gust.
With ivy now adorn thy doors, and wed;
Such is thy bride, and such thy genial bed.
Think'st thou one man is for one woman meant?
She, sooner, with one eye would be content.
    And yet, 't is nois'd, a maid did once appear
In some small village, tho' fame says not where:
'T is possible; but sure no man she found;
'T was desart, all, about her father's ground:
And yet some lustful god might there make bold;
Are Jove and Mars grown impotent and old?
Many a fair nymph has in a cave been spread,
And much good love without a feather bed.
Whither wouldst thou to choose a wife resort,
The Park, the Mall, the Playhouse, or the Court?
Which way soever thy adventures fall,
Secure alike of chastity in all.
    One sees a dancing master cap'ring high,
And raves, and pisses, with pure ecstasy;

348

Another does with all his motions move,
And gapes, and grins, as in the feat of love;
A third is charm'd with the new opera notes,
Admires the song, but on the singer dotes:
The country lady in the box appears,
Softly she warbles over all she hears;
And sucks in passion, both at eyes and ears.
    The rest, (when now the long vacation's come,
The noisy hall and theaters grown dumb,)
Their memories to refresh, and cheer their hearts,
In borrow'd breeches act the players' parts.
The poor, that scarce have wherewithal to eat,
Will pinch, to make the singing-boy a treat:
The rich, to buy him, will refuse no price;
And stretch his quail-pipe, till they crack his voice.
Tragedians, acting love, for lust are sought:
(Tho' but the parrots of a poet's thought.)
The pleading lawyer, tho' for counsel us'd,
In chamber practice often is refus'd.
Still thou wilt have a wife, and father heirs;
(The product of concurring theaters.)
Perhaps a fencer did thy brows adorn,
And a young swordman to thy lands is born.
    Thus Hippia loath'd her old patrician lord,
And left him for a brother of the sword:
To wond'ring Pharos with her love she fled,
To shew one monster more than Afric bred:
Forgetting house and husband, left behind,
Ev'n children too; she sails before the wind;
False to 'em all, but constant to her kind.
But, stranger yet, and harder to conceive,
She could the playhouse and the players leave.
Born of rich parentage, and nicely bred,
She lodg'd on down, and in a damask bed;
Yet daring now the dangers of the deep,
On a hard mattress is content to sleep.
Ere this, 't is true, she did her fame expose:
But that, great ladies with great ease can lose.
The tender nymph could the rude ocean bear:

349

So much her lust was stronger than her fear.
But, had some honest cause her passage press'd,
The smallest hardship had disturb'd her breast:
Each inconvenience makes their virtue cold;
But womankind, in ills, is ever bold.
Were she to follow her own lord to sea,
What doubts and scruples would she raise to stay?
Her stomach sick, and her head giddy grows;
The tar and pitch are nauseous to her nose.
But in love's voyage nothing can offend;
Women are never seasick with a friend.
Amidst the crew, she walks upon the board;
She eats, she drinks, she handles every cord;
And if she spews, 't is thinking of her lord.

. . .

This was a private crime; but you shall hear
What fruits the sacred brows of monarchs bear:
The good old sluggard but began to snore,
When from his side up rose th' imperial whore:
She who preferr'd the pleasures of the night
To pomps, that are but impotent delight;
Strode from the palace, with an eager pace,
To cope with a more masculine embrace;
Muffled she march'd, like Juno in a cloud,
Of all her train but one poor wench allow'd;
One whom in secret service she could trust,
The rival and companion of her lust.
To the known brothel-house she takes her way;
And for a nasty room gives double pay;
That room in which the rankest harlot lay.
Prepar'd for fight, expectingly she lies,
With heaving breasts, and with desiring eyes:
Still as one drops, another take his place,
And baffled still succeeds to like disgrace.
At length, when friendly darkness is expir'd,
And every strumpet from her cell retir'd,
She lags behind, and, ling'ring at the gate,

With a repining sigh submits to fate:
All filth without, and all a fire within,
Tir'd with the toil, unsated with the sin.
Old Caesar's bed the modest matron seeks;
The steam of lamps still hanging on her cheeks
In ropy smut: thus foul, and thus bedight,
She brings him back the product of the night.

Juvenal, *Satires* 6.50-102, 114-32 (John Dryden)

II

Nor always do they feign the sweets of love,
When round the panting youth their pliant limbs they move,
And cling, and heave, and moisten ev'ry kiss;
They often share, and more than share the bliss.
From every part, ev'n to their inmost soul,
They feel the trickling joys, and run with vigor to the goal.
Stirr'd with the same impetuous desire,
Birds, beasts, and herds, and mares, their males require;
Because the throbbing nature in their veins
Provokes them to assuage their kindly pains.
The lusty leap th' expecting female stands,
By mutual heat compell'd to mutual bands.
Thus dogs with lolling tongues by love are tied,
Nor shouting boys nor blows their union can divide;
At either end they strive the link to loose,
In vain; for stronger Venus holds the noose.
Which never would those wretched lovers do,
But that the common heats of love they know;
The pleasure therefore must be shar'd in common too.

Lucretius, *On Reality* 4.1192-1207 (John Dryden)

THE MERRY WIDOWS

You will find many so-called widows who were never wed, but wear
false mourning to cloak an evil mind; and, unless a big belly under the
cloak or a baby's persistent crying at home betrays them, around they
stroll, heads up, feet fluttering. Some woo sterility, and kill all at once

the unsown seeds of men within them. Others, when they realize their sin has made them pregnant, take abortifacient potions, and often enough poison themselves in the process, earning hell on three counts— for suicide, for adultery (since Christ is the soul's true husband), and for infanticide.

. . .

See how the eunuchs escort their roomy sedan chairs, and rouge covers their puffy cheeks. You would think they were trying to lure a husband, not mourn one. Their house is full of flatterers and hangers-on. Priests, who should carry authority and awe with them, come to kiss the forehead of their patroness, and extend a hand—to bless? No, to pocket a stipend. The patronesses grow more proud at this priestly dependence on them; and since they know that husbands exercise real authority, they prefer a widow's freedom, in which they have the name of chaste nuns, but stuff themselves with every imaginable viand before falling into a slumber to dream of—apostles.

St. Jerome, *Letters* 22.13, 16 (G. W.)

RELIGIOUS CASTRATION

Attis propelled by his swift ship through deep waves, set his
    quick feet upon the Phrygian shore;
entered the heavy sunless forest where his mind grew dark as
    shadows over him
and there, his blood gone mad, seized a sharp stone, divorced
    his vital members from his body,
then rising (the ground wet with blood) he was transformed,
    a woman with her delicate white hands
sounding the tympanum, the tympanum singing praise
    through sacred trumpets raised to goddess Cybele,
    mysterious mother of a sexless race.
Then in his sweet falsetto Attis sang: Now follow me, O priests
    of Cybele, come follow, we are creatures
of this goddess, wind, dance, unwind the dance again, O exiles
    from a far land, come with me
across the rapid salt sea wave. Your bodies shall be clean; no
    more shall Venus

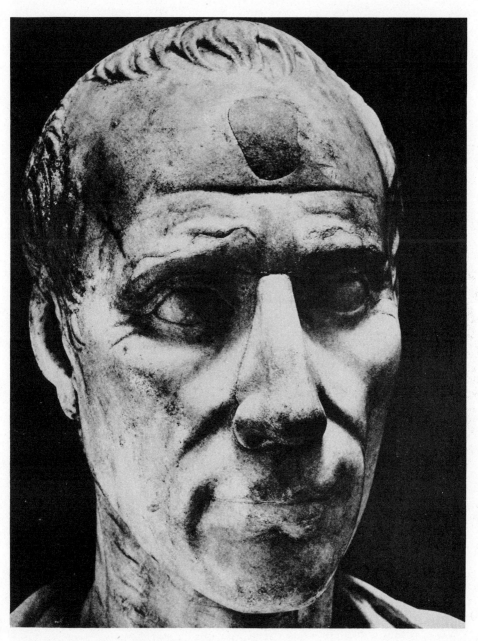

32. Portrait bust. Rome, Museo Vaticano.

The more lifelike and individual these busts become, the more are they death's-heads . . .

stain you with foul disease and move your limbs with power
       of love.
Now under my leadership (this mad delight) land in her rich
       dominions, sing you her praise
make her heart leap with the same joy that rises in your blood
       at this sweet liberty.
No longer wait for her, but come, follow my way that winds
       upward to her temple,
making glad noises with the pipe that plays a song to welcome
       her,
clash cymbals, dance and shake the earth with thunder, your
       quick feet sounding her glory, and like the girls
who follow Bacchus, toss your heads, shout songs in measure
       to the Phrygian pipes, come join her merry
company where drunken cries rise in a chorus. The sacred
       symbol of her worship trembles in air
that moves with noise poured from your lips here in this place
       where the great goddess wanders.

Now Attis (not quite woman) called her followers, leading
       them toward green blooming Ida where
his followers crowded, tongues trembling with shrill noises,
       hollow cymbals crashed and the tympanum rang again,
       again
the race sped forward. Then wavering exhausted, the ghost of
       their very lives issuing
from lips, circling in delirium they followed Attis through the
       green shadows, she who sprang
like a raging heifer freed from harness, till they sank, defeated
       (weariness in their eyes, and starved for lack of food)
       at the high temple of Cybele, their goddess,
then madness declined into a heavy wave of sleep, minds sunk
       in darkness.
But when the sun transformed the skies into a radiant heaven,
       his mighty rolling brilliant eye
disclosing hills, the savage sea all in clear outlines, and there
       was liquid peace within his mind, the horses
of dawn rose galloping, trampling night underfoot, and Attis,
       leaving sweet Pasithea wife of sleep, awoke,
looked back and saw what he had done, how his mad brain

354

deceived him saw how he lost

his manhood—all this in passionless clarity seized his mind,
and with his eyes turned homeward

across the sea, she wept, poor creature, neither man nor
woman.

Land of my birth, creating me, my fatherland I left you (O
miserably, a fugitive)

I have gone into this wilderness of snow to live with beasts
that circle Ida's mountain,

my brain in darkness—and where are you, land of my fathers,
for you have vanished and my eyes return

where you once rose before me. In this short hour while my
brain still welcomes sunlight,

I praise you—now shall I be driven back into this wilderness
where everyone,

my friends, my parents, and all I love shall fade. I shall not
walk again through the city streets, nor join the crowd,

(O glorious young men) who fill the stadium and who excel
in many pleasures.

Look at my misery and hear me cry my curse against this
miserable fate,

I am a woman, hear my voice and look at me who once walked
bravely hero of games, a boy who stood

rich flower of youth equal to all who challenged him. All
these were mine: friends crowding at my door,

wreaths of sweet flowers in my room when morning sun called
me away, and a welcome threshold that I left

behind me. Witness me, a girl, a slave of Cybele, dressed like
a girlish follower of Bacchus,

half my soul destroyed, and sterile I must live on this cold
mountain

and like all others in snow-bound Ida's province, follow the
deer and wild boar—a man undone,

longing for home again. And as these words flowed from her
glowing lips a prayer rose to the gods,

Cybele released her lions, driving one nearest to her side into
the forest saying:

Go follow him, he who is mad Attis, mangle his brain within
your claws, go follow

him who longs to leave my empire; give your rage to him,
    transmute your madness to his person,
lash tail and throw your rolling head, mane erect in fury,
    follow him.

At this the creature sprang through the deep wilderness, and
    on a glittering sunstruck beach found Attis
drove him back to Ida where now wandering forever Attis
    delirious, sings praise, a servant to the goddess Cybele.

Great goddess, spare me, never haunt my home—take others
    for your slaves, those creatures
that you have driven mad and those who in their madness
    wake again your passionate cruelty.

                    Catullus, *Songs* 63 (Horace Gregory)

CORRUPT PRIESTS

I

PAGAN

Bellona's priests, an eunuch at their head,
About the streets a mad procession lead;
The venerable gelding, large and high,
O'erlooks the herd of his inferior fry.
His awkward clergymen about him prance,
And beat the timbrels to their mystic dance;
Guiltless of testicles, they tear their throats,
And squeak, in treble, their unmanly notes.
Meanwhile, his cheeks the miter'd prophet swells,
And dire presages of the year foretells;
Unless with eggs (his priestly hire) they haste
To expiate, and avert th' autumnal blast.

          .   .   .

How can they pay their priests too much respect,
Who trade with heav'n, and earthly gains neglect?

With him, domestic gods discourse by night;
By day, attended by his choir in white,
The baldpate tribe runs madding thro' the street,
And smile to see with how much ease they cheat.
The ghostly sire forgives the wife's delights,
Who sins, thro' frailty, on forbidden nights,
And tempts her husband in the holy time,
When carnal pleasure is a mortal crime.
The sweating image shakes its head, but he
With mumbled prayers atones the deity.
The pious priesthood the fat goose receive,
And they once brib'd, the godhead must forgive.

Juvenal, *Satires* 6.511-18, 531-41 (John Dryden)

I I

CHRISTIAN

He is up with the sun, to consult his list of calls; he short-cuts his way along, to pop his head in while the ladies are still in bed. If he spots a pillow he likes, or a dainty fabric, or any fine piece, he compliments her on it, admires, fingers it, pities himself for not possessing its fellow—not really begging for it; why beg where he can blackmail? Everyone fears the city's most talkative busybody. He is the foe of chastity and fasts, the connoisseur of steaming luncheons, of succulent birds like that called (in Greek) a "chirping duffer." His tongue is rough and unrestrained, with a ready arsenal of insults. Wherever you go, there he is. Whatever is said, he said it first, or made it worse. He changes horses constantly, steeds so sleek and high-strung you would think him some rich brother of the king of Thrace.

St. Jerome, *Letters* 22.28 (G. W.)

GOSSIP

Full in the midst of the created space,
Betwixt heav'n, earth, and skies, there stands a place
Confining on all three, with triple bound;
Whence all things, tho' remote, are view'd around,

357

And thither bring their undulating sound:
The palace of loud Fame, her seat of pow'r,
Plac'd on the summit of a lofty tow'r.
A thousand winding entries, long and wide,
Receive of fresh reports a flowing tide.
A thousand crannies in the walls are made;
Nor gate nor bars exclude the busy trade.
'T is built of brass, the better to diffuse
The spreading sounds, and multiply the news;
Where echoes in repeated echoes play:
A mart forever full, and open night and day.
Nor silence is within, nor voice express,
But a deaf noise of sounds that never cease;
Confus'd and chiding, like the hollow roar
Of tides receding from th' insulted shore;
Or like the broken thunder, heard from far,
When Jove to distance drives the rolling war.
The courts are fill'd with a tumultuous din
Of crowds, or issuing forth, or ent'ring in:
A thoroughfare of news, where some devise
Things never heard; some mingle truth with lies:
The troubled air with empty sounds they beat;
Intent to hear, and eager to repeat.
Error sits brooding there, with added train
Of vain Credulity, and Joys as vain:
Suspicion, with Sedition join'd, are near;
And Rumors rais'd, and Murmurs mix'd, and Panic Fear.
Fame sits aloft, and sees the subject ground,
And seas about, and skies above; enquiring all around.

Ovid, *Transformations* 12.39-63 (John Dryden)

THE ALCOHOLIC'S END

The laughing sot, like all unthinking men,
Bathes and gets drunk; then bathes and drinks again.
His throat half throttled with corrupted phlegm,
And breathing through his jaws a belching stream,
Amidst his cups with fainting shiv'ring seiz'd,

His limbs disjointed, and all o'er diseas'd,
His hand refuses to sustain the bowl,
And his teeth clatter, and his eyeballs roll,
Till, with his meat, he vomits out his soul.

Persius, *Satires* 3.98-102 (John Dryden)

THE LECHER'S END

Another shakes the bed, dissolving there,
Till knots upon his gouty joints appear,
And chalk is in his crippled fingers found;
Rots like a dodder'd oak, and piecemeal falls to ground.

Persius, *Satires* 5.58-59 (John Dryden)

INSOMNIA

You god, most placid god, what fault is mine
that I alone have lost your gifts and weep?
O peace is on the beasts, the birds, the kine;
the sweeping mountain-tops are dim with sleep.
The truculent streams are faint; the wrinkled sea
falls smoothly back and lips the crooning land.
Now seven moons have risen quietly
and seen my lanking cheeks, the stars have fanned
their flickering lights, and dawn has pitied me
and touched me with the coolness in her hand.
What can I do? I'd fail, though I possessed
the eyes of Argus with their changing light,
the thousand eyes that took their turns for rest.
Perhaps some lover through the lengthening night
bids Sleep across his kisses take to flight.
Come thence. I do not pray that you will dip
your full wings in my eyes. The happy throng
may make that prayer. But gently pass along
and touch me with your wing's extremest tip.

Statius, *Stuff* 5.4 (Jack Lindsay)

359

TO ONE'S DYING SELF

Elusive self and soul-let, only you
could cheer my clay and keep it in repair—
(how send this laugher in me out of me,
to places alien, brittle, and moon-bare?)

The Emperor Hadrian, *To Himself* (G. W.)

"CAST OFFAL"

We, who are dead and gone, shall bear no part
In all the pleasures, nor shall feel the smart
Which to that other mortal shall accrue,
Whom of our matter time shall mold anew.
For backward if you look on that long space
Of ages past, and view the changing face
Of matter, toss'd and variously combin'd
In sundry shapes, 't is easy for the mind
From thence t' infer, that seeds of things have been
In the same order as they now are seen:
Which yet our dark remembrance cannot trace,
Because a pause of life, a gaping space,
Has come betwixt, where memory lies dead,
And all the wand'ring motions from the sense are fled.
For whosoe'er shall in misfortunes live,
Must *be,* when those misfortunes shall arrive;
And since the man who *is* not, feels not woe,
(For death exempts him, and wards off the blow,
Which we, the living, only feel and bear,)
What is there left for us in death to fear?
When once that pause of life has come between,
'T is just the same as we had never been.
    And therefore if a man bemoan his lot,
That after death his mold'ring limbs shall rot,
Or flames, or jaws of beasts devour his mass,
Know, he's an unsincere, unthinking ass.
A secret sting remains within his mind;
The fool is to his own cast offals kind.

He boasts no sense can after death remain,
Yet makes himself a part of life again,
As if some-other-He could feel the pain.
If, while he live, this thought molest his head,
"What wolf or vulture shall devour me dead?"
He wastes his days in idle grief, nor can
Distinguish 'twixt the body and the man;
But thinks himself can still himself survive;
And, what when dead he feels not, feels alive.
Then he repines that he was born to die,
Nor knows in death there is no other He,
No living He remains his grief to vent,
And o'er his senseless carcass to lament.
If after death 't is painful to be torn
By birds, and beasts, then why not so to burn;
Or, drench'd in floods of honey, to be soak'd;
Imbalm'd, to be at once preserv'd and chok'd;
Or on an airy mountain's top to lie,
Expos'd to cold and heav'n's inclemency;
Or crowded in a tomb to be oppress'd
With monumental marble on thy breast?

Lucretius, *On Reality* 3.852-93 (John Dryden)

WHY PRAY FOR OLD AGE?

"Jove, grant me length of life, and years' good store
Heap on my bending back; I ask no more."
Both sick and healthful, old and young, conspire
In this one silly mischievous desire.
Mistaken blessing, which old age they call!
'T is a long, nasty, darksome hospital,
A ropy chain of rheums; a visage rough,
Deform'd, unfeatur'd, and a skin of buff;
A stitch-fall'n cheek, that hangs below the jaw;
Such wrinkles, as a skilful hand would draw
For an old grandam ape, when, with a grace,
She sits at squat, and scrubs her leathern face.
    In youth, distinctions infinite abound;

361

No shape or feature just alike are found;
The fair, the black, the feeble, and the strong;
But the same foulness does to age belong,
The selfsame palsy, both in limbs and tongue;
The skull and forehead one bald barren plain,
And gums unarm'd to mumble meat in vain:
Besides th' eternal drivel, that supplies
The dropping beard, from nostrils, mouth, and eyes.
His wife and children loathe him, and, what's worse,
Himself does his offensive carrion curse!
Flatt'rers forsake him too; for who would kill
Himself, to be remember'd in a will?
His taste not only pall'd to wine and meat,
But to the relish of a nobler treat.
The limber nerve, in vain provok'd to rise,
Inglorious from the field of a battle flies:
Poor feeble dotard, how could he advance
With his blue headpiece, and his broken lance?
Add, that endeavoring still without effect,
A lust more sordid justly we suspect.

Juvenal, *Satires* 10.188-208 (John Dryden)

RESIGNATION

Maintain an unmoved poise in adversity;
Likewise in luck one free of extravagant
   Joy. Bear in mind my admonition,
      Dellius. Whether you pass a lifetime

Prostrate with gloom, or whether you celebrate
Feast-days with choice old brands of Falernian
   Stretched out in some green, unfrequented
      Meadow, remember your death is certain.

For whom but us do silvery poplar and
Tall pine conspire such welcome with shadowy
   Laced boughs? Why else should eager water
      Bustle and fret in its zigzag channel?

Come, bid them bring wine, perfume and beautiful

Rose-blooms that die too swiftly: be quick while the
   Dark threads the three grim Sisters weave still
      Hold and your years and the times allow it.

Soon farewell town house, country estate by the
Brown Tiber washed, chain-acres of pasture-land,
   Farewell the sky-high piles of treasure
      Left with the rest for an heir's enjoyment.

Rich man or poor man, scion of Inachus
Or beggar wretch lodged naked and suffering
   God's skies—it's all one. You and I are
      Victims of never-relenting Orcus,

Sheep driven deathward. Sooner or later Fate's
Urn shakes, the lot comes leaping for each of us
   And books a one-way berth in Charon's
      Boat on the journey to endless exile.

Horace, Songs 2.3 (James Michie)

INEXORABLE

   Alas, dear friend, the fleeting years
      In everlasting circles run,
   In vain you spend your vows and prayers,
      They roll, and ever will roll on.

   Should hecatombs each rising morn
      On cruel Pluto's altar die,
   Should costly loads of incense burn
      (Their fumes ascending to the sky),

   You could not gain a moment's breath,
      Or move the haughty king below,
   Nor would inexorable death
      Defer an hour the fatal blow.

   In vain we shun the din of war
      And terrors of the stormy main,
   In vain with anxious breasts we fear
      Unwholesome Sirius' sultry reign:

We all must view the Stygian flood
    That silent cuts the dreary plains,
And cruel Danaus' bloody broad
    Condemned to everduring pains.

Your shady groves, your pleasing wife
    And fruitful fields, my dearest friend,
You'll leave together with your life:
    Alone the cypress shall attend.

After your death, the lavish heir
    Will quickly drive away his woe;
The wine you kept with so much care
    Along the marble floor shall flow.

Horace, Songs 2.14 (Samuel Johnson)

NOTHING

After death nothing is, and nothing death—
The utmost limits of a gasp of breath.
Let the ambitious zealot lay aside
His hopes of heaven (whose faith is but his pride),
Let slavish souls lay by their fear,
Nor be concern'd which way, or where,
After this life they shall be hurl'd:
Dead, we become the lumber of the world,
And to that mass of matter shall be swept
Where things destroy'd with things unborn are kept.
Devouring time swallows us whole,
Impartial death confounds body and soul.
For hell and the foul fiend that rules,
    The everlasting gaols
Devised by rogues, dreaded by fools,
With his grim grisly dog that keeps the door
    Are senseless stories, idle tales,
Dreams, whimseys, and no more.

Seneca, The Trojan Women 397-408
(Earl of Rochester)

364

FEAR OF HELL

I

The old familiar heat buried in men's bones must make itself felt at times; but praise, but honor for him who, as soon as his thoughts turn this way, extinguishes them, dashes them on a rock. And Christ is the rock. How often in the desert—when I lived in that extended loneliness, that rugged sun-baked home of hermits—did I think myself back amid Rome's sensual solicitings. I sat alone there, and bitterness filled me. I was a shaggy lump, my limbs in a sack, my skin sun-rusted and scaly as an Ethiop's. Every day tears, every day sighs, and if sleep came on me as I fought it off, I banged my loose rattling bones down on bare ground. No need to mention food or drink; hermits drink nothing but cool water even when they are ill, and to take anything cooked would be a wild indulgence. I had put myself in this prison I shared with lizards and preying beasts because I feared hell. Yet I was often circled in by dancing girls. Under a face blanched, a body chilled, with fasts, my mind was all aboil; where all else was dead, the lively fires of lust bubbled on within me.

St. Jerome, *Letters* 22.6-7 (G. W.)

I I

Value a soul that has confessed. I curse my shaky
limbs, and silent regret is in me, and high fear
that hurts like the cross, forecasting the torments of Hell
at the last; and the wounded heart endures its ghosts.

Ausonius, *The Prayer* 54-57 (Richard E. Braun)

I I I

Here find your games of the circus,—watch the race of time, the seasons slipping by, count the circuits, look for the goal of the great consummation, battle for the companies of the churches, rouse up at the signal of God, stand erect at the angel's trump, triumph in the palms of martyrdom. If the literature of the stage delight you, we have sufficiency of books, of poems, of aphorisms, sufficiency of songs and voices, not fable, those of ours, but truth; not artifice but simplicity. Would you have

33. Tragic mask, colossal size. New York, Metropolitan Museum of Art.

. . . for all things, tears; a mind wincing at man's pain . . .

fightings and wrestlings? Here they are—things of no small account and plenty of them. See impurity overthrown by chastity, perfidy slain by faith, cruelty crushed by pity, impudence thrown into the shade by modesty; and such are the contests among us, and in them we are crowned. Have you a mind for blood? You have the blood of Christ.

But what a spectacle is already at hand—the return of the Lord, now no object of doubt, now exalted, now triumphant! What exultation will that be of the angels, what glory that of the saints as they rise again! What the reign of the righteous thereafter! What a city, the New Jerusalem! Yes, and there are still to come other spectacles—that last, that eternal Day of Judgment, that Day which the Gentiles never believed would come, that Day they laughed at, when this old world and all its generations shall be consumed in one fire. How vast the spectacle that day, and how wide! What sight shall wake my wonder, what my laughter, my joy and exultation? as I see all those kings, those great kings, welcomed (we were told) in heaven, along with Jove, along with those who told of their ascent, groaning in the depths of darkness! And the magistrates who persecuted the name of Jesus, liquefying in fiercer flames than they kindled in their rage against the Christians! those sages, too, the philosophers blushing before their disciples as they blaze together, the disciples whom they taught that God was concerned with nothing, that men have no souls at all, or that what souls they have shall never return to their former bodies! And, then, the poets trembling before the judgment-seat, not of Rhadamanthus, not of Minos, but of Christ whom they never looked to see! And then there will be the tragic actors to be heard, more vocal in their own tragedy; and the players to be seen, lither of limb by far in the fire; and then the charioteer to watch, red all over in the wheel of flame; and, next, the athletes to be gazed upon, not in their gymnasiums but hurled in the fire—unless it be that not even then would I wish to see them, in my desire rather to turn an insatiable gaze on them who vented their rage and fury on the Lord. "This is he," I shall say, "the son of the carpenter or the harlot, the Sabbath-breaker, the Samaritan, who had a devil. This is he whom you bought from Judas; this is he, who was struck with reed and fist, defiled with spittle, given gall and vinegar to drink. This is he whom the disciples secretly stole away, that it might be said he had risen—unless it was the gardener who removed him, lest his lettuces should be trampled by the throng of visitors!" Such sights, such exultation,—what praetor, consul,

367

quaestor, priest, will ever give you of his bounty? And yet all these, in some sort, are ours, pictured through faith in the imagination of the spirit. But what are those things which eye hath not seen nor ear heard, nor ever entered into the heart of man? I believe, things of greater joy than circus, theatre or amphitheatre, or any stadium.

Tertullian, *On the Games* 29-30 (T. R. Glover)

"WHY, THIS IS HELL . . ."

All things, like thee, have time to rise and rot;
And from each other's ruin are begot:
For life is not confin'd to him or thee;
'T is given to all for use, to none for property.
    Consider former ages past and gone,
Whose circles ended long ere thine begun,
Then tell me, fool, what part in them thou hast.
Thus may'st thou judge the future by the past.
What horror see'st thou in that quiet state?
What bugbear dreams to fright thee after fate?
No ghost, no goblins, that still passage keep;
But all is there serene, in that eternal sleep.
For all the dismal tales that poets tell
Are verified on earth, and not in hell.
No Tantalus looks up with fearful eye,
Or dreads th' impending rock to crush him from on high;
But fear of chance on earth disturbs our easy hours,
Or vain imagin'd wrath of vain imagin'd pow'rs.
No Tityus torn by vultures lies in hell;
Nor could the lobes of his rank liver swell
To that prodigious mass for their eternal meal:
Not tho' his monstrous bulk had cover'd o'er
Nine spreading acres, or nine thousand more;
Not tho' the globe of earth had been the giant's floor:
Nor in eternal torments could he lie,
Nor could his corpse sufficient food supply.
But he's the Tityus, who by love oppress'd,
Or tyrant passion preying on his breast,

368

And ever-anxious thoughts, is robb'd of rest.
The Sisyphus is he, whom noise and strife
Seduce from all the soft retreats of life,
To vex the government, disturb the laws:
Drunk with the fumes of popular applause,
He courts the giddy crowd to make him great,
And sweats and toils in vain, to mount the sovereign seat.
For still to aim at pow'r, and still to fail,
Ever to strive, and never to prevail,
What is it, but, in reason's true account,
To heave the stone against the rising mount?
Which urg'd, and labor'd, and forc'd up with pain,
Recoils, and rolls impetuous down, and smokes along the plain.
Then still to treat thy ever-craving mind
With ev'ry blessing, and of ev'ry kind,
Yet never fill thy rav'ning appetite;
Tho' years and seasons vary thy delight,
Yet nothing to be seen of all the store,
But still the wolf within thee barks for more;
This is the fable's moral, which they tell
Of fifty foolish virgins damn'd in hell
To leaky vessels, which the liquor spill;
To vessels of their sex, which none could ever fill.
As for the Dog, the Furies, and their snakes,
The gloomy caverns, and the burning lakes,
And all the vain infernal trumpery,
They neither are, nor were, nor e'er can be.
But here on earth the guilty have in view
The mighty pains to mighty mischiefs due;
Racks, prisons, poisons, the Tarpeian rock,
Stripes, hangmen, pitch, and suffocating smoke;
And last, and most, if these were cast behind,
Th' avenging horror of a conscious mind,
Whose deadly fear anticipates the blow,
And sees no end of punishment and woe;
But looks for more, at the last gasp of breath:
This makes a hell on earth, and life a death.

Lucretius, *On Reality* 3.968-1023
(John Dryden)

DESCENT

Dim shapes, they travel'd the dark way
through waste night, Death's ringing palaces,
an emptiness inhabited—
travel'd as men go through woods
foiled of light by an elusive moon
while Jove darkens heaven, and heaven's dark
erases many-colored earth.

Vergil, *The Song of Aeneas*
6.268-72 (G. W.)

INDEX OF AUTHORS AND TRANSLATORS

(Titles are given in Latin below, but are translated into English after each selection in the text. Authors are listed chronologically, and translators are given in parentheses).

373

INDEX OF AUTHORS AND TRANSLATORS